Sunset
on the
Clyde

For Wendy

Sunset on the Clyde

Duncan Graham

Neil Wilson Publishing • Glasgow

Published by Neil Wilson Publishing Ltd
Suite 303A, The Pentagon Centre
36 Washington Street
GLASGOW
G3 8AZ
Tel: 0141-221-1117
Fax: 0141-221-5363

A catalogue record for this book is available from the British Library.
ISBN 1-897784-44-9

Typeset in 10 on 11.5pt Garamond Book by The Write Stuff, Glasgow
Printed in Musselburgh by Scotprint Ltd

Contents

Introduction

Forty years have elapsed since the last fling of the Clyde Steamers in the fifties. I have tried to be as accurate as memory will allow, and apologise for the mistakes and errors which must inevitably have crept in. They are honestly made. I hope that I have done justice to the characters both human and ships, as I endeavoured to temper the judgment of youth with the experience of age. I apologise also to any of either set who might feel I could have portrayed them in a more favourable light. Above all I hope that for those who were there, happy memories will flood back, and for those who missed out, a little bit of our history will be recalled in a way more lively than the sort of text books we all had at school. There should be something here for those who are aficionados of steam and for the vast majority who simply experienced a day 'doon the watter'.

At the helm of Waverley, August, 1993. Just like the good old days ...

In addition to my own extensive resources built up over the years I have drawn on the many authoritative works which exist on the subject, some of which are listed in the suggestions for further reading. I should particularly like to place on record my gratitude to fellow members of the Clyde River Steamer Club (C.R.S.C.) and the Paddle-Steamer Preservation Society (P.S.P.S.) for their help, to those who were so willing to allow their photographs to brighten the pages, and whom I hope we have managed to acknowledge accurately and to my wife Wendy for many hours slaving over a hot word-processor.

Duncan Graham, CBE
Appleby,
Cumbria.

The Die is Cast

The least original way to begin is to say that the war changed my life. Unlike the comedian Robb Wilton I am not entirely clear as to where I was on the day war broke out but I do know that shortly thereafter my parents made an eccentric decision. The phoney war was a period when for the average civilian, and indeed for the ordinary serviceman little took place and there was more boredom than excitement. I suppose this gave a great deal of time for the imagination to run riot. My mother assumed, as no doubt did every other mum, that wherever she was with her infants was where Hitler would unerringly strike. We took him very seriously and I suppose with good reason. It was not until long after the war when I first saw the Charlie Chaplin film, *The Great Dictator* that I realised that there could be a funny side to the grimmest of events.

My mother decided unilaterally on an evacuation from Rouken Glen, in the suburbs of Glasgow, to Dunoon where aunt Peggy, who represented the upper-class end of our decidedly mixed family, held both ownership and court at the Cowal Hotel in East Bay. It had to be the East Bay because what little sand there is is in the West Bay and the East Bay is therefore infinitely higher class. The Cowal Hotel shone forth like a beacon because it was and still is quite the tallest building in the East Bay topped with distinctively Scottish dormer windows, and just where, if you stagger out from the bar on the boat, you cop your first eyeful of Dunoon. This is ironic because the Cowal Hotel was *the* temperance hotel in Dunoon as its publicity literature made proudly clear. It was many years later that I discovered that other hotels had cocktail bars and lounges. Temperance, by the way, is an odd euphemism for abstinence. The visitors to the Cowal Hotel neither expected nor received even the smallest of sensations.

Behind the scenes I have no reason to doubt that in an atmosphere reminiscent of the prohibition, illicit brews passed furtively amongst the inmates. I never worked in a hotel kitchen where the staff were ever less than half-cut. It would be too much to say that I had evidence that my

11

*The PS Ivanhoe leaving Corrie, Arran at the turn of the century. Presumably
the followers of the Temperance Movement had got off at Dunoon.*
MCLEAN MUSEUM, GREENOCK

uncle was more temperate than abstinent, but after he retired, his wine
cellar was extensive.

There was a Clyde paddle-steamer, the Ivanhoe which in the 1880s
was a temperance ship. No alcohol was served on board. Anyone who
'visited the engines' on her was not making the time honoured excuse
for nipping below to the bar. It was claimed she was successful, but an
'Ivanhoe Flask' with a suitable capacity for a day's cruise could be purchased in Glasgow before going aboard! I'd like to think that her more
sober passengers, who prized her yacht-like looks, her decks scrubbed a
snowy white, and crew in white blouses with navy blue collars, came
ashore at Dunoon and made a bee-line for the Cowal.

In other ways the Cowal Hotel was typical of its time. On the ground
floor to the left of the front door lay the public rooms and to the right a
resplendent dining room. Here were waitresses with spidery black legs,
their black uniforms relieved only by white aprons and little caps of the
kind which nurses used to wear before the NHS cuts. There was a head
waiter; he seemed formidable to me but then any man dressed in tails
might seem so to a three year old. He was to become my friend, as even
in the darkest days of rationing he conjured Scotch trifle from the
recesses of the kitchen. Even paying guests found him forbidding and as
was the way in those days they had to compete for his favours. He
reminds me now of that famous head waiter in New York whose obitu-
ary was said to have been... 'At last God caught his eye'.

Upstairs on four floors were the 30 or so bedrooms which could be reached by the kind of lift which was all the rage in Hollywood movies and department stores such as Copeland & Lye and Pettigrews & Stephens in Sauchiehall Street. The well in which it ran was an open tracery of girders and wire netting. Its expanding metal doors echoed throughout the hotel and its interior was dark wood and mirrors. It broke down daily, much to the distress of the more aged permanent residents. They had placed their faith in it and taken rooms on the top floor at the front for the view across the Clyde to the Cloch Light and the steamers, cargo ships and liners which thronged the Clyde in the thirties. Behind the lift shaft lay my aunt's office, a visit to which, at a tender age, put me off the idea of office work for life. It fostered a distaste for bureaucracy which has grown apace.

My aunt was a semi-invalid, a martyr to asthma and spent most of her time either in the office or in her splendid bedroom-cum-sitting room on the first floor just above the canopy of the entrance, where chauffeurs handed out the guests from their splendid cars. There were more Armstrong-Siddeleys and Daimlers than Austin Sevens. At that time the room fascinated me. It was not because the furnishings were so opulent or the view so splendid but because it uniquely had a washhand basin surrounded by all the appurtenances normally seen in bathrooms. There was nothing en-suite about hotels in 1939. Nowadays every B&B boasts of it on the little signs which are covered with a binbag when they are either full up or the owners have gone out for a night on the tiles.

That unique washhand basin was still there when I made my first professional visit in 1974 to what had been the Cowal Hotel. It was now the Education Offices of Argyll County Council. That year saw the setting up of Strathclyde Region, a move so unpopular that when out for a pint I had to conceal the fact that I had become second in command of an education department which spread from Iona to the Gorbals. That very room had become the office of the Director of Education and I went there to meet Charles Edward Stewart. In the reorganisation he had become my Divisional Education Officer. Years later he told me that I appeared even odder than he had been led to believe. Instead of delivering an inspirational speech about the future of education, I had apparently banged on about the plumbing arrangements!

Dunoon was close to the Tail o' the Bank which was to become one of the greatest concentrations of military and naval activity in the whole of the UK. It was from here that the great convoys were to issue forth through the boom which was constructed between the Gantocks close to the pier at Dunoon and Cloch on the other side. The gates were drawn open and shut by dumpy boom defence vessels attached to them at bow and stern. The fear of submarine attacks on the myriad of ships which lay within was palpable — even more so after Gunther Prien in U47 sank the Royal Oak in Scapa Flow. Records show that U-boats were put in to penetrate the Clyde estuary and that early in the war at least two laid a significant number of mines. In reality, however, a much greater threat lay in bombing — or blitzing as it was to become known. More experienced students of war than my parents might just have worked out that there was more chance of a stray bomb landing on Dunoon than at Rouken Glen — although it's fair to say that the famous Glasgow park was used as a lorry dump for most of the war, ruining what had been the finest turf in any of the parks in the 'dear green place'. The grass has not recovered even yet.

Perverse as it may seem, it was to Dunoon that I and my sister were borne in the autumn of 1939 aboard the turbine steamer Queen Mary II. I have no recollection of the 20-minute voyage but I do have a clear picture of Rory, my aunt's chauffeur standing on the pier with his skip cap and black leather leggings. If he had met more important and prestigious people at the pier over the years he did not betray it. Rory and I were to become firm friends and I was to become accustomed to riding in the Alvis. This splendid car had replaced an even more magnificent one built in the early twenties at the Arroll Johnston works in Paisley. The coachwork was carried out by a relative, a skilled craftsman, James Turnbull.

Petrol rationing did not seem to curtail the goings-on at the Cowal Hotel. On one occasion my aunt set off for Glasgow by car, the long way round. Presumably this was because she did not wish to risk the 'planks' which had to be braved in taking a car across the Clyde by steamer. Today one can reach Dunoon by road in a couple of hours; in those days it was an epic journey and could easily take seven or eight hours. The roads were largely single track winding past Loch Eck through Strachur and up the eastern side of Loch Fyne with grand views across to Inveraray. Nowadays one has to remind oneself of just how remote these places were and how much more accessible by steamer than by road. Then there came the Rest and be Thankful. To today's tourists the name must seem quaint as they belt over the top in fifth gear. In 1939 and for a long time thereafter cars had to turn round and reverse up the trickiest and steepest part because their reverse gear was lower than first. On a good day passengers could stay aboard while this manoeuvre was carried out. Cars tended somehow to be at their most temperamental on the wettest days. Safely arrived at the top there were more than the usual reasons for 'resting and being thankful' and unless you were bound for a temperance hotel a small sensation was most definitely in order! How on earth my frail and ailing aunt survived this and the return journey I suppose only Rory knows. There is little likelihood that she was revived with a drop of the hard stuff.

Cars were hardly used by ordinary folks like ourselves in the thirties, I was 14 years old before my father acquired his first car. It was a black

14

The Arroll Johnston, c1923, coachbuilt in Paisley by James Turnbull for the Cowal Hotel

secondhand Standard 14 which came from Prossers of Stirling — where he knew 'a man'. Between Rory and the Alvis and my father's pride and joy I can only recollect a hurl in an affluent neighbour's Humber Super Snipe to the Dutch House near Prestwick for afternoon tea. That one afternoon was as novel then to a 12-year-old as I suppose is the first package tour for today's youngsters. In the days before motorways Troon and Prestwick seemed as far away as Malaga is today and the Dutch House was just as exotic. Afternoon tea seemed to me just as splendid as the one I had some years ago in the Mandarin Hotel in Hong Kong. Hong Kong is now the last bastion of afternoon tea as it used to be served in the Cowal Hotel. I hope the Chinese appreciate this when they take over in 1997, but somehow I doubt it.

Life for a child of tender years in the Cowal Hotel was not lacking in interest. For one thing there was an early insight into the class system in the West of Scotland. My mother, not by nature in awe of anyone, knew her place in the pecking order. I learned mine the hard way at the hands, or should I say fists of my cousin whose natural superiority was reinforced by the extra strength of three years age advantage. There was little point in complaining as it was assumed that in the prevailing order of things he could do no wrong. I grew to detest him as privilege conveyed him smoothly to a prestigious public school, to university and inevitably to become a doctor. My mother was never to forgive me for failing to follow in his footsteps. Even at that time she could envisage the brass plate in Harley Street and the hyphenation of my middle and surname to the prestigious Gilmour-Graham. When I met that cousin 30 years later he turned out to be civilised and affable and a pillar of the medical establishment of the university in our capital city. It was to be many years before I lost that inbuilt respect for rank and privilege and it was only after mixing with the cream of the English public schools and Oxbridge in Whitehall that I finally concluded that there was no correlation at all between upbringing and being a gentleman. Burns got it right as ever — 'The rank is but the guinea's stamp, the man's the gowd for a' that'.

The war years were spent substantially in Dunoon with periods back in Glasgow, one of which was neatly timed for the Clydebank blitz. I remember only too vividly being allowed out from under the shelter of the dining room table to stand at the back door of our bungalow, staring at the droning German bombers. An errant bomb neatly halved a bungalow in Etive Drive in Giffnock and we all traipsed down to marvel at the crater. My father, whose job as a maths teacher kept him out of the services, manned the stirrup pumps on the roof of Shawlands Academy from where he brought home a piece of precious shrapnel which had landed in the playground. We visited relatives at Clydebank and I can well remember marvelling how odd the tenements looked when the outer walls were removed and you could see right into each room. Furniture lay at crazy angles, curtains and light fittings flapped in the wind and I almost expected to see the tiny tenants going about their business in these curious dolls houses in the sky. The post-war clearances in Maryhill surreally created much the same impression.

We also spent an increasing amount of time at Bannockburn where my mother had been brought up. Her unerring ability to choose a dangerous place at a dangerous time took us for a short time to relatives in Methil in Fife and a house within 100 yards of the docks. Perhaps she knew that the Germans would not come! I think this skill may be hereditary. When I became Depute Director of Education for Renfrewshire, I was sent on a course at the Nuclear Defence School at Easingwold in Yorkshire. On the first night the colonel blimp in charge unfolded a map of the world with circles around the three places which were bound to be obliterated first in a nuclear war. Number one circle contained Greenock, Gourock, Dunoon and the nuclear submarine bases at Faslane, Coulport and the Holy Loch! My future civil defence career involved the notional evacuation of the entire population of Paisley to Greenock by train — surely an odd assumption in high command that the Buddies would co-operate in being evacuated to the disaster area from which Greenockians would be fleeing on the 'up' line. I found too that I had assumed an awesome responsibility for a very considerable number of piles of Heinz bean cans. These rusted away gracefully in a location which even now is too secret to mention: suffice to say it is not too far from a famous football ground in Paisley. It would have been bad enough in the aftermath of a nuclear explosion, without having to survive exclusively on beans. Headier responsibilities were to come in due course including a nuclear headquarters in Humberside which had been made significantly less radiation-proof than originally planned. One of my predecessors, feeling that it lacked certain airs and graces had thoughtfully provided it with windows which were not even double-glazed.

But by far the most exciting thing for me about Dunoon was the Clyde and the ships which sailed on it. Since that time every day spent away from the Clyde has a sense of deprivation about it. I knew nothing of the splendours of the thirties with the vast arrays of steamers of rival companies conveying throngs of people doon the watter, but I soon fell for the Queen Mary II. Her wartime days took her to and fro between Gourock and Dunoon with a regular monotony, relieved only by serving as tender to the troop ships which lay at the Tail o' the Bank.

With the movement of military personnel to the Holy Loch, combined with the normal day-to-day traffic across the Clyde even the Queen Mary's great capacity was taxed. Her decks were strewn with cargo, mysterious boxes guarded by sentries and the odd motor car — usually a military one since cars for civilians were few and far between. How on earth those who came over in the dark managed around the single track roads of Cowal with their headlights covered by those daft dishes with slits in them, God only knows. Dunoon Pier was alive with folk going back and forth. As far as I can recall the Town Council did not waive the pier dues so somebody must have made a small fortune there. Heart-rending farewells and departures were an everyday occurrence as men left, some of them never to return. On a jollier note liaisons were quickly formed which seemed, for reasons which escaped me at the time, to continue under the pier and be consummated in ways at that time beyond my ken.

The Queen Mary II started the war in battleship grey — a far cry from the resplendent white and black hull and white funnels with black tops of the Williamson Buchanan Line who were her first owners. Later on in the war she had a black hull with her upper works in a rather dingy ochre and towards the end of the war she was painted in an overall light grey which in some conditions gave her an eery silver, almost ephemeral appearance. None of this disguised her sheer beauty and I spent hours tracing her path back and forth, as she laid her trail with plumes of heavy black smoke from her coal-burning boilers.

I badgered my parents and anyone else who would listen to me for the reason why the Queen Mary had those roman numerals at the end of her name, and what she had done before she became Dunoon's lifeline. I learned that she had been built in 1933 by Denny's of Dumbarton, probably the most famous of all the builders of coastal and cross-channel ships. Her owners had run sailings from Glasgow's Bridge Wharf to the Clyde coast. In the days before trains reached Princess's Pier in Greenock and the other railheads at Gourock, Craigendoran and so on, almost all the traffic between Glasgow and the Clyde went on the steamer and

The Queen Mary II returning to peacetime duty after World War Two

Bridge Wharf and the Broomielaw witnessed more than a dozen departures per day. By the thirties it was the Glasgow working man and his family and the works outings which kept the steamers in business. It is hard nowadays to appreciate the affection with which Glaswegians regarded the boats which transported them from the smoke and grime of industrial Glasgow to the most beautiful estuary in the world.

The Mary was quite the most splendid vessel ever to have been built for this traffic. She was launched by Lady Colquhoun of Luss on Thursday, March 30, 1933. The papers were full of tales of her size and the splendour of her fittings. By no means the fastest vessel on the Clyde she could turn in a handy 18 knots and although not the longest, she was certainly the broadest thus making her incredibly spacious and well able to cope with more than 2000 passengers. Billed as 'Britain's finest pleasure steamer' she left Bridge Wharf every day promptly at 10am calling at Dunoon, Rothesay and Largs before cruising to a different part of the Arran coast every day. Sometimes it was to Brodick and to Corrie where a rowing boat came out to carry passengers ashore. On other days it was Whiting Bay or to Skipness and around the Island of Inchmarnock. 'German' bands played on the decks on the days when it did not rain and when it did there was plenty to enjoy below decks. I did not know why these bands were so-called. The name was obviously less popular after the war — perhaps they should have been called Empire Bands in the way that German Biscuits were renamed! The first class dining saloon was beautifully panelled, the tables covered with crisp white tablecloths and napkins, silver cakestands and teapots all engraved with the company crest — a Turkish crescent and star, and stewards dressed in black waistcoats and bow ties. First class passengers could have the whole cruise, including lunch and high tea for 10/- and they could save a shilling if they made do with a plain tea. The steerage passengers (equivalent to third class passengers on a train) had far more shelter than on any other boat. Steerage passengers were by custom confined to the stern of a ship where they had to suffer the noise and vibration of the screws. However, the Queen Mary was the best in the fleet for this class of passenger. They had their own tea-room, the quaint 1930s feature of a soda bar, a smoke-room and of course a bar for those who were not of the temperance persuasion. It is not surprising that under the command of Captain Donald McKinnon, who stayed with her until her wartime years, the Queen Mary was thought by many to be, in the words of Para Handy, 'the smartest vessel in the tred'.

The story about her name is a curious one. Each day during the 1934 season as she made her way down the Clyde she passed the shipyards, doing their best to survive in the depression years. At John Browns of Clydebank lay the increasing bulk of the vessel known as yard No. 534 enveloped in the deafening clatter of the riveters. Despite the depression Cunard were engaged in building the ultimate transatlantic liner. According to the story the directors had decided to name their ship Queen Victoria. They were given audience by King George V — who incidentally had had a steamer named after him in 1926. The story goes that they told him that they proposed to name their masterpiece after 'the world's greatest Queen'. To this King George allegedly replied: 'Why, certainly I am sure my wife will be delighted!' Confusion, embarrassment and consternation ensued. Now the Queen Mary along with her fellow Bridge Wharf steamer the King Edward had been transferred from Williamson Buchanan to the Caledonian Steam Packet Company and so it was to that company's directors that the Cunard counterparts had to come cap in hand mumbling as to whether or not they would have the good grace to see their way etc, etc... It has always seemed more likely to me that Cunard all along wanted to name their ship Queen Mary but the tale is always worth the telling and a deal was struck. The Queen Mary, the 'real' Queen Mary as I see her, became Queen Mary II and a portrait of Queen Mary (the lady) soon adorned the walls of the lounge complete with a brass plaque signifying Cunard's gratitude. The Queen Mary II was incidentally to revert to plain Queen Mary in 1976 after the Cunarder had departed for her berth in Long Beach, California.

In any case it would appear that consulting royalty about the names of ships is a risky business. The story is told of the audience given by the King of Belgium in 1895 to the director of the navy. He asked him what name was to be given to a new paddle-steamer for the Dover/Ostende route which was markedly slower than her two sister ships. On learning that no name had been agreed, the King whimsically suggested 'Rapide!' — and Rapide it was for the 30 years she sailed slowly back and forth across the Channel, although all things are relative — she could top 20 knots. She at least avoided the fate of one of the flyers, Princess Henrietta, which sliced a smaller paddler clean in two on a foggy day off Dunkirk.

I have had links with the Queen Mary ever since 1939 — even to this day when the Queen Mary is a floating restaurant on the Thames embankment. During particularly important meetings with Kenneth Baker, the Secretary of State for Education in the Department of Education in York Road, it was a great comfort to me to be able to look beyond the massed ranks of civil servants to the Mary floating serenely on her berth. She kept me sane.

I was lucky enough to see both the 'big' Queen Mary and the Queen Elizabeth slip in and out of the Clyde as they made their unescorted dashes across the Atlantic as troop ships. It says something for the camouflage that such great vessels could seem almost unobtrusive. They were a poignant sight. I remember grown-ups telling about the time when the Queen Mary arrived after she had cut right through HMS Curacoa, her escort vessel for the last stage of her voyage, with a great number of fatalities. Queen Mary II served as tender to both Queens and although I cannot claim to having seen her alongside, I can imagine how diminutive she must have looked. Later on I was to serve on steamers which acted as tenders to the great Empresses as they called en route from Liverpool to Canada — it was like being in a cup floating alongside a barrel.

There were other Clyde steamers around in the war years. The Lucy Ashton which was quite the oldest of them and thus not called up for war service, did sterling service from Craigendoran around the piers in the Gareloch and once or twice a day to Dunoon. She was ancient and tiny — a sort of living museum-piece. She had been built in, of all places, Rutherglen in 1888 and until painted wartime grey she had a 'wee red lum'. She was to survive the war and with so many steamers lost in active service, she paddled on until 1948. Thereafter, incredibly, her hull was stripped of its paddles and she was used for experiments in jet propulsion. For a boat that could, in her hey-day, give the illusion of going backwards at full speed ahead this must have been a highly satisfactory way to bow out. Experiments, however, could hardly have been a success as the Clyde is notably lacking in jet propelled ferries and not one of today's can manage more than a modest 16 knots with the wind behind it. The Lucy Ashton's siren was bought by a firm in Chile, and its notes for many years summoned the workers to their shift in a factory in Santiago.

Outside the boom, danger money was paid to the crews and those of a nervous disposition frequently confused any suspicious object with a periscope. There is no history of submarine attack on a Clyde steamer but it has to be said that in post-war years when testing torpedoes in Loch Long our own lot managed to torpedo the Countess of Breadalbane when making her full 9 knots towards Arrochar. The warhead was a dummy but the same description could not be applied to the master of the Breadalbane whose comments added greatly to the already extensive repertoire of the seamen on the bridge and shocked a number of maiden ladies taking light refreshments below. The purser, who was a mate of mine at university, pulled the birds at many a dance at Rothesay on the basis of his experiences under fire! As usual the Navy denied all knowledge although the tale was confirmed by Erchie the diver whose job it was to retrieve the torpedoes that got lost in the loch. Erchie was a real character whom I got to know later when I was a purser on the Maid of the Loch. He was constantly torn between revealing the latest idiocies of his employers and the constraints of the Official Secrets Act. A pint or two of McEwan's heavy always tipped him towards treason. Erchie's bald head had assumed the shape of the diving helmet he wore as, torch in hand, he clumped along the bottom of the loch which he claimed was littered with all manner of embarrassing and expensive debris. It probably still is.

I was nine years old when the war ended, had attended more primary schools than I could count up to and was to spend less and less time in Dunoon and on my beloved Clyde. I can recall being taken by Rory to the new promenade on the top deck of Dunoon pier where one had to pay extra to view. From there at 10am one could witness a whole parade of steamers as the Clyde came back to peacetime life. Propellers and paddles churned the waters. There was a loudspeaker announcing departures and destinations and blurting out Jimmy Shand's ubiquitous accordion music between sailings. There was another flurry at lunchtime and then the return of the great paddlers and turbines in the early evening — it was a far cry from the Mary in her wartime grey disgorging drab civilians and uniformed troopers against the backcloth of the boom and the mass of war and merchant vessels at the Tail o' the Bank. By then she had resumed the 10am sailing from Bridge Wharf — at last things were really getting back to normal. But sadly temperance hotels were going out of fashion, my aunt had succumbed to her asthma and my uncle had sold the Cowal Hotel to Argyll County Council.

Tantalising Glimpses 1946-52

The years between the war and my student days were spent not unprofitably in educational terms and might have been even more so had my thoughts not wandered so often to the Clyde. Girls were to figure only later. Fortunately the school I attended believed in the generous application of physical stimuli to encourage study. Today it is fashionable to spare the rod and send for the psychologist but not at Hutchesons Boys Grammar School, Gorbals, Glasgow in the late forties. Six out of ten for spelling was the threshold, — five marks were likely to lead to five marks on the hands, administered with clinical, magisterial efficiency. In the Latin class the slowest division of four at declensions and conjugations got three apiece on a good day. As seats varied daily there was a hideous scramble to avoid the row with the spotty youth who stuttered — the stopwatch the size of a turnip was not calibrated to allow for human frailties.

Hutcheson's Boys Grammar School was a hard school in every way. It was fee-paying but £2. 10/- a term was affordable with the result that pupils were drawn by ability alone, from the leafy suburbs of Glasgow's south side, the aspiring housing estates like Kings Park and from the Gorbals itself. There were few snobs since their parents preferred to pay much more for what was possibly much less at Glasgow or Kelvinside Academies. Contempt was mutual. Today's rugby players could teach us nothing about the black arts. We usually lost to these schools in scoring terms, but not at maiming and gouging. I suspect that if we had been better off, my outlook would have been different.

My parents used to explain that the building in Crown Street had been there before the Gorbals, when the city was still 'dear green fields' — on the south bank at least. I have to say that it was very hard to envisage this. Both Crown Street and Cumberland Street, which I walked every day from the tramstop in Bridge Street, and the Gorbals Cross area provided a vital part of my education. It was that last sordid, decaying but vital phase before the planners and 'improvers' shook the life out of the place. But it was the people who walked and shuffled along Crown

Street who were my real education. Together we slipped on the cobbles trying to avoid the 'Silent Death' — the trolley buses which had come to oust the much-loved trams. What a climb-down they were. Rail-less, they were much less predictable, and accidents were frequent. Not for the first time new technology proved incompatible with the old — there were still plenty of horses and carts wending their eccentric way. Coalmen still shouted up close-mouths, their prices chalked on boards stuck on the back of their carts. Flittings were still done by horse-drawn van and Steptoe & Son could have passed by quite unnoticed. Collisions and altercations led to the fruitiest of exchanges which mingled interestingly with the wise words of the principal teacher of English and author of the grammar book used in most Scottish schools, Daddy Knox — whose room was on the front overlooking Crown Street. Iron discipline prevailed: years later he confessed to me he had often heaved the tawse with suppressed laughter too. He did not do so the day he found the initials DG carved on a desk in Room 9, his wee empire. I was modestly proud because John Buchan, the author of *The Thirty-Nine Steps* had left his initials embedded in Crown Street wood. Lord Byron had left his on the stone ramparts of the Chateau de Chillon on Lake Geneva; I had seen them there, protected by perspex and I had written an article for the school magazine, *The Hutchesonian*, about him. Now I had made my mark on Hutchi at last. It is best to draw a veil over what happened next.

'Who has the initials D.G.?' he enquired mildly.

'Me sir, me sir,' I cried, anxious to please and to serve.

'Step this way,' he said in markedly steelier tone...

Later in the staffroom under the stairs, where the fags were lit from a bare gaspipe, perpetually alive like the flame at the tomb of the unknown warrior, Daddy Knox probably gave a victory display of targetwork with his Lochgelly. He was long past the stage of practising his aim on a stick of chalk on the table to avoid missing the crossed hands (the way I eventually learned as a tyro-teacher, in order not to welt my own shins instead). When that happened before 30 boys, steely self control was essential. If one lad in one school anywhere had ever guessed, the image of a profession would have been ruined for ever.

Culture was acquired more by accident than design in Hutchi. The curriculum was narrow. English, Maths and History for all. Then the class-system operated — Latin and Greek for the high fliers, Modern Languages for the middle of the road, and Science for the positively obtuse. They had the best of it, becoming doctors or accountants — in one case Glasgow's biggest turf accountant, and all made money. The top lot got arts degrees and were living proof that you do not become richer by degrees. Real education was largely accidental — absorbed from a few Mr Chips who had seen life and been in the war. The history master had been captain of a destroyer in the convoy battles in the North Atlantic. When he was demobbed and recruited to Hutchi, he was adjudged too inexperienced to run the school book-store! Today's educationalists who talk of curriculum breadth and studying ten subjects at least, will note that we made do with no more than a passing acquaintance with the arts or even DIY skills. The only visual aid I ever saw was a tattered wall map of ancient Greece, from which either the mice from the open fire-place or an errant youth had amputated the Peloponnese. In spite of that, Ninian Jameson, the classics master, brought alive a world so remote from our own lives as to seem quite unreal. Alexander the Great, Dionysius in his tub, Socrates philosophising — he had met and interviewed them all. If he knew about the custom of Greek men to take boys as their 'companions' he forbore to mention it, although he was less restrained about how badly the mother of Parliaments in London compared with democracy in Athens in the third century BC. Looking at what passes for debate in the House of Commons today, he'd be even more disillusioned.

He would stand in Room 19, toothbrush moustache bristling and Brylcreemed hair glistening, his ample posterior bent into the fire toasting while we shivered. To get the best of the heat as the coals glowed less and less, he would turn his gown into a huge ball which he pushed up his back almost to neck level. He had never once visited Greece which was as remote to him as the moon to us. When, after retirement, he took his first package tour, courtesy of Thomson's, it was said he was disappointed beyond measure, complaining bitterly to the Greek government about tourists being allowed to desecrate hallowed sites. Even so, like so many of us, he must have been thrilled to stand on the Acropolis on a bright summer's morning visualising his heroes gliding in and out of the Parthenon, ogling the Cariatyds. Mark you, the last time I went, it was more like a Glasgow Corporation building site.

Long before I left the place I had resolved that no child of mine would endure the ordeal of a Scottish classical education but looking back I can see the gains — an ability to work hard under pressure, and a lively social conscience. However, memories of my life and privileges compared with the boys and girls I saw every day in Cumberland Street, shoeless and inadequately clad for the ravages of a Glasgow November have left a lasting impression. Children from whatever background deserve the best of educations. Sadly even today it is better to be born with a silver spoon in your mouth!

Nowadays both the Gorbals and Hutcheson's have changed beyond belief. In both cases much of the poverty and the bleakness have gone. Both have lost something too. The new Gorbals could be anywhere, the new 'Hutchi' is just another over-sized good school in a characterless building in Pollockshields. When I delivered the Founder's Day Address

The turbine Glen Sannox approaching Ardrossan in the 1930s and about to take on holidaymakers for the return to Brodick

in Glasgow Cathedral a few years ago, I tried to remind today's pupils that without daily immersion in the Gorbals of the past, their experience of life was sadly lacking. Collecting for charity is a poor, if worthy, substitute for seeing poverty and fortitude at first hand.

What kept me going was the prospect of escape to the Clyde coast — not as easy as it is nowadays with our cars and our affluence. For me it was to Arran for a few brief glorious weeks each summer. Arran was paradise and so was getting there. Where now stands the largest glass-covered shopping precinct in Europe overlooking St. Enoch's Square, there then stood St. Enoch's Station, with its imposing facade, its grey sandstone hotel, and the smell and grime which we conveniently manage to forget when we romanticise about steam engines. It could turn a shirt collar black at a hundred paces. At the bottom of the carriageway which led up to the main entrance were two tin enamelled advertising boards; the art of selling was direct and simple. One said 'A boon and a blessing to men, the Pickwick, the Owl and the Waverley Pen'. The nibs were illustrated. The other said 'Don't be misled, Camp Coffee is the best'. It was years before I realised that misled meant 'mis-led'! The journey to Ardrossan was full of excitement, perched in non-corridor coaches, piled with luggage, dying for that first sign of the sea (and for a loo!) as the train crept down the branch line to Winton Pier, clattering across the level-crossing and into the platform from which tantalising bits of steamer could be glimpsed. It was usually the Glen Sannox. The old lady lacked the space and the cover of Queen Mary II, but she was a flier.

We were hustled aboard, father puffing and grunting under the weight of the cases. Gangways were lowered and we were off to Brodick and another world. Our ultimate destination was Corrie and at Brodick it was Ribbeck's bus we made for. I can vividly recall those little Bedfords with their protruding snouts, the sliding door and the whining gears. Forty miles per hour was beyond their reach and the slightest incline reduced them to crawling pace. Nowadays lovingly preserved survivors take well heeled tourists on exceedingly leisurely vintage tours of the Highlands and Trossachs. Other rival-owned buses were parked at the pierhead with message-boards leaning against the bonnets declaring destinations from Lagg to Blackwaterfoot. Passengers for Lamlash and Whiting Bay stayed on the Sannox. At the frustrating pace of the slowest passenger down the gangplank we were finally off. It was agony waiting for what seemed hours. If you weren't seasick on the Sannox, you could be sure to be bus-sick on the six miles up the coast, but it was worth it.

Those who had filed off with us were quite a different breed from those who went doon the watter from Bridge Wharf. Arran was the playground of the West of Scotland middle-class. They exulted in healthy pursuits — walking, cycling, golfing, tennis, swimming in the sea. They wore shorts to a man, and tennis dresses to a girl. They abandoned Bearsden and Whitecraigs for the 'Fair', and sometimes longer with father 'commuting' at weekends. Few 'took' a house; most made for the same boarding house year after year, ranging from half-a-dozen up-market ones in Brodick in a row near the pier, with names like Kingsley and Gwyder Lodge, to the smaller ones with tomato sauce bottles peeking out behind the curtains. In them all, meal times were fixed and woe betide those who missed them. In Black Rock in Corrie, meals were removed after ten minutes if not eaten. There were positively no seconds — portion control was not invented by MacDonalds but by Arran landladies. The island was apparently deserted at lunch and high tea time. While you had to book the first tee on the golf course three days in advance for 9.30am you could have it to yourself at 12.30pm. If the steamer was late, as it often was, no allowances were made and pies from Woolley's Bakery were the only answer.

Our destination was Lichfield, the name oddly chosen for what was a tiny red-sandstone cottage which had once been the foreman's house for the quarry. One of the windows was still adapted for dispensing wages on Fridays. It belonged to my great-aunt Grace upon whose generosity we depended entirely. She was the widow of Archie, my great-uncle who had been a sea-captain sailing to the Far East. He had come to Corrie to visit my grandfather, a quarryman who had forsaken the slate of Luing for the sandstone of Arran, and had there cemented a relationship with Grace Watson which gave us our links with Arran. It was never clear how long he had been dead, but it was a long time ago.

The Watsons were, and are, typical of many Arran families. They spend the winter in Craegard, an imposing house, standing high above the shore where the road goes up to the artists' colony of white cottages at High Corrie. In summer they retreat to the outhouses at the back so that the house can be let. The contrasts in convenience were stark in the fifties. The outside loo was perched precariously above the burn. Excessive heaving caused it to tremble alarmingly — all the better to go quietly!

The retired generation looked after chickens, reminisced, and ate pancakes made in prodigious profusion by aunt Grace on the open range and covered in butter churned that day. In the corner beneath the waggity clock sat Hamilton, near to 90, his eyes twinkling through the haze of black plug smoke from his pipe. Hamilton had been the engineer of a puffer — a real-life Dan Macphail. The last of the line, The Roman, still lay at Brodick Pier. Hamilton was as equable as Dan was morose. He was at pains to disown Para Handy and the Vital Spark. Nevertheless as tales unfolded of an evening, it became clear how close to the mark Neil Munro had been. Hamilton had never married, but he'd been ashore in his best rig at many a dance and ceilidh from Lochranza to Crarae and Furnace. His puffer had been on the 'Secret Service' during the war. He'd been to Scapa Flow. His engines had always been immaculate, his haystack boiler in finest nick. One only had to glance at his pride and joy for confirmation. It was an ancient Velocette motorcycle, gleaming from cylinder to brass paraffin lamps, their wicks trimmed to perfection. It purred into life with the first thrust of his rheumatic foot. No museum could rival its perfection of preservation. It never left the yard; just before he turned his face to the wooden wall at the back of Craegard for the last time, he broke it into pieces — an uncharacteristic gesture from such a quiet gentleman. He it was who first took myself and my sister mackerel fishing of an evening in his wooden boat. In those days, you could fill a boat in an hour, and row back knee-deep in fish. Sadly mackerel are only at their best within hours of being caught and freezers for domestic use were unheard of. Cold larders were the only refrigeration we knew. Hamilton let us overdo it once, and then we learned to take from nature only what we needed. To this day I put back almost all the trout and salmon that I catch. I went back to school and won an essay competition — the only bit I can remember was about 'the pelucid water chuckling beneath the keel as Hamilton rowed without apparent effort a boat whose varnished hull reflected every ripple'.

None of the younger generation at Craigard had married. George was the butcher. He had no shop. He had a blue Fordson van of uncertain vintage. George never walked; when his van stopped he ran to the back, and in one movement threw open the doors and pulled out a board to give some shelter to his customers. The shelves groaned in the morning at 7am when he left on his rounds. Heaven knows at what time he got up to prepare in the meat-store behind the house. There was nothing fancy

— mince, braising steak for boarding house landladies, popeseye for the gentry, lamb and pork chops (with spice as an optional extra shovelled from an oversized tin pepper-pot) and sausages. It was plain fare augmented by tins of spam, Jean McGregor's Scotch broth and beans. George doubled as lifeline and town-crier in one. Corrie had no pier to act as a focal point. No longer did rowing boats from Ferry Rock put out to meet the steamer. By the time George had progressed from Craegard to Sannox and back, all that was worth knowing was known.

On Sundays he rested, and the Sunday paper van took over. It did not reach Corrie until noon. A fishing boat brought the papers to Brodick leaving Ardossan at dawn. There were even juicier tit-bits in Corrie than in the pages of the *News of the World* and *Reynolds News* — the former never referred to by its proper name but by euphemisms such as 'the journal'. It was frequently read concealed within the more seemly pages of the *Sunday Post*. I read it avidly — in today's terms it was gloriously coy... 'Female undergarments were found in a bush... intimacy then took place'. My imagination ran riot.

Apart from the excitement of the papers, there was much church-going in Corrie. It was always a surprise to see folks in their Sunday best — they looked so different as they walked to church. There was but one bus on a Sunday and few cars. The bus left Corrie Post Office at 2pm for Brodick and returned at once, then lumbered off on another round-trip at teatime. Apart from the odd visitor its occupants were entirely male and still dressed in their suits and ties. Queries as to why they went to Brodick were met by the baffling explanation that they were 'bona fides'. In time I learned about the idiosyncrasies of the licensing laws — only those 'travelling in good faith' were entitled to refreshment on the Sabbath. The definition of travelling was, I think six miles. Thus, the drouthie men of Corrie were transported to Brodick for a half and a half pint (or several of the same) and, in order to maintain a seemly social balance, the good men of Brodick paid a weekly exchange visit to the public bar of the Corrie Hotel. Everyone seemed happy with this cordial arrangement, from the busdriver on overtime and a snifter to those who had had their vision so thoughtfully broadened by the government legislation. Similar arrangements no doubt existed in Lamlash and Whiting Bay, Lochranza and Blackwaterfoot.

George had been in the RAF and retained a services haircut. His immaculate striped apron was complimented by shining black boots, all spit and polish. His way with the young was leg-pulling backed up with an uncanny knowledge of the teenage island romances of the day. However discreet, the participants could not fool George. Odd that a man of such humour and energy appeared to us at least to have no private life of his own — or did he?

George was a man of the world. Donald, his brother, was a shepherd. He was shy and reserved but not withdrawn. He worked with uncle

The 'bona fides' bus at Whiting Bay, c1948 with the Jeanie Deans at the pierhead. GRIMSHAW COLLECTION

Sandy at the steading across the burn. They seldom spoke. Sandy was in any case in some kind of permanent disgrace. Annie his wife was not approved of in the village. Heaven knows why — in her printed dress, inch of knee and black wellingtons (in those days, like Fords, you could have any colour you liked as long as it was black), she worked from dawn to dusk with the cows. The byre was whitewashed and clean, the straw sweet and fresh, and the Ayrshire Cows, which came in brown and white, were milked twice a day by hand. Annie taught me to milk — perched on a three-legged stool, dodging the swishing tail, and jamming my knee against its leg. 'Cows kick forward and horses back', she explained. At first my hands ached with pain and frustration. I just could not match those solid rhythmical spurts from the udder which soon filled the galvanised pail which Annie gripped between her knees. Later I could cope with my share — six beasts or so; it was oddly satisfying sitting in the byre, head resting against a warm flank, hands pulling almost expertly. The product went to the kind of spotless dairy you now see in museums, with butter churns, milk-churns and coolers that looked like mangles with wash-boards incorporated.

Sandy hefted a pair of the churns into the back of the milk cart every morning (except Sundays). On a summer morn at 7am one could invariably see Sandy three houses ahead of George. Sandy was taciturn and no rival to George as a gossip. His horse shared his temperament — it had an evil rheumy eye, and was reputed to bite. It stopped unbidden only at the houses where Sandy did business. Sandy dispensed milk into an assortment of receptacles, none of which was a milk bottle. They ranged from tin jugs to white enamel ones with lids, and at the big house one which looked like pewter with brass handles. Cats popped out to lick up the spillings from the tap. Unlike today's milkmen, Sandy had no side-lines, neither bread nor orange-juice. His milk tasted like no milk does nowadays — creamy, defiantly unskimmed and to the healthy eaters of today — lethal. Sandy was not all that keen on visitors even if they were paying customers. His party trick was to fumble pathetically with the can as he handed it back, spilling some milk, which almost always had the desired effect of extracting profuse apologies from the more gullible ladies from Milngavie while increasing sales at the same time.

Sandy and his horse had much in common with his bull. Ayrshire bulls with their dark red skin suffusing the white are notoriously fickle. Sandy's had eyes which turned to white ice at a hundred paces. Fortunately this did not seem to have an adverse effect on the cows of Corrie and surrounding district. Discreet and not so discreet calls were paid by lovelorn heifers driven along the road by owners who had to withstand the jibes of George from behind the van. The action was suitably shielded from public view in the yard and satisfaction guaranteed. It was inevitable that at too tender an age I should hide in the hayloft to spy on these clandestine proceedings. These lessons would have rendered any 'facts of life' lectures at Hutchi redundant had the school had the temerity to provide them. I also learned some non-classical words the day the bull escaped and went off to sow some of his oats under private enterprise. It was later said by George that the widow Carlin's cows halfway to Brodick had thereafter had a smug look about them which spoke volumes. By the time Sandy retrieved the beast it had managed to sit on and squash a motorbike and then meander aimlessly into Ribbeck's bus giving it a good dent in the process. I wonder if the Freisians you see in fields today with yellow electronic collars and numbers on their rumps have as much fun with the bowler-hatted artificial insemination 'bull' from the Ministry of Agriculture and Fisheries. I doubt it.

Donald had an altogether more peaceful life. He set off at 6am every day, summer and winter, for 'the hill'. He climbed the 2618ft to the top of Cir Mhor along the ridge and back down. By 3pm he was back after the sort of trip for which climbers with ropes and Austrian mountain boots would have set up base camp, taken two days to complete and boasted about for months. His equipment was a shepherds crook and a parcel on a string containing his rough-hewn sandwiches. He drank from the clear, soft mountain streams. He covered miles with his two dogs, tending to his sheep, rescuing them from all sorts of pickles. Sheep have only one aim in life and that is to die as quickly as possible. Nothing pleases them more than lying on their backs with their feet in the air like a Thurber dog. Donald was dedicated to their survival physically, and his own economically. It was hard. When I was 16 I spent a summer as his apprentice and consequently I have never lost my love/hate feelings for sheep. I only have time for real black-faced sheep, not those effete southern softies, which now seem so much in favour. When I was responsible for an agricultural college in Suffolk in the eighties, the staff pandered to me by putting six black-faced sheep amongst the Suffolks so that I could lean on the gate and bore them stiff with half-baked advice.

On clear days Donald and I were rewarded with a view which made all the hardship worthwhile. This vista stretched from the Argyll hills, Bute and Cumbrae in the north to Holy Isle lying below on the eastern side of Arran at the mouth of Lamlash Bay, and on to Ailsa Craig due south in the far distance. There were whole weeks when we saw none of this and the mainland could have been as far away as America, except that the Glen Sannox seemed too small to be a transatlantic liner as she passed back and forth. Real liners did pass on their way to Canada; I was to see them at much closer quarters when I achieved my dream of working 'on the boats'. In the meantime I learned how to care for ewes and lambs, rubbing pitch into sore hooves and cuts, and applying the age-old remedies which have since been replaced by antibiotic injections. No wonder shepherds now need these shrunken bicycle tractor-things to carry their portable pharmacies around. Sheep still seem to die just as happily, if anything ewes look even more harassed as they care for the twins and triplets which selective breeding has brought upon them. In the hillfoots near where I live, shearing and dipping is still a communal activity as it was in Arran, and it is still backbreaking work. Have you ever tried hefting a reluctant ewe into a dip it doesn't fancy and then getting on with the next couple of hundred? No wonder Border farmers make such good rugby players. Even I made the Second XV the next season and found the training dead easy. I might not have done if, on my last day with him, Donald had not sheared the head straight off an adder which was poised to strike at my bare ankles. I was to learn again and again how courageous and calm these quiet diffident men are. I have also a healthy contempt for all those naturalists who tell you how inoffensive adders are.

The serious life of Corrie went on largely beyond the visitors' ken. Where village and visitor came together was at the ceilidhs in Corrie Hall. Officialdom seemed to have decreed that from the Butt of Lewis to Arran these buildings were to be constructed of corrugated iron, walls cream and roofs red. Inside, Corrie Hall was spartan with a trestle-table for the tea-urn, a rather rickety platform and round the walls a motley collection of chairs for the combatants! Records were the source of music, from a distinctly unreliable gramophone which gave a whole new meaning to the Hesitation Waltz. The more enthusiastic the dancing, the more likely was the needle to jump. I knew something about what was quaintly described as 'ballroom dancing' having gone — as did all those from the Glasgow fee-paying schools — to McEwens' School of Dancing in Sauchiehall Street. There were two such institutions — according to legend Roger and Alice fell out 20 years before. Roger's was for me a heady mixture of excitement — girls and humiliation — adolescent lust tempered by two left feet; when I reached Corrie the records were the same — Victor Sylvester 78's, but the approach and execution were a mite more robust.

I learned Scottish country dancing from Annie Watson, the sister of

George and Donald. The cares of Craegard were shed in Corrie Hall on Wednesday and Saturday evenings. She danced like gossamer and was inexhaustible. She it was who told me that my grandfather, the quarryman, had been known as 'Dancie Graham' and deservedly so. We made quite a team, with background support from Jimmy Shand, Bobby McLeod and Will Starr. We quenched our thirst on orange juice and Ir'n Bru — Corrie Hall was temperance too.

Occasionally the Shiskine Band came to play live and clearly brought their own booze — they had to be helped on and off the platform, and seldom made it out of the village without ending up in the ditch. In full flood they never missed a note or a beat and I never heard them play sober. Their accompaniment to Strip the Willow inspired us to prodigious feats. At the end of every progression along the line, the aim was always to birl the girls as high into the air as possible. Due to this practice I once 'joined' the band on stage as I misjudged the centripetal forces my own energy had created; I lost my grip on Annie and plummeted headfirst into the inebriated musicians. On the whole we were rather well behaved. We did not need to act like teenagers because the phrase was not coined, allegedly by James Dean, until 1955. If it was not a golden age, it was at least uncomplicated. Girls were to be kissed on the way home, after a squeeze or two on the dance-floor. The goodnight kiss was not a prelude to anything more significant.

On Thursday night the hall was transformed into a cinema. An aged projectionist appeared from Brodick in an asthmatic Austin Twelve packed with shiny circular filmreel containers. The projector and screen were slowly assembled then came the bit it was worth coming early for — putting up the black-out — summer evenings were long in Corrie. The curtains and boards had first been put up in wartime. Either they had not worn well or else Corrie Hall must have been an excellent reference point for the Luftwaffe. We watched our epics in twilight. The things in which I later indulged in the Golden Divans at the Elephant in Shawlands were strictly not on in Corrie. The back row of the Corrie Hall was where the sun set just as it did in the movies.

I wonder if the great producers of Hollywood and Elstree ever grasped the danger of their masterpieces coming in reels. In halls throughout the Highlands their purple patches could be ruined if one ended in the middle of the great drama as it unfolded. There is nothing worse than 'denouement interruptus'. Breakages of film were more random, but five restless minutes punctuated only by sighs and muffled curses from the projectionist was something not even *Gone With The Wind* could survive intact. Ronald Reagan became President in spite of it. The closest we came to riot in Corrie was the night on which the final reel of *The Cruel Sea* turned out to star Groucho Marx. Jack Hawkins apparently inadvertently starred as a Marx Brother in *Catacol* on the other side of the island. The Austin Twelve left Corrie in record time that night.

It is difficult on an island like Arran to remember that everything supplied or consumed has to come by boat — everything from buses and tractors to the contents of the Miss Logans' 'Jennie'a Things' at Ferry Rock — an emporium which could then supply everything from a tin of Zebo or the Glasgow Herald to an umbrella or an oil lamp and which is today, inevitably, a bijou craft centre. All Arran's coal came to the stone pier at Brodick on the puffers. At this time it was the Roman which had been built in 1904 and survived until 1958. She had been built for the firm of John Hays, but by this time had been acquired by the Kelso family of Corrie whom we knew slightly. They had an elegant house at the Sannox Burn, where my father visited Ebbie (Ebenezer no less) with whom he had taught in Glasgow. My sister visited grandson Willie with whom 'she walked out' for a time thus raising hopes of a suitable marriage. I encouraged her on the basis that I might become a deckhand on the Roman.

Puffers got their name because their primitive engines expelled steam in audible puffs through the grimy funnels which sat right in front of the wheel-house near the stern. Below was the engine-room where engine-men like Hamilton Watson ruled. They seldom had or needed paper qualifications, but they were skilled and ingenious men, who had to make-do and mend far from their base in the Glasgow docks. In time many of them became skippers where again knowledge and experience mattered more than certificates and fine uniforms. Boats like the Roman had a total crew of three. Only the seagoing ones rated a cook/deckhand as well. The great thing about them was that they could beach themselves alongside a pier or on the shore and float off on the next tide. We can all remember the clouds of steam from the engine for the winch as the crew toiled on a summer's day to unload coal or to load sacks of Arran Pilots for the potato market. Peering through open doors, as far as one could see, the living space was primitive with a coal-fired range to provide heat and cooking. Crews had to supply and cook their own grub. The loo was in a small hut up by the mast — public, draughty and primitive like the rest of the vessel. The men who sailed in these boats had nerve, skill and character — they were indeed, in the words of Para Handy 'Bruttain's hardy sons'.

Heavier goods came from Ardrossan in the cargo-boat Arran later renamed Kildonan to free the name for the first ever car ferry which proved to be far too small for the growing trade of the fifties. Kildonan looked like an overgrown puffer. She was twice as long at 120 ft and had diesel engines which thrust her along at a breakneck speed — by puffer standards — of 10 knots! She could carry ten passengers who were invariably locals or visitors who had missed the Sannox. She left

The PS Glen Sannox in the 1890s at Brodick Pier. MCLEAN MUSEUM, GREENOCK

Ardrossan before 7am with mails, newspapers and cargo, and was in Brodick soon after 8am. As the Sannox did not appear until 11am her arrival was much appreciated. Things appeared much earlier than they might. Letters could be delivered and answered on the same day, though I doubt if that degree of urgency was typical of the natives. Tycoons in shorts, cut off from the office in St.Vincent Street, or Blythswood Square, probably appreciated it more.

I once stood on the pier watching the Arran/Kildonan loading for the return trip. Mailbags, luggage, a bent Fordson tractor were followed by cattle being driven down the ramp, over the gangway and into her hold — some of them sired by Sandy's Bull; what a hosing out there had to be at Ardrossan and woe betide those downwind on the way over.

Apart from the daily call at Lochranza by the Duchess of Hamilton on her way to Campbeltown, everything happened when the Glen Sannox reached Brodick at 11am and 3.20pm. Nowadays the sense of occasion is missing as cars pour off and on with monotonous regularity from slab-sided ferries berthed in seconds with bow-thrusters and fancy rudders. It took real skill to coax the Sannox alongside in all weathers; like most of the turbines of those days, it took all the experience of the great masters with little margin left for error. Finally gangways were on and organised confusion ensued. People poured down the gangways, young and old, tripping over pets and suitcases, into the embraces of relatives or, more affectionately, friends. Bags of mail whizzed over the rails, boxes and trunks were loaded on handbarrows and the turnstiles clanked — even going on to greet the boat rated the full tuppence. Later the returning crowds which had poured off the Bedfords of Ribbeck's and Gordon's to make way for the new arrivals, made their way sadly and soberly aboard and she was off, usually late but relying on her 20 knots to let her catch up. She looked elegant but old-fashioned. It was rumoured that she had been built in haste for the railway company in 1925 by Denny's of Dumbarton. She was almost identical to the first ever of the turbine steamers, the history-making King Edward, built in 1901 and the Duchess of Argyll of 1906. Perhaps they were in too much of a hurry to up-date the plans. She spent most of her life on the Arran run, even through the war and became a great favourite. The most exciting thing that happened to her was having one of her saloon plate-glass windows shattered by a basking shark in Brodick Bay. Fortunately it was before the war or else they might have thought it was a U-boat or even an escaped torpedo from Loch Long! Her saloons and dining-room were as elegant as you could wish, but there was little cover on the decks for traditional Glasgow Fair weather. It took strong men to brave the decks in the 'death boat'. This left Whiting Bay at 6.25am. and Brodick at 7.05am designed specifically to get father into work in Glasgow by 9.02am at St. Enoch's. There were of course no boats, bona fide or otherwise, on Sundays.

Much is written nowadays about declining standards of service, and the value of competition, and the Arran run bears this out. In August 1892, Caledonian Steamers boasted Arran to Glasgow in 80 minutes, leaving Brodick at 8.05am. The train alone took 70 minutes in the 1950s. 1892 was the year in which Caledonian's paddler Duchess of Hamilton was challenged by the Glasgow and South Western's elegant Glen Sannox, one of the fastest and most elegant steamers ever to grace Clyde Waters. Built in Clydebank she was claimed to have achieved 20+ knots in trials — a prodigious speed for a paddler, probably unsurpassed by any other and barely matched by her turbine successor. The eyes of Hamilton, the Corrie puffer engineer, positively glowed as he described her to me — 'the loveliest vessel of her age'. G&S.W's colours were red funnels with black tops, white upper works and light grey hulls. There were gold crests on her paddle-boxes and with her great length and twin pencil-thin funnels what a sight! Hamilton also remembers the passengers being virtually frog-marched up the gangways and bundled into the train — 80 minutes left no time for stragglers or even luggage. Today the average journey time by car ferry and train is two hours and ten minutes.

Even this looks good when compared to the winter timetable in the early fifties. Ardrossan was often storm-bound for vessels lacking today's power, and so the winter-base was Fairlie in the shelter of Cumbrae. This meant an extra 20 minutes in the boat — no laughing matter for the weak of stomach, and of course the train had to puff all the way back

35

along the coast to Ardrossan before turning towards Glasgow. The compensation was that the winter-boat was the Marchioness of Graham. We tended to claim a family connection, as my father maintained, quite without proof I may say, that we were Grahams of Montrose and not of Monteith, and 'belonged' to the clan whose chief now owned Brodick Castle and had steamers named after his wife! She (the steamer that is) and I were both of 1936 vintage. She was built at Fairfields in Govan, and was the only turbine at that time to have only one funnel. She succeeded a similar vessel, the Atalanta, whose engines were said to have been working models for the Cunarder Lusitania alongside which she was built in the famous John Brown's Yard at Clydebank in 1906. The Marchioness was small and intimate and her 17 knots were fast enough for winter. She was a grand seaboat, with good steam-heating in the saloons.

In the winter youngsters could hide below decks and peek out of the openings in the sides beside the engine room. She had an empty space behind the funnel for the stowage of motor cars, eased aboard over the perilous planks. She was an odd forerunner of today's car ferries. She had an unfortunate liking for the Isle of Cumbrae; twice to my knowledge she managed to run aground near Keppel Pier, fortunately with little damage other than to her dignity and the master's reputation. She spent most of her summers as the Ayr excursion boat and in 1954 when the Glen Sannox was towed off forlornly for scrap, she took over the Arran summer run on her own. The coming of the new Glen Sannox in 1957 heralded the end of her winter work on the Arran run. A year later, as the last coal-burner left on the river, unglamorous but friendly, she was withdrawn. Happily, as with so many Clyde boats she found a new life in Greece. I sailed on her, much altered and modernised, on a sun-drenched day trip from the Piraeus in the late sixties. To me she will always bring back happy memories of a winter's trip across steel-grey white-capped waves to an island devoid of its summer trippers, dominated by a snow-covered Goatfell, and with Ribbeck's faithful Bedford Duple at the pierhead.

Inversnaid

In the spring of 1954, and almost 17 years old, I acquired sufficient highers to guarantee admission to university. That one of these passes was in mathematics is a perpetual source of wonder to me, matched only by my surprise the day the Secretary of State asked me to conduct a national investigation into this very subject in England in 1988. This confirmed my father's fairly low opinion of both the English and myself. With entry to Glasgow University secure, and parents struggling financially to pay for a university education, conscience drove me to seek gainful employment for the summer vacation. It was easy to get casual jobs then, with the sole exception of the one I coveted — student purser on the Clyde. These were reserved for the sons of senior railwaymen and were, to put it mildly, rare. It was therefore suggested that hotel work in a congenial spot was worth trying. There was a vacancy at Inversnaid Hotel on Loch Lomond for a hall-porter: one of the duties jumped out from the details — catching the ropes and pulling on the gangways for the steamers. I signed on.

Rather later I consulted a map of central Scotland and found that Inversnaid had much in common with Dunoon; although on the mainland, geography had made it virtually an island. To get there by road involved going first to Aberfoyle, then taking a beautiful, winding single-track road past Loch Ard to Stronachlachar near the head of Loch Katrine, and then continuing for four or five miles over the hills on an unmade road down a series of hairpin bends to the hotel — the only building in the hamlet. The road stopped dead at the pier, although there was a footpath round the lofty falls of Inversnaid and down the lochside to Rowardennan, where the youth hostel lay at the foot of Ben Lomond. Once you had arrived and the car had left, there was no escape other than by small boat across the loch to pick up the Alexander's Oban bus to Glasgow, or by steamer to Balloch and the train. I was fated to join a closed community.

The owner of the hotel had suggested that rather than risk the perils of the long way round we take the Oban bus, alighting at the jetty on the opposite side of the loch from the hotel, where we would be picked up by boat. I was to be accompanied by Noel, a fellow sixth-former, who had also secured a job at Inversnaid. My father, no doubt anxious to make sure that we at least got off to a good start, volunteered to drive us to the jetty in the Standard Fourteen. In pouring rain and with a cloudbase at loch level, we made our way from Balloch, through Luss and Inverbeg. Having negotiated the hairpins of the Bonnie Banks we at last reached Tarbet, where we paused at the hotel for afternoon tea, served by students like ourselves. We paid close attention. Reluctantly at 4.30pm, the appointed hour, we made for the jetty. The rain had if anything intensified and we were soon soaked to the skin, as we cowered beneath the silver birches on the lochside. In a sodden suitcase was my 'uniform' of black trousers from someone's old dress suit, two white jackets with stud-like detachable buttons to facilitate washing, and a black tie. Noel and I stood for half an hour in damp, miserable silence, rain dripping from the trees, waves slapping rythmically onto the shore. Half a mile across the loch which lay below a blanket of impenetrable mist, Inversnaid was totally invisible. When the sun did shine the hotel was a magnificent sight set on a little promontory above the loch, gleaming white with slate-grey roof and black window surrounds. It has been greatly extended in recent years and is now rather out of sympathy with its surroundings. It lies in the heart of Rob Roy country with his caves to the north and his prison to the south. I had taken the precaution of reading all about the legends and managed to make a few bob later from the tourists as I regaled them with stories of cattle rustling, claymores, and derring-do.

Eventually a 30ft launch with shelters fore and aft materialised out of the gloom, steered by a spectral figure who turned out to be Willie. His appearance had more to do with drink than with death and with the deliberate movements of the advanced alcoholic, he moored up, beckoned us on board and cast off. I later learned that he was only in his forties, but the white hair, bloodshot eyes and the shaking, nicotine-stained fingers curled around the Woodbine told a different tale. As we beat out way across the stormy waters it transpired from the conversation that he was half-boatman, half-busdriver and the first inkling of what lay ahead dawned upon us. Willie was simultaneously half-gentleman and half-maniac depending upon the alcohol level in the blood. I had met my first Highland Jekyll and Hyde, but certainly not my last.

As we staggered ashore at the jetty which lay beside the pier and close to the fall, I carried my case up 39 steps to the hotel, wondering at the top whether whether it was here that John Buchan had been inspired. It was back-breaking work. Next day I was to carry no less than 40 cases up those wretched steps and then up three flights of hotel

The Sir Walter Scott at Trossachs Pier, Loch Katrine in 1950

stairs. It was Thursday and Glenton tours had arrived. Their bus, an odd muddy-brown in colour, lay across the loch. One of the great novelties of Glenton's five day tour of bonnie Scotland was a sail to a remote and romantic hotel across a Highland loch. I carried the cases back down on Saturdays, before the Sunday lot arrived from Chorley and Batley cracking jokes about kitchen sinks in their portmanteaus but always stopping short of active help. Inversnaid Hotel was one of the first bus-party hotels in Scotland. It was to be good practice for women's outings on the steamers: callow youths grow quickly into men when those ladies are bent on a good time! Male drunks are a pushover by comparison. Willie's job was subject to demarcation rules — navigation and banter yes, humphing the cases — no. The portering was in my job title. I protested albeit weakly that I was a hall-porter and not a pier-porter — for beneath it all the pier had very obvious attractions for me.

Willie's imbibing pattern had to be carefully controlled to ensure that he was, loosely speaking, at his most sober about 1.30 in the afternoon. The steamer disembarked each day at 1.15pm a small group undertaking what was known in the trade as Tour No.1 as well as the usual hikers and the honeymooners. Loch Lomond, Loch Katrine, The Trossachs and Callander was the itinerary and the key link in a complex chain was yet another decrepit Bedford, driven over the hairpins and the potholes past Loch Arklet to Stronachlachar by Willie. Once there the tourists were safely in the hands of normality again in the shape of the crew of the Sir Walter Scott, the tiny steamer which would

39

The Maid of the Loch in 1954 at Inversnaid. Willie's launch Rob Roy is in the foreground. Grimshaw Collection

take them to Trossachs pier. The bus to Callander was a model of dull conformity after Willie and the blue Bedford.

While the unsuspecting tourists had a quick gin and tonic in the cocktail bar, Willie would back the bus out of its battered shed beside the bothy where we all slept and edge it down to the door of the hotel. At that stage you could detect whether this was to be a journey of uncontrolled bravado or white-knuckled concentration. Depite his disposition, Willie never lost a passenger on the way over. On the way back empty, he was liable to lose bits of the bus on rocks or in ditches. If he wasn't back by 3pm we sent out the search party with the tractor and a nip or two to keep Willie quiet. Thank God that due to the steamer times, Tour No.1 could only be undertaken in one direction.

On the only occasion I went to Stronachlachar, I walked. The call by the Maid of the Loch had been cancelled due to high winds, and as a result the hotel was deserted. Willie's bus lay silent in its shed. I tossed a coin with Noel, and won. He would cope with any stray customers for afternoon tea and I would satisfy my curiosity about Loch Katrine and its steamer, which I had never seen. It was an invigorating stroll to say the least, but at walking pace I had ample time to savour the wild beauty of a grey Loch Arklet flecked with white by the winds. I was more than ready for a quiet sail on Loch Katrine. The wind had dropped and the loch was at its inimitable best.

The Sir Walter Scott whose namesake had done so much to bring the beauties of the Trossachs to public attention was, and remarkably still is, a little gem. Built in 1900, she is a real steamer, lovingly preserved and modernised. She patrolled the loch during the war in camouflage in case German paratroopers landed and now she belongs to the Strathclyde Region Water Authority who are responsible for ensuring that Glaswegians get the purest possible water from the loch. At Stronachlachar she passes the rather splendid houses where generations of Glasgow councillors, exhausted by their administrative labours, have had luxury holidays at the expense of the grateful citizens.

Assisting with the passenger launch and tying up the Maid of the Loch and the Prince Edward were by far the best things about working at the hotel. I used to stand in the front porch watching for the first sign of smoke coming round the little island just north of Tarbet pier. I then had precisely ten minutes to unlock the turnstiles, bring out the gangway and perch on a bollard with studied nonchalance. The Maid was new and very grand, the Edward an exquisite piece of Edwardiana. We soon got to know the crews and sometimes earned a word of praise from the skippers for a smart piece of ropework. They brought news of the outside world and of the gossip in the other tiny lochside communities. How I envied the pursers in their white officers' caps and navy tunics, counting the passengers and collecting the tickets. The nearest I got to that sort of thing was counting the hapless, unsuspecting souls onto Willie's bus. The rest was hell without respite from 6am to midnight.

It is hardly possible for me to do justice to the Naishes who owned the hotel. In their mid-sixties, they made a remarkable pair. Mrs Naish had the bulk and the firepower of a battleship. Her voice was louder than a foghorn. She was the first of some redoubtable women who cropped up in my career, long before the days of womens' lib. Such women do not need the assistance of feminism to terrorise the weaker sex. Even now the recollections induce a cold sweat. I spent one Christmas stocking the shelves of a pioneering supermarket — Goldberg's Discount Warehouse in the Candleriggs. Miss Brown, the manageress, was more of a torpedo boat, slim, fast and deadly. The food shortages were lingering on and she had laid two cases of tinned salmon aside for the directors' wives. I discovered the cache in the storeroom and in all innocence sculpted them into a most tasteful mini-pyramid. Like seagulls detecting a field being ploughed, women appeared from Argyle Street and Auchenshuggle and the pile crumbled before my eyes. The inevitable aftermath did little for my self esteem and clarified my ancestry to Miss Brown's satisfaction.

But Mrs Naish comfortably topped the lot, especially when supported by her red-haired daughter Lucy. If those casting for the ugly sisters for the Pavilion Christmas panto had had to make do with a mother and daughter, here was the perfect pair. Nothing pleased them. The chambermaids, douce lasses from Lochboisdale, South Uist, were held in a constant state of terror, the waiters were cowed and the kitchen staff sullenly rebellious. I learned fast at Inversnaid.

'Daddy' — as both women called him — had been a fighter pilot in the First World War. He confined his activities to the cocktail bar, behind which he cut an impressive dash. His silver hair, the bristling handlebar moustache and the synthetically anglified accent (unless he had downed a couple of sly drams) lured many an unsuspecting visitor to ask him about the war. There was then no escape for them over the course of the next two hours of utter boredom. Naish simply bludgeoned them into submission with his stories. Only drink could dull the pain. He had fought duels with the Hun in the days before machine guns. The form, according to Naish, was to fire off revolvers at each other, miss, and come as close as possible to shaking hands with the enemy before flying off into the sunset with honour satisfied on both sides. But he was no match for his good lady. In the cockpit of the cocktail bar he felt secure; he ventured beyond its protective ambience only on rare occasions. One such was when he fired me. It was the only time I have seen a grown man literally dance with rage.

A typical day went like this. Up at 6am, dust the entire set of public rooms, in the sure knowledge that a sterile finger would be smoothed along every ledge to detect skimping. The floors were vacuumed next. Then it was into the kitchen to wash up after breakfast. I discovered then how important status is. The chief washer, a surly refugee from Govan, specialised in cutlery. Crockery was beneath him and plainly only worth the attention of the likes of me. To this day I still feel superior washing up the forks rather than the plates. After that it was the suitcases, the fond farewells to the blue-rinsed septuagenarians (and perchance a few welcome tips), in with the first steamer and then back to the kitchens for the lunchtime debris.

Thereafter I literally came into my own. It was siesta time for the Naishes, the waiters, and the kitchen staff. But some cars would struggle through from Aberfoyle, their occupants bent upon afternoon tea, often shaking uncontrollably after an encounter with Willie and the bus.

I have seldom seen my mother at a loss for words. Revelations of Willie's drinking sprees and about the kitchen porter who topped up with meths and set after Lucy with a carving knife, she could take. However, the news that I personally was making sandwiches, buttering scones, and setting out cakes on stands was too much for her. What I made sure she was kept in the dark about was the innards of my sandwiches. I processed through a hand-mincer all the scraps of congealed fried eggs and bacon left over from the kitchen, including those from the guests' plates. The outcome was surprisingly attractive to look at and simpering matrons in cloche hats from Kelvinside used to single them out for particular praise. A stray fingerprint in the butter would create outbursts of disapproval in comparison. I seldom risk eating minced items in catering establishments now, although I am sure that at Inversnaid and elsewhere today hygiene is beyond reproach. These ladies were good tippers once they learned that I was a poor student and I managed to keep these tips too because no-one else was around. All other declared tips went into a kitty from which, such was the way of things, the Naishes extracted 60%, most probably in recognition of the fact that they realised everybody was on the make. All the staff in the hotel excelled at being tipped surreptitiously. Absolutes about honesty are harder to define in the real world than in the theoretical world of the classroom.

I inadvertently reserved my grandest appearances for dinner. I was not permitted to serve at table, but the clearing of tables was my task. I used to drop everything and was only saved from the wrath of the Naishes by a lovely lass from South Uist who took pity on me and adopted the role of sweeper as I made grandly from table to pantry with the clatter of cutlery on parquet the audible betrayal of my incompetence. I did, however, master pouring coffee and milk simultaneously from two huge silver pots. Then it was the washing-up again, augmented by the glasses in the bar. When honeymooners were resident, and they did appreciate the solitude, we had a rota for the bedroom door vigil. This could be very educational. Fortunately I was not there the night a bridegroom opened the door without warning and two eavesdropping maids fell into his arms. It was not clear who was most embarrassed. Years later when it came to my own wedding night, I confused my bride by opening the bedroom door at regular intervals and peering out suspiciously into the corridor .

I got 25/- a week and my keep in the bothy in return for virtually ceaseless labour which not surprisingly promoted a deep sense of injustice in my near-manly breast. Watching the chambermaids, far from home and homesick with only a little English to augment their natural Gaelic was hard to take. Their life was, if anything, worse than mine. They were comely as well, but I swear this had nothing to do with it. It happened the day the Americans came in a Buick. At the pierhead there was a solitary petrol-pump with Benzene emblazoned on a globe at the top, but it did not have the benefit of an electrical power source and had to be hand-pumped. You will be ahead of me on whose job it was to fill the tanks of the occasional visiting Wolseley or Lanchester. It was 16 strokes, up and down, to the gallon. The Buick, it has to be said, was rather splendid and had reached us intact without having encountered Willie. 'Fill her up, boy!' the American said leaning on the trunk (the boot, of course) which was as long as a yet-to-be-invented Mini. I dimly heard the response to my anxious query — around 37 gallons! After ten I could hardly stand and the American lasted another two before we collapsed in a mutual heap. He had, we agreed, now taken enough to get back to Callander and modern pumps. As he tackled the hairpins, Lucy tackled me. She had witnessed from afar; profit from a lush 25 gallons had been squandered. At this moment, and this is absolutely true, as some kind of omen, a headless chicken sped between us and leapt over the end of the pier. It was never entirely clear if it was the kitchen porter with the carving knife, who had decapitated it, and whether he had perhaps had Lucy in mind. Even the dead were quick in Inversnaid..

The summons came and I made my way solemnly but with great, one might say, foolhardy courage, to the drawing room of the Naishes; for in my undoing I had formulated a plan of which Ray Gunter, the formidable Secretary of the TUC at that time would have surely approved. I would negotiate revised conditions of service and remuneration for the entire staff. The only terms revised that day were my own. I would receive £1 in lieu of notice and Willie would convey me in the launch Rob Roy to the other side of the loch in ignominy. The flag, if it had had one, would have flown at half-mast. Willie had grown quite fond of me. Later in life I became an ACAS arbitrator in many acrimonious disputes. I never forgot how little can be achieved by reasoned argument in the face of naked power.

As I stood at the front door awaiting Willie's pleasure, with my suitcase, still in my black trousers and white-jacket, The Maid of the Loch hove into view. I was ordered to get her alongside. I was too stunned to rebel. I caught the heaving line, hauled up the hessian rope, hooked it over the bollard for the last time, and positioned the gangway. As I stood there disconsolately, the purser beckoned me on board. I stumbled up the gangway, caught my foot in the planking and my left shoe joined the headless chicken in the depths. I hopped on, all the way across the deck — conscious of the skipper's eyes piercing my neck from the heights of the bridge — and into the ticket office. Alistair Brown, the head purser turned to me with a smile. 'The assistant purser of the Prince Edward has been taken to hospital. Can you start tomorrow morning or do you have to give notice?' I hopped off, hoping to heaven he would not ask the Naishes for a reference. My belief is that virtue had at last met its just reward. I was drunker than Willie when we finally reached the other side of the loch. It had taken 40 minutes to cover half-a-mile.

Loch Lomond and the Last of the Edwardians

There were drawbacks to the new life and these were not lessened by the hangover resulting from my abrupt departure from the employ of Inversnaid Hotel. I found to my dismay that I had to leave home before 7am to reach Balloch by nine 'o clock each morning, seven days a week. The concept of 'days off' had not percolated to Balloch. The theory was simply that there was all winter to recover.

I was the proud possessor of a free BR pass from Glasgow (Queen Street or Central — both low level) to Balloch but I had myself to find the fare, fivepence I think, for the red number 8 tram from Rouken Glen to Renfield Street. The most suitable train turned out to be the 7.50am from the Stygian hell of Central low level. After being condemned and closed for many years, it is now unrecognisable since it was modernised and electrified. Today's commuters have little idea of what it was like. It was the Cinderella line to the coast and only the most asthmatic of engines in the running sheds were used to puff and wheeze their way through. The whole scene was quite literally breathtaking. You could barely see across the platforms, let alone along them. On this first morning I travelled in a third class compartment, resplendent in a white shirt, black tie, my school blazer stripped of the badge and the rugby colours. The trousers from the Inversnaid dress suit completed the ensemble. Uniforms were not supplied by the marine arm of BR and a late night debate with my parents had resulted in a deal — if I survived this job, next year I could go to Paisley's merchant navy section round the corner in Clyde Street and purchase battledress and trousers.

By the time I reached Balloch the shirt was somewhat less than pristine. Steam buffs always conveniently forget the grime and filth. The train had escaped from the tunnel into the sunshine somewhere near Partick after passing through Anderston and Stobcross — two miles of smoke and gloom. Following the interminably dreary tenements and factories of Yoker and Clydebank, we reached more open country at Bowling, where one could spot the entrance to the Forth and Clyde Canal, its basin in those days always with a puffer or two. Then came a glimpse of Bowling Harbour, now deserted, and views across the Clyde to Langbank. With luck a large ship with attendant tugs could be seen moving slowly up the dredged channel marked with stone buoys. Dumbarton was where the line turned inland again, and at Dalreoch the Balloch train branched off to make its way through the Vale of Leven. At this point I would see for the first time Ben Lomond and the surrounding hills. Hugging the bank of the river Leven, we passed Renton and Alexandria, and reached Balloch where the river was alive with small boats, like a stretch of the Thames misplaced in Scotland. From there it was half-a-mile through the woods, craning for the first glimpse of the Prince Edward. The journey took an hour on a good day.

It was a glorious morning as I climbed out at Balloch Pier. As instructed I made my way to the Maid of the Loch which lay alongside a rickety, narrow jetty used by the stand-by vessel. I could see the inky depths beneath the piles where the planks were missing. The Maid was in her second season — huge and resplendent, the ultimate evolution of the paddle-steamer and as events were to prove, the last of the line. She might not even have had paddles if the water at Luss Pier had not been too shallow for a screw vessel. As it turned out, life being what it is, Luss Pier had been closed in 1952 while the Maid was still on the stocks in A & J Inglis' yard at Pointhouse on the River Kelvin. It did not reopen until 1980. The Maid was dismantled and rebuilt a section at a time on the side of the loch in the same way that so many ships had been built for the vast inland seas of Africa by the Clyde yards. Later on when I joined her crew, I was to wonder if a few screws had gone missing on both boat and crew.

I was issued with an officer's cap and two white cotton tops which were to be washed and worn in sequence. The cap had the slightly smaller diameter of the old NB cap, and the badge was not BR issue but LNER. When wearing it the next year I was to be very well received at Craigendoran where subjugation to Caley rule from Gourock was still resented some six years after amalgamation. I soon learned how to bash and abuse the cap until it took on — in my imagination at least — the romantic U-boat captain's rake which student pursers sought to emulate in the fifties.

Soon it was back over the gaping planks and round to the railway pier where the Prince Edward lay in the sunshine, steam simmering gently and paddle-wheels creeping round, straining herself against the ropes as she warmed up for the morning sailing to Ardlui. Behind her the loch lay mirror-flat with the islands and the shore of Balloch Park reflected in a technicolour perfection. The contrast with the Maid of the Loch was extreme. The Prince Edward was the last of the old slender graceful

Donald McDonald on the right, later to become captain of The Maid of the Loch, at Balloch Pier before the Second World War. GRIMSHAW COLLECTION.

steamers. She reflected an elegance and a pace of life which was beginning to slip away. Until the Maid came, 20 feet longer and nearly twice the tonnage, the Prince Edward had been the biggest, the fastest and the most richly furnished.And she remained the fastest because the Maid seldom made more than 12 knots — and indeed had only managed 14 knots on her trials.The Edward's days were clearly numbered but fortunately I did not appreciate that then.To match the new Maid for her last season, her sleek hull was painted white as were her upperworks and paddleboxes — the latter embellished with a gold and black nameplate and the traditional loch-style horizontal slats.The saloons were white, the funnel buff with a black top. It was quaintly placed smack in front of the bridge which did little to help the view forward. The bridge was wide open to the elements and dominated by a huge steering wheel against which the skipper leant with calculated nonchalance.

He had a buccaneering look about him and a U-boat skipper's cap. He studied me quizzically for some time and in silence. I must have passed muster — just. With a wry smile and a greeting in a rich Skye accent, he welcomed me aboard. I signed the articles which indicated that I would obey orders and refrain from mutiny. I was then warned precisely which parts of my anatomy were at risk and specifically to what, if there was any slackness in my gangway work. Like all of the loch skippers, he had come through to command from the lower decks, with no master's ticket and with a vocabulary bilingual in abuse, both Gaelic and English. I soon learned from his brother, still just a seaman on the waistrope, that he was an inveterate student-baiter with some 30 years practice of the black art. It would have broken his heart to admit that he was really quite proud of 'his' students, many of whom had gone on to be doctors, lawyers and teachers. That first day he seemed to me as formidable as both the Naishes put together. While I never entirely lost my fear of him, I grew to admire not only his skills at handling his vessel but also the masterly exploitation of his image as an attraction to the ladies. On a fine day the bridge was seldom without a merry widow or a rich, awe-struck spinster.

Soon it was down to the purser's office to meet John. His post was one of only two full purser's jobs on the West Coast open to a student. Oddly the other one was on the tiny Countess of Breadalbane which having started life on Loch Awe was moved to the Clyde and later sailed on Loch Lomond as successor to the Maid of the Loch. John was a delight-ful fellow, four years my senior and had been around on the loch for some years. This was to be his last summer. The walls of the office were full of ticket cases, carefully locked at night. These were full of tubes con-taining stiff board tickets the like of which you now only come across as souvenirs on preserved railways. These covered hundreds of different destinations. I was therefore relieved to learn that for the time being John would sell them, and I would check and collect them. I could not even get the old-fashioned ticket-dating machine to work. That was a skill that had to be acquired with time. Virtuoso pursers were reputed to be capa-ble of punching both ends of six tickets in less time than it takes to read this sentence. In comparison today's booking clerks are sadly deskilled, restricted to the mere pressing of so many buttons on keyboards.

John gave me my first lesson in the subtleties of command. As an offi-cer I had nominal rights which in reality could only be exercised with tact. While in charge of gangways, ticket collection and counting passen-gers, I could technically exercise control over the seamen. Seamen of West Highland origin do not take kindly to such duties which they regard as beneath them, a necessary indignity. They have an infinite capacity for disobeying a direct instruction while evading any kind of disciplining. You worked with the grain or not at all. If you were 17 years old, you walked as if on glass. Purser legend is rich with tales of what befell those who tried it on. It was not long before I was to find out for myself.

A tour of the Prince Edward then followed, as the first passengers trickled aboard: most would come by train in those days, ten minutes before we sailed. Below decks West Highland accents were noticeably absent. The rich distinctive dialect of 'the Vale folk' prevailed; the natives of the Vale of Leven are a race apart with an accent all their own. In the dining saloon the waitresses were matronly, designed for endurance rather than speed, and with strong mothering urges. I was to prosper in girth from their kindly instincts. Their patter was the raw material for Tommy Morgan and his skits at the Metropole. The dining saloon was on the main deck forward, the usual arrangement on the loch. On inland waters ships can risk bigger windows at the front and lower down.

Passengers partook of lunch or high tea in panelled luxury at tables with crisp white cloths, bedecked with silverware bearing the company crest. At the same time they enjoyed the panoramic, ever-changing views of one of Britain's longest lochs as the Edward slid along at a brisk 15 knots.

Just as the saloon was luxurious, the galley was tiny and primitive with a coal-fired range. The resident genius was Gordon, a huge gallus youth, living testimony to the excellence of his own cuisine. The only complaint he had ever received was from officers who had tired of too much fresh salmon and agitated for bangers and mash. In this they echoed the famous complaint of the folk of Renfrew that their employers gave them too much salmon from the Clyde in the 19th century! At the after end on the same deck was the tea-room presided over by Kate. Cakes and sausage rolls came daily from HQ bakeries in Gourock. The former were set out in silver cakestands just as in Miss Cranston's Tearooms in Sauchiehall Street, Glasgow. Tea came from a huge urn which was filled in the morning and topped up throughout the day. By afternoon it had the consistency of tar and I became addicted. To this day I cannot face weak tea or the effete Earl Greys and Darjeeling's — I must have tar. Obviously times and fashions change; I have no recollection that she sold coffee at all. Kate's brew found its way to the crew quarters in the focsle, to the depths of the boiler room, and into the open bridge, where its main purpose must surely have been to stave off hypothermia on the wet days. Over the weeks I became accustomed to visiting Kate after we left Balmaha on the up-run. When I could see Pulpit Rock from her pantry window (where an early steamer perished in the 1840s) I had just enough time to drink up and dash to the paddle-box to cope with the hikers for Rowardennan and the youth hostel.

It was time to go to work; the steam of the approaching train could be seen through the trees and I could meet the chief steward, the redoubtable Bob Swann later. I was issued with my hand-counter or 'clicker' as the seamen called it. In those days they were beautifully made of brass and capable of counting to 999 — we did have more at times, but how could we know? Rather like the Falklands, I learned to 'count them out and count them in'. In those happy days it was a fairly nominal duty — tragedies due to over-loading were for the corners of the fading empire and the distant future and happily not for the Clyde or Loch Lomond. The first count I ever did was 217, no more no less.

For the first day I watched the seamen unlash the gangways and heave them ashore. Gangways at railheads were heavy and handling them was another skill to learn to the accompaniment of bruises (mine) and curses (Gaelic). Later, I was given lessons in balancing and lashing gangways and tips on how to liven up the pier staff if they did not punch their weight at their end. This was followed by the etiquette of ticket inspecting. Below decks the cap was doffed and placed under the arm.

49

This did not make punching tickets any easier but it had an old-world charm appropriate to the Edward. Uniquely, her pursers took off their caps on the open foredeck too; this had something to do with the high rate of cap loss on windy days.

At 11.25am the skipper took a last look up the pier — there was always at least one straggler. On his better days he waited. On others it was a fine art to get them galloping before you threw off the gangways just before they made it. A blood brother, master of the car ferry Cowal, used a stopwatch and could cast off with hapless souls still clinging to the gangways. Passengers were clearly for sport as I gradually came to realise. We backed slowly out in a gentle curve, then the telegraphs clanged for full ahead. That always led to much noise, spray and thumping as the paddle-wheels changed direction and began to claw their way forward. We gathered way and my new life had begun. Already I had some qualms about berthing at Inversnaid, but before then there were other piers to visit for the first time.

As at Inversnaid, each visit was an event for the hamlets on the lochside for in the distant past the steamers had been the only link with the outside world. Even the roads were mere tracks and the steamers ran — as many as four of them in those days — summer and winter. It was only in 1933 that winter sailings were abandoned. In the fifties the roads to Balmaha and Rowardennan were single-track and hardly better surfaced than the Stronachlachar road Willie knew so well. Even the main road, the A82 was tortuous and dangerous. Those who now enjoy the new road which extends as far as Tarbet should sample the bit from there up the loch on to Invernarnan to get a clue as to what it all used to be like. No wonder goods still came by steamer in the fifties . In any case with fewer cars on the roads, public transport dominated. If you did not come by steamer, it had to be the West Highland rail-line to Tarbet and Ardlui. In those days a train with only two carriages and a tiny tank engine worked between Craigendoran and Arrochar serving communities along the Gare Loch and Loch Long and both the train and steamer journeys had an air of intimacy and adventure impossible to recreate today.

After leaving Balloch the first call was Balmaha, which was reached by sailing along the base of the loch amongst the islands which included the largest, Inchmurrin. There was a nudist colony there, and when the word spread on a sunny day, the Edward used to heel alarmingly to port as the would be voyeurs lined up for a look. The skipper who normally dismissed all navigation aids as unmanly, nonetheless adjudged Inchmurrin worthy of closer scrutiny through the 'glasses' which were normally left neglected and ignored in the wooden box on which he sat.

Balmaha pier is tiny, projecting from a rocky point into deep water. It is situated on a bend where the steamer passes between Clair Inch and

Inchcailloch. This makes manoeuvring a mite tricky and all the rope work needs to be crisp. The pier master was up to the task. Alec MacFarlane's family was and is a legend, with the boatyard close by and a job as one of the few water-postmen in the UK. If he was not on the pier himself, you would surely see his launch nipping between the inhabited islands in the south west corner of the loch. He was a cheery soul with a lively wit and I came to know him well enough to accompany him on his rounds after the season was over.

After Balmaha, it was all of 40 minutes until Rowardennan. In time, but not this first trip, that meant a visit to the bridge, and a 'shot at the wheel'; after all there was less to hit on this stretch. The seamen were happy to surrender the wheel, making it clear that anyone who wanted to wrestle with it for fun was a penny short of tuppence. There was no such thing as power-steering — it was a system of chains directly linked to the rudder you were moving. I quickly learned not to oversteer: it was too exhausting and gradually the wake resembled a 'dog's hind leg' less and less as the weeks passed. Then it was tea with Kate, and the pier. As there was no tide and little traffic, the gangways were light at Rowardennan, which was just as well since there were no regular pier hands. I found out that if no-one turned up it was my job to leap ashore, catch the ropes and lift up the gangways before attempting to re-assume the dignity befitting an officer. Apart from hostellers the passengers were either lusty mountaineers with hairy legs or folk walking up the path to Inversnaid — much more genteel and given to collecting wild flowers. From here there was a ferry across to Inverbeg which was just as well because many of the climbers and walkers miscalculated and got back just in time to see the Edward leaving on the last run — a small, disheartening speck topped by a plume of black smoke.

Another 25 minutes steaming lay between us and Tarbet. On this part of the voyage I used to pay my respects to the chief engineer. The engine room was on the main deck flanked by the paddle-boxes and open to public view. The chief was an amiable man from Clydebank, who was only ever ruffled by the odd dispute with the skipper if we hit a pier too hard. It was then a matter of fine judgment whether the skipper had 'rung down' on the telegraph too late, or the chief had pulled the wrong lever. The engines of the Edward had two huge cranks which were fascinating to watch. After a while their movement had a mesmerising effect. As she moved there was a perceptible stop-go motion which one soon became used to. It had been much more pronounced on the old-fashioned boats on the loch which had only one crank. Crack ships on the Clyde were 'triple-expansion' types with three cranks on the shaft which resulted in almost turbine-like smoothness.

Tarbet was always busy. Student porters hurried from the hotel to greet us. On this first call I treated them with what I considered a commensurate degree of condescension. Here there was a mass exodus for Tour No.5 — the famed Three Lochs Tour — Loch Lomond, Loch Long and Loch Goil. In the words of the brochure passengers 'find their own way from Tarbet Pier to Arrochar Pier and board steamer for sail down Loch Long via Loch Goil and thence to the rail-head at Gourock or Craigendoran'. For a cost of 14/6d second class you could be back in Glasgow by 5pm having seen some of the finest scenery in the world in a trip lasting six and a half hours. This was naturally a very popular trip for families. One could see little groups toiling away over the hill — it must be a good two miles up and over, with a boat to catch at the other end. You could also do the tour in reverse, so we got the reciprocal load when we got back to Tarbet later in the day. The next year when I worked on the Maid of Argyll on the Clyde, I experienced the complete steamer part of the tour. On a good day and at weekends four to five hundred was a not unusual number for us to disembark at Tarbet. The Three Lochs Tour had started in 1867 but sadly it ceased just over a century later when the pier at Arrochar was allowed to fall into disrepair. What had been a daily service in the thirties had dwindled to once a week as habits changed. It was too easy to cover much of the ground by car, although hardly as much fun.

After Tarbet, it was round Tarbet Isle and the short dash to Inversnaid. As we approached on this first day, I was given the option of staying below, but decided to get it over with. Willie took the ropes with his customary aplomb. Beside him, resplendent in white jacket and black tie, stood a new student on his first day in my job — an early illustration for me of the fact that no-one is irreplaceable! Behind him in echelon stood the three Naishes, looking indefinably smug. Then they saw me — clearly Willie had not enlightened them. They stiffened visibly, turned as one and marched off up the rise to the Hotel. I never set eyes on them again.

In another half hour or so we reached Ardlui at the head of the loch after that beautiful sail past the narrowing fjord-like crags and Inch Vow. On this last leg, I sat at the officers' table and partook of a Prince Edward 'luncheon'. It was hearty fare — soup, meat and two veg, followed by Scotch trifle. It would have been well worth the 6/6d which the passengers paid for theirs. I was now ready for a rest but we had only five minutes to turn round at Ardlui. I noticed that on Fridays we 'lay over' there until 4.10pm and remarked to John that this must be a glorious chance for a break. He gave me a rather old-fashioned look and indicated that I should wait and see! Friday is pay-day he said; the full significance of this remark escaped me until the end of the week.

I remember little more of that first day. We were back in Balloch at 4.10pm having cut the corner by missing out Rowardennan and Balmaha. Then we did the whole voyage again. I remember the evening sun on the loch, that glorious sail past Luss and on through the narrows at full speed — an act of sober bravado by the skipper — and myself beside him sensing the ready acceptance by the crew of the new boy. A very shy seaman from Staffin in Skye sidled up to me and asked if I would do him a favour in the morning. Naturally I agreed, but little did I know what this would entail. I was home just in time to get the next day's tram into Glasgow but precious little left in which to go to bed.

My second journey to work started a tradition. I sauntered up the platform to examine the engine at Central Station. The driver had watched me at Balloch the day before and, flatteringly, recognised me as a fellow-railwayman. He asked if I wanted to travel down with him. No second bidding was required and we made our way to Balloch with an overjoyed student purser on the footplate. Until then I had tended to ignore the tunnels which make up most of the line as far as Partick, reading the much lamented *Bulletin,* little sister of the *Glasgow Herald,* until daylight appeared. On the footplate it was very different. The tunnels were constantly smoke-filled from the sturdy tank engines used on suburban lines at that time. Passing through them with the driver, red-rimmed eyes peering ahead for signals, the fireman sweating at the fire-box to keep up a head of steam for the incline, was an experience which made Dante's *Inferno* look like a barbecue in the back garden of the manse. Quite apart from the smoke, the heat was intense, and it was terrifying to be rushing blind at even 20mph headlong into the inky darkness on a bucking, shaking monster. For the crew all this was routine: it was a signal at red that they really feared. A long stop could reduce driver and fireman to sinking to their knees gasping for air at foot-plate level. So much for the glamour of steam!

It was Bowling before I recovered and began to positively enjoy it although I had not yet had a look at my white shirt. Bowling was where the original line to Balloch had started, passengers coming from Glasgow by steamer and also along the Forth and Clyde Canal. It was the place where the Craigendoran steamers spent the winter in the days before nationalisation. Soon after 1948, they were transferred to Greenock's Albert Harbour nearer to the HQ at Gourock. This meant a long daily trek, via Glasgow, for crews who lived mainly in Dumbarton and the Vale. The rest of the journey was pure joy — Dumbarton Rock, Denny's Yard — the cradle of so many Clyde steamers, and on through the Vale of Leven. Whenever Callum and Archie were on the roster, I travelled on the footplate — with an old pullover on and my shirt in a paper bag!

It was from Callum that I finally found out why the fogged glass windows on the Captain's cabin of the Edward and the Purser's Office bore the mysterious legend 'D.& B.J.L.'. The North British railway had extended the railway from Bowling to Queen Street in 1858 and acquired the Loch Lomond Steamboat Company 30 years later. Soon the rival

Caledonian railway had built the Central line to Dumbarton. The prospect of two railways through the Vale of Leven was narrowly averted by the agreement to set up the Dumbarton and Balloch Joint Line Committee in 1896. The line and the steamers on the loch were separately administered until the full amalgamation process was complete many years later. The Prince Edward was the committee's biggest and last purchase in 1911, although she did not sail on the loch until the following year. Like the Maid 40 years later she was built by A&J Inglis, but unlike her she was floated up the Leven, minus her bridge, funnel and mast. Or at least that was the plan. Unfortunately the river was so low that she stuck fast on a sandbank at Dillichip. Horses were brought down and set to work, heaving and panting, but they could not budge her. Steam traction engines puffed and blew and fared no better. To the great embarrassment of all, this fine vessel was stuck there until the spring of 1912 brought high water. They finally got her off, but their joy was short-lived because she was now too high to get under Bonhill Bridge and became wedged beneath it! This had happened once before to a new steamer and the same solution was applied. A holiday was declared in local schools and the kids traipsed down to become human ballast and so, at last, she made it. The tearoom and galley were as busy that day as her older sister's must have been in the winter of 1894-5 when the loch froze from Balloch to Luss and the crowds who descended from Dumbarton and Glasgow were fed and watered by the iced-in steamers. Even in the fifties there were many folks around in the Vale who could remember both events.

Somewhere along the line, the Prince Edward had lost her mast which detracted from her appearance a little. While the hulls of the steamers lasted for ever in fresh water, apparently not so the woodwork. There were never enough masts to go round. In the days of four steamers they could only muster three masts amongst them. When there were only three steamers there were only two masts to go round, and the Prince Edward and her consort the Princess May — the last two of the old guard could not muster one between them! It seemed too much of a good thing when the new Maid came complete with no less than two of her own. In due course the dreaded rot was to claim one of these too.

That second morning Balloch Pier was a hive of activity The Edward was at the jetty and the Maid was on the early run. The baker's van was disgorging its load and beside it lay a small white van bearing the legend 'S.L. Neill'. Behind this in conclave were the chief stewards Alan Rennie of the Maid of whom more anon, and Bob Swann. Neither was tall but they dwarfed a tiny man called Sammy. I never learned whether he was S.L. Neill or merely an employee. His van was to roll up to every steamer I worked on from Balloch to Millport. He was ubiquitous, a purveyor of haddock for high tea and gossip for high table. If Sammy didn't know it, it wasn't worth knowing. What deals were struck between him and the masonic order of stewards one can only surmise. Sammy prospered and so did they. As recently as last summer a white van with the same name rolled up to the Lord of the Isles at Oban and I almost expected Sammy to emerge. Clearly the contract has outlasted him, and now embraces MacBrayne as well as Caledonian!

Bob Swann had a shock of white hair — parted in the middle, gleaming teeth trimmed in gold, and looked like a prosperous middle-aged undertaker. The smile was just as disconcerting. There was an evening cruise that night, he was short of staff and importuning the innocent. I qualified. Without thought to new-found status, I soon agreed that once the passengers were all on board, with three hours and no piers, I could spare an hour or two. Clearly he had had his eyes open at Iversnaid Pier. Two evenings a week for the rest of the season, it was on with the white jacket and the bow tie, behind the bar pulling pints of McEwans' Heavy which of course had to be sampled to ensure consistency. I had entered into a world which guaranteed free meals for girlfriends and the occasional parent, in return for services rendered. These included drafting letters to the bosses in Gourock to obscure the dividing line between their legitimate business and Bob's private enterprise which involved sundry meat and vegetable contractors and whisky smuggled aboard to be sold as nips at 25% profit via the company's optics. We had a wee embarrassment the night he fell down the gangway and his attaché case flew open to reveal an extremely fetching leg of lamb. I have noticed since that stewards seldom go ashore without a case or a holdall.

Little love was lost between skippers and chief stewards, perhaps because the opportunities for the former to speculate were rather limited. I never saw one with the courage to insist on opening a case, although they complained and muttered behind their backs. Stewards had to be treated with respect. They could bring even a skipper to his knees. A mild rift in relationships could mean a drying up of the supply of tea and scones to the bridge. A confrontation could mean requests for high teas for a skipper's hungry relatives being met with advice as to how tickets were available from the purser in the normal way. One beleaguered skipper at war with both steward and engineer had been forced to seek a transfer for himself!

The reward for my Nelsonian outlook was a winter job as a waiter on Friday nights in the Cameo Ballroom in Shawlands. It was an adjunct of the Elephant Cinema whose 'golden divans' (for two) could be hired for 3/6d, well beyond my means if not my inclinations! I had to acquire in the Barras a decidedly seedy set of tails — in the fifties wine-waiters had presumably to look vaguely like Fred Astaire. The deal was three quid a night plus tips. You paid for drinks at the bar, then conveyed them to the customer and recouped yourself. You've guessed it in one. The barman 'did' me and I 'did' the elegantly attired customers by increasing amounts as the evening progressed and alcohol dulled the arithmetical processes of the dancers. I remained very sober indeed. In his winter guise of maitre de at the Cameo, Bob Swann looked on approvingly. It helped to pay my way through university and I learned that custom and wont and absolute honesty are not comfortable bedfellows. Later in my career when errant schoolmasters were wheeled before me for punishment, I like to think that judgment was tempered by conscience!

As I stood in the morning sun at Balloch Pier, watching the catering tableau, the seaman who had spoken to me the evening before hovered in the background. We sat under the station canopy on the wrought iron seat with 'Balloch Pier' emblazoned on the back. There were long pauses, lapses into the Gaelic, shuffling of feet and lowering of eyes. John, it emerged, could neither read nor write. My predecessor had both written the weekly letter to Jean on the croft at Staffin and read to him the reply. Would I take on the task together with getting the postal order each week on pay day? Of all the taxing and rewarding things I have ever had to do, composing those letters in a style which John could conceivably have used to convey the week's news and his clumsily expressed but sincere affections to Jean was the hardest and the most satisfying. I felt as though I was maturing quickly in the school of life. I visited them on the croft many years later and Jean took all those letters from a brass-bound oak box, complete with envelopes, held together by a rubber band. When she told me she'd never been closer to John than when he was away that summer, the tears were in my eyes as much as hers.

As the summer passed, I made a daily cycle-run up to the bank in the village with the takings — the steward's in one leather bag sealed with wax and the purser's in another with a brass plate bearing the words 'North British Steam Packet Company'. This was also an occasion for posting letters to all parts of the Hebrides and returning with requisites such as Thick Black Tobacco, which some smoked and others chewed. When I returned one day I found the purser's office transformed. We had a carpet on the floor and pictures in the spaces between the ticket cases. Closer inspection revealed that the carpet, a floral silver grey bore the imprint 'LNER First Class'! John had been waiting patiently for first class compartment carriages to be left overnight in Balloch sidings. The pictures in their wooden frames with screw holes at each corner looked oddly familiar too. Over the next few summers, I took part in a number of evening forays to the sidings in various places, to furnish offices and cabins. It was exciting, dangerous and exhausting. You could heave yourself up onto many carriages before finding one with a door left open. Assistant pursers today are not subject to the same temptation and compartment carriages are but a memory. They were great fun if you could get one to yourself with the right company.

Friday at Ardlui

The days passed quickly and I acquired the necessary skills of a proper purser. The culmination of each day was the 'scroll' balance which was done in pencil in a rough book. On each third day it was the ink one, which was subject to closer scrutiny by 'them' — in our case the railway purser on the Maid of the Loch. It was a lengthy process — more so on the Clyde cruise boats which had even more tickets. The tickets were kept in 'tubes' — 30 or more of each type for each destination — first, third, three-monthly, excursion, half-day — dogs, privilege (for railway employees) — the list was endless. In addition tickets for meals were sold by the purser. The dining saloon seated 70 and tickets for several sittings could be sold on busy days. Chief stewards would have much preferred to handle all this themselves.

The bottom ticket in each tube protruded so that its number was exposed. The assistant called these out and the chief entered them in his book. Due note was taken of tubes which were nearly empty which then had to be replenished from the stock cupboard in time to ensure that we did not run out at busy times. Popular destinations were allocated several tubes just in case. Behind this seemingly straightforward logistical process was a massive printing and distribution organisation which beggared belief. You could literally buy a printed ticket from any pier on the loch to hundreds of destinations in Scotland and England. There were also blank cards to be filled out by hand but they were seldom needed. After all the numbers had been entered in the book, subtraction of the previous day's final number gave the number sold. Then it was out with the battered blue 'Ready Reckoner'; much muttering of 'Fifteen at three and six' etc, liberal use of rubber and a final total emerged. Only then was the money counted with bated breath. The banknotes were attended to first, separated into the different Scottish banks which were the Bank of Scotland, the Royal Bank, the Clydesdale, the now-defunct British Linen Bank and one whose name I have sadly forgotten. The remaining notes after all this made up the English pile. Almost all were £1 notes with the occasional large white Bank of England fiver. Only when the Colquhouns of Luss travelled did I cast an envious eye over a crisp tenner. If the cash matched the scroll, joy was unconfined. It was seldom far out, but even a discrepancy of half a crown or so at the end of a long day meant doing the whole thing again. There was frequently an element of 'honest cooking' — a pound or two over one day was stored away for the inevitable day of shortage. It was felt wise to show minor discrepancies occasionally to demonstrate that we were not suspiciously perfect; but if the loss or surplus was inexplicably huge — say £10 or so, we were in real trouble.

Apart from occasionally being allowed to sell tickets, my duties on deck consisted of gangway work, and changing what were known by the crew as the 'fans'. Each set of fans consisted of a vertical pole a few feet high, with pivoting boards attached at the top bearing the names of the piers. Spread out like a fan, they read Balloch, Balmaha, Luss (unused) Rowardennan, Tarbet, Inversnaid, Ardlui. After each pier they had to be adjusted by doubling up the boards no longer required. As there was a fan on both the port and starboard sides of the bridge and you could not always predict which way we would come alongside, you had to look lively. Although a more sophisticated system was by then employed on the Clyde, they were still referred to as the 'fans' to the immediate confusion of all new assistant pursers, to whom the instruction to 'change the fans' came as something of a shock! The word is still used on the Waverley even today.

The other main task was collecting and cancelling tickets. Each ticket, from wherever it originated, was sorted in number-sequence into bundles, after cancelling with a neat, triangulated punchmark. By this time I was not surprised to find that the cancelling process was the exact reverse of the distribution system. There were large bundles collected for Glasgow Queen Street and small ones for, say Kilmacolm or London Euston. The tickets were bound with string, tied with a special slip knot and despatched to Gourock. How they checked them, interpreted them and disposed of them I never did find out, nor did I desire to. It was an effective sanction. I envisaged some bespectacled, gimlet-eyed, inexhaustible inspector checking every single ticket. I hope the knots slipped on them, spraying tickets in all directions. There was also a critical height for each bundle, beyond which it became decidedly unstable. The worst were the Tour Tickets which had not two but three 'halves'; each one being tiny and fiddly. We often set little traps for the head office collectors, for example, every second one upside down and the wrong way round. Nothing ever came back, although I have heard since that in the sixties 'they' were fussier and sent back scolding letters, especially if they found among the 'mis-collections' the wrong half of a ticket to somewhere as far away as London. This was easy enough to do, if passengers handed

*With the entire crew either playing football or in the Ardlui Hotel, some
hopeful passengers await their none too steady return!*
DUMBARTON DISTRICT LIBRARIES

over say four tickets at once, and you failed to note that one was the
wrong way round.

By now you may be wondering why Fridays were different. For a
crew which worked a minimum 12 hour day, seven days a week the
'oasis' of four hours at Ardlui was longed for each Friday. Each department celebrated in its own way. The skipper and the mate (it was he
who piloted the boat into piers while the skipper rung up the movements on the telegraph) took off their caps, replaced their uniform
jackets with sports jackets, and ambled as unobtrusively as possible up
to the Ardlui Hotel which lay 200 yards away through the trees beside
the main road to Crianlarich. It must have been hell for them resisting
the desire to break into a run. Such were the licensing laws in those
days that the bar was shut during the duration of our lie-over. This was
not a problem. Miraculously a side door opened silently as they
approached and then closed behind them. Inside they found foregath-
ered the stationmaster from Ardlui and conveniently, the local consta-
ble, tunic open, cap set aside, his bicycle carefully parked out of the
way of prying eyes behind the beer barrels at the back. As it was Friday,
in the morning the crew had queued at the window of the office for
their pay, in cash, and I had taken the relevant envelopes to the bridge,
the chief steward and the chief engineer. Now there was fuel to feed
the flames! The bar was cool and shady, the lights out, the company and

the crack were good. They enjoyed themselves, with little heed to the return trip.

About the same time a small group emerged from the stokehold, eyes blinking in the sunlight. They were pale-skinned beneath the soot and the grime, their bare arms tattooed and massive. I had only once ventured below through the double pressure doors beneath the huge pistons in the engine room, and into the boiler room. If these doors were left open, any flashback could result in the flames from the furnace filling the whole stoke-hold with fatal consequences. Extreme care was exercised by otherwise totally laconic, laid-back stokers and greasers. Inside was the haystack boiler — that was literally its shape — upright and tall in complete contrast to the horizontal cylindrical boilers of modern vessels. The funnel sat on top of it and a huge furnace glowed at its base into which two stokers threw coal from the vast, black piles trimmed and stacked behind them. Many years later I had to train my wife to do the same task in miniature when we kept our own steam yacht Galatea on Ullswater in the Lake District. Each morning seamen opened manhole covers in the deck and barrows of best Welsh steam coal were poured down the chutes; after this operation the decks had to be hosed down. Illumination in the stokehold came from the fires and one or two naked bulbs. There were also portholes on the waterline, which meant that they had a water-worm's eye view of the world — until, that is, the ship started to move and then the wake plunged them into a world of green water and foam.

At Ardlui they damped the fires down, and made for the football field. This was a rough patch of meadow, studded with boulders and thistles and thoroughly manured by the black-faced sheep and their sturdy lambs. There they found Gordon the cook, who looked after the ball, the galley-boys, a few locals, occasionally a foolhardy passenger, and usually John and myself. No seaman would even dream of demeaning himself by joining in — perhaps had there been shinty sticks, things would have been different. With the hotel effectively out-of-bounds, they wandered off, trousers bulging and clinking gently, revealing that 'arrangements' had been made with Bob Swann. They returned just in time to cast-off.

The youngest, Dougald, once missed out and had to thumb a lift to Tarbet from a foreign tourist whom he managed to convince that he was a customs officer. Dougald had Friday trysts with a lass at the farm up the road. Unfortunately she was married. After her husband found out, he applied for, and was granted, an immediate transfer to the Arran run!

The football matches were epics, every single one. Scoring was high, injuries many and inflicted as much by the terrain as the tackling which settled scores which had simmered all week. Breathers were gained by kicking the ball into the loch or taken while it was wiped down after contact with a cowpat. Until then my football career had been as a rather orthodox left-back with Giffnock North Amateurs. After Ardlui, and a first class degree in mayhem, it was clear that I would never be permitted to satisfy my ambition to turn out for Queens Park, whose matches my father still attended wearing his bowler hat. I suspect that it was as a direct consequence of my Ardlui matches that I was later sent off for maiming the goalkeeper of the Govan Police Team in a late tackle. In the greatest miscasting of all time, I had turned out for the Govan Clergy Select in what was hilariously billed as a charity-match!

It was while recovering from injuries inflicted in retaliation for an injudicious tackle on a stoker, that I decided to have a swim instead. Oh dear. Loch Lomond was, and is, not for the fainthearted. It is a very, very, cold and forbidding piece of water and judged by the annual drowning tragedies, highly dangerous. A man whom I still admire once swam its entire length — 21 miles of sinister malice; when stepping ashore at Balloch, he managed a celebratory jig before collapsing into the arms of his retainers.

John, the seaman whose letters I ghosted, advised me to go round the top of the loch to the Falloch River where the inflow of water had built up a shingle-bank of shallow water. On a warm day the sun could raise it to a bearable temperature. I picked the right day and the right company — she looked very fine in her pre-bikini 'swimming-costume'. Among the more intriguing things we discovered that day was that the mouth of the Falloch looked as if it were man-made. Detective work was called for.

No-one aboard the Edward whom I questioned had a clue. A chance remark from a passenger led me to Inverarnan Hotel which is some two miles up Glen Falloch from the head of the Loch, on the road to Crianlarich. When you first see this old drover's inn in its beautiful setting amongst the trees close to road and river, your suspicions are aroused. You begin to wonder why such an inn, at such an isolated spot? I managed to piece the story together. The road above Ardlui in the mid-nineteenth century was particularly bad, boggy and virtually impassable in winter. In 1847 a rudimentary canal was dug, using the river bed and cutting off the corners where it meandered. At Inverarnan a little turning basin was constructed, together with a slipway for maintaining steamers.

In 1848 the paddle steamer Waterwitch, iron-hulled and built by Denny's, was advertised as sailing to Ardlui, calling at all today's destinations (Luss and Balmaha had only ferries and no piers) and continuing right up the canal to Inverarnan. One can imagine the scene there as passengers and cargo were transferred, the former no doubt suitably refreshed in the inn, to stagecoaches for the journey on up the glen. At Crianlarich one coach turned west to Fort William — what a journey across Rannoch Moor that must have been! The other made east and down to Loch Tay at Killin, there to connect with the steamers which

The Prince Edward under 'full' control again on our way back from Ardlui!
GRIMSHAW COLLECTION

would convey travellers to Kenmore at the northern end of the loch, and thence to the north -east. In time the canal silted up, steamers grew too big for it and the road improved. Soon Ardlui was once again the steamer terminal.

But my curiosity was sufficiently aroused as to what evidence remained. That would need a boat. Today with a flotilla of small craft in the marinas along the loch shore, it would be easy. In 1954 the only rowing boat within sight was the ship's boat on the Prince Edward. This had not been launched to anyone's recollection for years — so much for the Board of Trade safety inspections. It had literally been painted and rusted into its davits. One shuddered at the prospect of it ever having to be launched in an emergency. For reasons which will become clear, John had a certain amount of influence with the skipper. As a result, one sparkling Friday afternoon in September, after a lot of huffing and puffing on a trial lowering at Balloch earlier in the day, the boat was launched and John and I made our way up the Falloch with an oar each.

It was an unforgettable experience. We had to push our way through branches, hack back the jungle and manhandle the heavy boat over the shallows. We had entered another world. We disturbed wildfowl and trout which had probably never seen man. We admired the simple and effective beauty of the early Victorian brickwork on the embankments, still well preserved, but covered in moss and lichen. We got nowhere near Inverarnan, but provisioned by the ladies of the Vale, we were amply regaled as we lay nestled in a tree-lined bower. Eventually we returned triumphant to the Edward where the boat, which had leaked like a sieve due to its dried out planking, was hauled back on to the davits. History had been made, but like so much of the loch's history, it remained discreetly unrecorded. I could not cancel the tickets on the way down the loch for blisters on my hands.

All good Fridays draw to a close. We were due to sail at 4.10pm and in good time the footballers trickled back to flashup the fires and cook the high teas. The seamen checked over the gangways and the fenders. The pursers reopened the office, but kept a wary eye on the side door of the Ardlui Hotel. About 3.55pm it opened and the skipper and mate emerged. Even on calm days they appeared to lean into the wind. Occasionally they stumbled on the rough path. With a supreme effort in full view of the public, the last 50 yards was covered slowly and with dignity. Dressed in civvies, it was not clear to the passengers who they really were. Rejecting any kind of assistance up the gangway the skipper passed our window and into his cabin which conveniently possessed opaque glass to conceal him from view. He would re-emerge in uniform, before slowly ascending to the bridge, his face a mask of concentration. Once seated on his box, he relaxed visibly — fortunately invisible to the passengers. Sometimes he fell off it; sometimes he appeared to sleep. The mate had a tendency to smile inanely.

It was time to act. We knew all the signs. Things were going to get worse before they got better. The skipper's natural bravado was likely to be inflated into quite extravagant views of his own ability At 4.10pm or thereby, he set the cap at a rakish angle, mopped his brow with a large handkerchief and made his way unsteadily to the telegraphs, which he jangled fiercely to waken the engineer. The mate and the wheel appeared to offer each other a measure of mutual support.

While most of the seamen could perform most of their duties at most of the piers, there was no certainty There was little prospect of one of them at the wheel much before Rowardennan. John would have to 'supervise' the telegraphs and I the wheel. On good days we left Ardlui astern perfectly, but at a remarkable rate of knots. On the others, we had several goes at leaving the pier. On one occasion, owing to a little misunderstanding over casting off the mooring ropes, we tried to take it with us. We wove our way down the loch with the skipper slumped on the box, John on the lookout, and myself at the wheel. Skipper and mate were propped up to appear to be ready and present for the piers. On the last Friday of the season, two students virtually singlehanded took a 300 ton steamer alongside at Inversnaid. After a while, fresh air and the passage of time tended to restore the professionals, but a helping hand was still in order. On that same Friday we were much involved all the way down. The skipper insisted on bringing her into Balloch on his own which he performed impeccably, apart from an understandable oversight. He failed to ring down for 'slow astern'. We slid gracefully part way up the beach and the bow stopped just short of the station building. The skipper, with great presence of mind and a remarkable sang froid, mopped his brow with the handkerchief kept up his sleeve, then rang 'slow astern'. We slipped back, tied up, and disembarked the passengers. Not a word was said. It was assumed by the absence of leaks that the flat bottom was intact. The engines and boiler seemed OK. The consensus seemed to be that the authorities had no need to be bothered about such a trifling incident. We completed the remaining days of the season with great circumspection, and without a public enquiry. It is rumoured that many years later, on the last Friday of the season the Maid of the Loch was part way up the River Leven before it was noticed in the dark that the light on the pier was on the wrong side of the boat. It was explained as a perfectly understandable human error — a brief confusion of port with starboard!

Quite abruptly it was all over. There is nothing more desolate than the scene after the last sailing of the season. Only the deck and engin-room officers were retained for the winter. They laid away their uniforms and donned boiler suits and dungarees for the slipping of the boat for painting, scraping, and refurbishment. The seamen took the ropes and deck gear ashore, stowed the seats and lifejackets in the station building and left for the fishing and the croft. The ladies of the saloon became housewives again or worked in local restaurants; Gordon became chef in a hotel and Bob Swann made for the Cameo Ballroom and other such venues.

The Prince Edward looked desolate and forlorn, and although as sound in hull and machinery as when new 50 odd years before, we realised her time had come. The Maid of the Loch was proving too big, too costly. Scarce resources would have to be concentrated on maintaining her alone. Ten years before in wartime, four steamers had been full every day, the only excursion steamers left sailing in Scotland. Changing habits, the motor car, and better roads were tilting the balance.

After we had locked up the ticket cases and taken them ashore and had drawn up the season's balances John returned to university for his final year and I went up to Gilmorehill as a 'fresher'. We were not to sail together again. The Prince Edward, the last of the great Edwardians was broken up on the slipway at Balloch in the spring of 1955. I knew that the assistant purser of the Maid of the Loch, a medical student on a six year degree course, was certain to do another season at least. I faced a whole winter on tenterhooks, wondering if I would be transferred to the Clyde or found surplus to requirements.

I awaited impatiently for the letter from the 'Kremlin' at Gourock due in the early spring. The visit to Paisleys' for the uniform was left pending.

The Cowal and Transition

L ate in the spring of 1955, the letter from Gourock arrived — a flimsy British Rail 'economy' sheet in a buff envelope. 'You are to report
to the Purser of the MV Cowal in time for the 9.20am sailing on a
date in June to be arranged. Your travel pass from Glasgow Central to
Gourock is enclosed.' This was good news with a tinge of bad. I was
going, in spite of an absence of railway ancestry, to be a purser on the
Clyde. Not surprisingly I was to start at the bottom. There were to be no
cruises to exotic places on Loch Fyne, no German Bands, not even lunch
and high tea in a panelled saloon. The Cowal was the hardest working,
most utilitarian vessel in the fleet. Her route never varied — ten return
trips a day between Gourock and Dunoon, with an occasional call at Kirn
the only variation to the routine. She was in service from 6.45am to
8.55pm although as a 'non-resident' I would miss the quiet first run of the
day. The Cowal was only a year old, had diesel engines, and was a car
ferry. I had only the dimmest awareness of what she looked like and of
the life I could expect to find.

The Cowal was part of a revolution taking place on the Clyde in the
fifties. Whereas on Loch Lomond the new boat, partly by accident in a
sense, had been a paddle-steamer carrying on a tradition, things on the
Clyde were to be very different. It is only in retrospect that old-fashioned
steam can be seen to have tourist potential. Paddle-steamers are still popular and heavily patronised on rivers and lakes throughout Europe but
there was to be no future for them on the Clyde estuary.

The Caledonian Steam Packet Company, on amalgamation of the
London Midland and Scottish Railways, and the London and North
Eastern Railways in 1948 would become responsible for all the railway-
owned steamers in the company's Scottish region. This signalled the
nominal end of the rivalry between the steamers based on the north side
of the river at Craigendoran (LNER) and those on the south (LMS) with
headquarters at Gourock. By 1951 the three remaining LNER paddlers
had been absorbed, and their red, black and white funnels painted in the
familiar Caley buff with black tops. The human relations side of things

SUNSET ON THE CLYDE

was to take much longer to sort out. There was an air of unconcealed triumph in Gourock, and well founded apprehension at Craigendoran. The sop of a houseflag based on the LNER St. Andrews Cross and the BR lion and wheel emblem was shortlived. By 1955 all the vessels sported the now-familiar yellow pennant with red lion rampant.

The amalgamated company inherited a largely ageing fleet consisting of coal-burning turbine steamers and paddle-steamers which had survived the war, together with the novel diesel electric paddle vessel (DEPV) Talisman, a unique curio on which I was later to serve. Their dates of building ranged from 1888 (Lucy Ashton) to 1947 (Waverley, the only post-war vessel). Their average age was 22 years. The only motor-vessels were cargo vessels or small ferries. The fleet was strong on glamour and tradition, short on operating efficiency. With rivalries gone and only a single 'interloper' on the Clyde in the shape of David MacBrayne's 'Royal Route' to Tarbert and Ardrishaig, wasteful duplications could be eliminated. Words like 'rationalisation' and 'cost-effectiveness' were being heard for the first time; the age of the grey accountant was at hand. The fleet was too old for doing nothing to be an option. Two other factors were at work, one technical, and the other, for want of a better word, sociological.

The war had seen, as wars do, great advances in technology, not least in the development of the diesel engine. MacBraynes had experimented with motor-vessels in the thirties, but not for their prime summer routes on the Clyde or to Iona and Staffa. It was the less glamorous places which were served by vessels which, while grudgingly admitted as being cheap to run, were slow, noisy and wracked by vibrations and rattles. They were not to be compared with the paddle-steamers, still less with the 'turbines'

The TS Duchess of Hamilton turning into Dunoon, 1955.
GRIMSHAW COLLECTION

66

The MV Arran at berth at Dunoon as the Lochfyne comes in on the Royal Route to Ardrishaig. GRIMSHAW COLLECTION

which could glide along at more than 20 knots in virtual silence. Steam paddle-engines revolve at a speed of about 50rpm and it is possible to feel the 'surge' as the two or three cranks turn the paddles. Turbine engines, in which steam is forced through a cylinder containing hundreds of tiny blades on a shaft which the steam drives round as it expands, and in their marine forms spin at 500rpm plus in silence and without vibration. Their successors now power jumbo jets and nuclear submarines. The turbine engine was the work of the Irishman Charles Parsons in the 1890s and his vessel Turbinia caused consternation at the Spithead review in 1897 when it sped through the fleet at 34 knots leaving the pride of the Navy limping along in its wake. The first commercial application was on the Clyde with the King Edward of 1901, referred to later in this book and built inevitably by Denny's. Her trial speed of over 20 knots and her lack of vibration marked her as the forerunner of not only the greyhound turbines of the Clyde and the English Channel, but also of great transatlantic liners such as the blue riband Mauretania. In the fifties I remember placing a glass of water on the deck of the Duchess of Hamilton at full speed; there was not a trace of a ripple. On the MacBrayne's Lochnevis, you could get a free face-rinse while trying to down a pint in the bar.

By the fifties, it was argued that at least some of the snags associated with diesel engines had been overcome. From now on new vessels would be diesel-powered. The claims made for them in terms of economy were fully justified. No longer were watchmen required to tend the boilers overnight, and stokers to be on duty for hours before sailing, raising steam and turning over engines. Idle and unprofitable days to 'clean the tubes' and clear the furnaces were not required. In an emergency vessels could be at sea in minutes, not hours. Fuel costs were cut dramatically and in an age where strikes were plentiful, oil was less vulnerable than coal, and cheaper.

Where things fell down was over the problems of noise, vibration and speed. The new breed of car ferries such as the Arran, Bute and Cowal, and smaller passenger boats — the Maids — can still be remembered by all who sailed on them for their less desirable features. Conversations were virtually impossible near the engine-room or the funnels. Every knife, fork, spoon and plate, shaked, rattled and rolled its way across the table; in the pursers office, books and papers could vibrate onto the floor. Engineers emerged from the bowels of the ship with an advanced case of St. Vitus dance. In terms of speed they were literally left standing by the vintage vessels; consequently their timetables had to be eased. With an untypical mastery of propaganda it was put about that speed was unimportant and uneconomical. We moved even further away from the days of 80 minutes from Glasgow to Brodick.

The relative unpleasantness was probably partly a function of size. When larger car ferries appeared later, the vibration and noise were less. In more recent times the speed problem has been overcome too. The elegant Tor Britannia which, when living in Suffolk, I used to watch slipping in and out of Harwich en route to Sweden, could manage an effortless 23 knots, with neither noise nor vibration from her powerful diesels. As far as passenger comfort was concerned these drawbacks and their alleged lack of character made them easy targets for the romantics and the traditionalists. Lively correspondence filled the pages of the *Glasgow Herald* and the *Greenock Telegraph*. A debate started which has gone on ever since. Ironically some of the motor vessels were in time to become just as much 'characters' as the steamers. The same has happened with railway engines. The move to diesel on the railways took place at the same time, and no doubt the arguments for diesel vessels were strengthened by railway owners who had embarked on the replacement of the Pacifics with Deltics on the main lines. Nowadays there are as many societies devoted to preserving diesel engines as steam locomotives.

Other changes of a more profound nature were taking place. Holiday habits were altering and while the era of the package tour was still in the future and Majorca and Benidorm had not yet entered the Glaswegian vocabulary, folk were increasingly turning to the brighter lights of Blackpool, Southend and the Isle of Man. As paid holidays became the norm, limited horizons were expanding and requirements grew more sophisticated than those on offer in Millport or Rothesay. While day trips were still in order and many families made the annual pilgrimage to the Clyde resorts, there were undeniable and irresistible signs of change.

An increasing number of people were managing to acquire their first car, my own family among them with the Standard Fourteen which took us to parts of Scotland which had only been place-names on maps before. Brand new cars were just becoming available; after the Second World War the Standard Vanguards, the Hillmans and the Austins had virtually all been for export. The relative prosperity of the fifties brought the new Morris Minor and Austin Sevens within the reach of many families of moderate means. This had a double impact on the Clyde. Numbers of passengers began to decline and the demand for cars to be transported across the Clyde grew in contrast. Dunoon for example could be reached in half the time from Glasgow by crossing the Clyde. If holidaymakers could take their cars, they could also take their luggage with them rather than sending the traditional trunks in advance to be stored by the landlady until they arrived — how much more convenient. The demand for efficient economical services to Dunoon, Rothesay and Brodick grew beyond the capacity of the few vessels which had space on deck. There had to be something better than the dreaded 'planks' which were thrown out from the side of the vessel onto the pier and driven over blind by petrified drivers.

The company was slow to respond. Just before the war there had been plans for a service to Dunoon and designs for a suitable vessel were investigated. The outbreak of war brought this to a halt. The problem was that the piers on the Clyde are all of differing heights and the tidal range is considerable. Many of them are very exposed. There was also the problem that they were mostly privately owned; getting agreement to add ramps would be difficult. The solution adopted was to design vessels with lifts which could hoist cars a few at a time from the car-deck to the pier and vice versa. The vessels would lie alongside and this inevitably meant intricate manoeuvring of cars from the deck onto the ramp of the lift. This was accompanied by much cursing from the seamen as they guided the cars onto the turntables and swung them round by hand to the great danger of chrome and paint work. For proud car-owners it was a heart-in-the-mouth experience. The lifts, based on an idea borrowed from aircraft carriers where lifts were used to bring aircraft up and down, could only move up and down painfully slowly. As I was soon to learn on the Cowal, it took much longer to load and unload at Gourock and Dunoon than it took to cross over — the whole process could take an hour with only 20 minutes at sea. The busier they were, the worse it got; it was quite common for the car ferry to be a whole 'run' behind which meant that a family could arrive at Dunoon and find the Cowal in, only to learn that they would have to wait for their booking until she had been to Gourock and back! But the new services were undoubtedly successful; in its first month the Cowal carried 400 cars compared to five the month before. Neverthless it has to be said that for lack of foresight and investment, a heavy price was paid. Roll-on, roll-off (RoRo) ferries were becoming commonplace in Scandinavia and Denmark at the same time. The introduction in 1972 of the Western Ferries from Hunter's Quay to

McInroy's Point, using retired Scandinavian vessels from the Oland Sound was a clear indication of what might have been. The problems with tide and wind put about as a justification for the decisions of the fifties seem flimsy in the light of the reliability of Western Ferries. Even now Gourock/Dunoon services are side-loading at Dunoon, with much shuffling and turning of cars and lorries. The decision taken in the early fifties, meant that for the first time, Clyde vessels were to be followers rather than leaders of change.

With the first set of degree exams behind me, I reported to the Cowal on 4 June, 1955 at the start of what was to be a glorious summer for weather. I was, without appreciating it, witnessing one of the last great summers on the Clyde. The weather brought passengers in abundance, the great names were still there, and the new generation had arrived. There were eight of the traditional steamers in all their glory. These were the two turbine 'Duchesses' — the Hamilton and the Montrose — engaged in day cruises from Gourock to the lower firth, the former being most associated with the voyage to Lochranza and Campbeltown, while the latter steamed all the way up Loch Fyne to Inveraray. Queen Mary II sailed daily from Bridge Wharf in Glasgow to Tighnabruaich, and the fourth turbine steamer, the Marchioness of Graham, was on the Arran run. Of the paddle-steamers, the Jeanie Deans sailed round Bute from Craigendoran, while the Waverley sailed to Arrochar (the 'Three Lochs Tour'), 'Round the Lochs' and to Arran. The Caledonia gave excursions from Ayr and assisted on the Arran run, while the Jupiter served Wemyss Bay and Rothesay, with a daily 'Cumbrae Circle' cruise. The Talisman wove her eccentric way from Wemyss Bay to Largs and Millport. The timetable of day, afternoon and evening cruises ran to 47 pages.

In these same pages were the rosters of the seven new motor vessels which were the product of a modernisation programme set in train in 1951. There were four almost identical Maid class vessels and three car ferries. In December 1952, it was announced that the Maids would be passenger-only vessels of 509 tons, capable of carrying more than 500 passengers in the upper firth. They would cost £1,000,000 in total and would be in service in the summer of 1953. Although small by Clyde standards — 165ft long when compared to the Queen Mary's 263ft with half her tonnage, they were trim little vessels with pert modern funnels. They had been planned only for shuttle services, but a change of plan saw them fitted out to do ordinary services and even some limited cruising. There was much criticism in the early days. They would not be able to cope; they would sink in the first decent gale; things were not the way they used to be. In fact they proved, as I was to find out shortly, excellent if lively seaboats, quite well adapted to half-day cruises — especially the forenoon Cafe Cruises, billed as attractive short cruises at a popular price

70

The Maid of Argyll, one of the four new Maids built in 1953. CRSC

of 3/3d which included cup of coffee and chocolate biscuit.

It was said that their names were lacking in imagination, but there had been other Maids in the history of the Clyde. Each managed to have a character of its own and to be identified with particular services. First to appear was Maid of Ashton, the first-ever ship built for the Clyde by the Yarrow Yard, much better known to this day for its warships, especially destroyers and frigates. Like the others she could carry 627 passengers, and her British Polar engines gave her a speed of about 15 knots. She became the boat for the Holy Loch run shuttling on a kind of bus service from Gourock to Kilcreggan and the little piers at Hunter's Quay, Kilmun, Strone in the Holy Loch and Blairmore in Loch Long. It was a purser's nightmare with a pier every five minutes. She was considered well built, reliable, but not the smartest or the fastest of the sisters. She entered service in May 1953.

Ten days later came the Maid of Argyll, built by A&J Inglis from whose yard at Pointhouse so many Craigendoran and Loch Lomond boats had come. Fittingly she was based at Craigendoran and carried out two busy round trips to Rothesay each day with a flourish on Saturdays when she undertook the Arrochar sailing. On this run her tearoom was set out for dining and she became a mini-cruise ship except that the vibration usually piled crockery and cutlery in a heap on the floor. As you will soon learn, I was to fall in love with her and my assessment of her may be biased. She wasn't the smartest or the fastest or the best built, but she cut a dash to match that of her captain, the redoubtable Donald Crawford.

Third to appear later in June was Maid of Skelmorlie, also from the yard of A&J Inglis. She specialised in Cafe Cruises and afternoon cruises from Largs and Rothesay. She was harder to pin down than the others and seemed less of a character. The same could not be said of Maid of Cumbrae, built by the Ardrossan Dockyard Company. Perhaps they wanted to make a name for themselves and secure further orders. She was the best appointed — noticeably better than the other three in terms of woodwork, saloons and finish. Although we of the Argyll were loathe to admit it, she was also marginally the fastest. She had the most interesting mix of service runs and cruises and she was the only Maid apart from the

Argyll to berth occasionally at Craigendoran. Her assistant purser gained some notoriety on the grounds that he tended to be seasick on rough days. His frequent trips to the rails on the leeside were wont to provoke a sympathetic epidemic amongst the more nervy passengers who thought he might be the captain! Mere mention that the Cumbrae was rostered for the 'Dunagoil Bay Cruise' was enough to turn him pale. This destination was too close for comfort to Garroch Head, the most exposed point in Bute, looking across the main shipping channel to the lighthouse on Little Cumbrae. Beyond this was deep-sea. In later years he became ship's doctor on a Cunard cruise liner, so he must have found the cure for the dread malady in the nick of time.

All the Maids gave good service before passing on to other things. They were reliable, safe, and so easy to handle that their skippers would take them into piers in all weathers which in similar circumstances would drive the big boys to omit piers or run for shelter. The Maid of Cumbrae was converted to a mini car ferry on the Clyde as a stopgap in the seventies before being retired in 1978. When last heard of she was in the bay of Naples serving the Isle of Capri, as the Capri Express, reunited in partnership with her sister the Maid of Skelmorlie, renamed the Ala. The Maid of Ashton now called Hispaniola is a luxury restaurant on the Thames at the embankment, close to the Queen Mary and a retired Humber paddle-steamer. The Maid of Argyll, withdrawn in 1974, was bought by Greek owners and renamed City of Piraeus. Some years later I was able to enjoy an idyllic day cruise on her to the island of Hydra — sundrenched as she seldom was on the Clyde. Appropriately, the purser's office had been converted into a bar.

The car ferries which appeared a year later were called rather baldly Arran, Bute, and Cowal — soon nicknamed the 'ABC vessels'. Although only 14ft longer than the Maids, they were much broader and higher, almost cut in half by the electric lift hoist with the passenger accommodation perched high above the car-deck. They could carry 650 passengers and were fitted with huge derricks which looked like goal posts at the stern for cargo loading . These were soon removed when it became clear that it was easier to tow on trucks of cargo behind little diesel 'doodlebugs' — the forerunner of containerisation. Like the Maids they could make about 15 knots and their British Polar diesels were every bit as noisy. Their tearooms were spartan with formica instead of wood and the saloon seats were fixed in rows like bus seats — reminiscent of a bingo hall according to a local newspaper of the day. Gone were the days of basket chairs in the forward lounge.

The Arran was built by Denny's, the most prolific of all the Clyde steamer builders and was originally designed for the Arran run. She was hopelessly small for the job and far from replacing the Marchioness of Graham, she came merely to support her with additional runs and also undertook relief work on the Dunoon and Rothesay runs. It took a much bigger and more celebrated car ferry, the third Glen Sannox of 1957, to cope with the Arran run. The Arran was converted to stern loading of cars in 1973 and then served on the Islay run until August 1974 when she was replaced by the Pioneer. Bute and Cowal were built by the Ailsa Ship Building Co. of Troon — now gone like all the other yards which built the new vessels; the exception being Yarrows. Appropriately they became the Rothesay and Gourock stalwarts respectively. Although there seemed little to choose between them the Cowal became the more celebrated. She handled the Dunoon run, non-stop all day, with no shift system for the crew. She held the record for squeezing in the highest number of cars, reputed to be 34, and also had the skipper with the stopwatch! Where other vessels left within five minutes or so of time, under John McLeod the Cowal left to the second and would-be passengers were faced with the prospect of a gangway being whipped away literally from under their feet. Assistant pursers who showed finer feelings for those passengers sprinting up the pier at Dunoon were liable to have their ancestry questioned in two languages from the bridge. It was to him I reported in June 1955. This was the big league. The purser, Jimmy Gracie, was a lovely man, kind and tolerant. He had to be. I collected more tickets on the first day than on a month on the Prince Edward and slumped back on to the train exhausted, arms limp from hoisting gangways up and down to that high passenger deck. I had also made the acquaintance of the notorious Mr Beattie, piermaster at Dunoon for many a year. His temperament was as mercurial as his face was florid. He was the scourge of student pursers; even his nephew becoming one in the sixties did not soften the attitude. But then he even charged his wife pier dues!

He liked it to be thought that he was an ex-captain, but in truth he had merely been a purser. His nautical instructions with language to match were also a well-rehearsed fake. I took him at face value as did many an intimidated passenger. He particularly disliked passengers leaving the pier down the way reserved for goods and cars. He would pursue them down the full 100 yards and force them to retrace their steps, back down the full length of the pier along the road and down the 'proper exit' to pay their pier dues. Woe betide the latecomer who tried a shortcut to catch a steamer. It took me five years and promotion to junior purser before I dared to pull his leg — but only as the gangways were down and we were leaving on the last sailing of the season.

My second day brought the worst gale of the summer. Our call at Kirn I remember vividly — we were 20 feet above the pier one moment, as far below the next. The skipper regarded all passengers who refused to 'walk the plank' as wimps and after a couple of refusals from frail old ladies, took the boat off for Dunoon in high dudgeon. Things were little better there. Meals on the Cowal were taken with a rush — 20 minutes being the maximum time between piers. That day I seemed not to mind missing out. A combination of the Cowal's lively gait and cancelling tickets at a little desk amidst the fumes on the car deck, close to an open porthole through which we were shipping it green, all but reduced me to mal-de-mer and disgrace. I found my sea-legs just in time. By the next day the sun shone and I began to enjoy it. I discovered that on the approach to Dunoon, when I could see the Cowal Hotel through the porthole, it was time to dash for the gangway. I soon learned to part the crowds around it with an authoritative push, and a shout of 'Gangways!'. Even now, I still tend to push through crowds without thinking.

Although one could only guess at what life was like on the crack steamers, at least the Cowal was a great place from which to view them. Such was the Cowal's timetable, and so often were we late, that most ships gave way to us and in so doing left the top berth vacant for us at Dunoon, and the end berth at Gourock. We saw off the morning rush of turbines from Gourock before we left at 9.20am and mixed with them on their return in the evening. At lunchtime we witnessed the stately progress of the Queen Mary downriver from Bridge Wharf, and the Jeanie Deans off to Rothesay and round Bute. Wherever they went, we never deviated. In later years the practice was adopted of changing the car ferries about which brought some welcome variety and relief — the Rothesay run had only six round trips a day and the passage lasted for a whole half-an-hour.

After a week, I was getting acclimatised. The only problem was the travelling. Even with the dispensation of missing the first run, and sometime the last, I was hardly home before it was time to leave again. Unknown to me, Jimmy Gracie bent a few ears in Gourock and the upshot was a transfer to the Maid of Argyll. She sailed most days at 10am and tied up at ten to six in the evening. In between sailings on the Cowal I walked with Jimmy up Gourock Pier to where the Maid of Argyll lay below. Admittedly it was low-tide, but she looked tiny — I could see right down her funnel. Was this wise, I asked myself? Was there a fate worse than the Cowal? The next morning it was the tram to the other low level station in Glasgow, Queen Street, thence to Craigendoran and into one of the best seasons of my career. I had been on the articles of the Cowal for exactly one week and since the seamen handled all the cargo on her, my battle dress uniform, purchased in Paisley's was still immaculate. The Maids were altogether different.

Maid of Argyll

As I walked down to the pier at Craigendoran, through the station and past the abandoned offices, relics of the days when these were the North British Headquarters, I wondered what lay in store. The morning was perfect — the precursor to a spell of unbroken sunshine which was to last the season and beyond. I swear to this day that there is nowhere better in the world to be on a fine June morning than on the Clyde estuary. The Jeanie Deans lay at berth 'A', the ripples glinting on her hull with the gangways roped off. Hers was a late start. Each day she left for the Round Bute Cruise at 12.35pm. The Waverley was at the next berth, ready for Arrochar and the Three Lochs Tour. She would leave at the same time as the Argyll. With extra headropes on to restrain her, her paddles were turning slowly so that the engines would be warmed up for the off. Many years later I had to go through the same procedure with my steam yacht Galatea on Ullswater.

The Waverley and the Jeanie Deans, similar at first glance, made an impressive sight. It was low tide and I had some difficulty in spotting the Maid of Argyll on the other arm of the pier. I could, however, hear her clearly. The Maids even in repose, had a deep throaty beat which rose to a full roar when 'full speed ahead' was signalled. If you have ever heard an InterCity 125 leaving a mainline station, you'll have some idea of what it was like.

She was a trim little craft with the lines of a small liner. At first all I saw was a squat funnel, cased in aluminium to save weight and buff-coloured tripod masts, fore and aft. Above the purser's office and behind the bridge was a high platform which was used for the gangways at low tide. It was chained off when she was moving because it was felt that the weight of passengers up there would make her unstable. It was a silly ruling. By far the best view forward for passengers was thus obscured. The only way left for passengers to look ahead was to press against the doors to the bridge wings. She was not in the slightest unstable and when, years later, she sailed in the Aegean Sea where a boat can take a fair pasting, they put an extra deck her full length at that level without any trouble at all. At least the steps up were a good roosting place — there were not many seats on the deck. Under these stairs, and facing the main companion way below was the window of the purser's office — a good vantage point but overshadowed by the stairs.

I reported to the purser John Brewster. He hailed from Stirling and was fairly new to the job. His accent endeared him no end to my mother with her Bannockburn ancestry. Like most full pursers he returned each winter to duties as a booking-clerk on the railways. John could be abrupt, sometimes tense, but he had a good sense of humour and knew his job. The balances were seldom far out. He relaxed over the years and became one of the senior permanent staff at Gourock. I could not have learned my trade from a better master.

He took me round to the bridge to meet Donald Crawford and an exceedingly young-looking mate in his first season, who 40 years later returned as a senior and much respected master in the fleet. It was the custom to entrust new mates to Crawford to be broken in. For my money he was the most skilled handler of a ship that I ever saw — and I saw some good ones. He was genuinely fearless, which is quite different from being reckless. Robin Hutchison, the mate, will not mind my saying now that at that stage he was decidedly inclined to the reckless and yet possessed a great skill in the making. It was to be a joy watching that pair in action. Twelve years later Robin was to achieve his first command, and appropriately it was Maid of Argyll.

Crawford would lean on the edge of the bridge, looking aft and appear to bring us alongside as if in a fit of absentmindedness. This could trap the unwary into conversing with him at critical moments thus earning a sharp rebuke, as did any pursers using the loudspeaker while he was coming alongside. Although from the bridge he could virtually touch the seamen handling the bow-rope on the tiny foredeck, when in formal mood he would ring the berthing telegraphs loudly to give instructions. The seamen always replied with an 'Aye, Aye, Sir!' which made it all rather amusing.

I came to worship Crawford, though my leg was pulled incessantly. It was impossible to twig when he was at it. When I brought my girlfriend, Margaret, aboard for the first time, I was in a hopeless rash of fear and confusion. He simply swept her off her feet, took her to the bridge and regaled her with tales of his past. I reclaimed her with difficulty a whole round trip and four hours later. In the summer she lived at a house just round Toward Point which we passed, half-a-mile offshore four times a day. He never missed a blast on the horn and responded to the towel she waved from the shore with a handkerchief the size of a small sheet. There is even today an echo of this to be witnessed. Once a week Waverley cruises to Pladda at the south end of Arran. Captain, crew and passengers wave to the widow of Captain McNab, a famous Clyde skipper. She responds with a towel in a way that takes me back almost 40 years in an instant.

Soon after my arrival, we were off and as the day progressed I met the rest of the crew — 13 in all. On weekdays the Argyll did two round trips to Rothesay leaving Craigendoran at 10.05am and 2.05pm returning at 1.45pm and 5.50pm. We called at Gourock, Dunoon, Innellan and occasionally Kilcreggan. Apart from the call at Gourock, this had been the basic bread and butter run of the North British Steamers for many years. There were no quiet spells. We caught the morning rush at both rail termini, the 'Cafe Cruises' from Dunoon and Innellan and on the first run back, the lunchtime trade from Rothesay and Dunoon. The afternoon run was perfect for those looking for a shorter sail than those available on the big all-day cruise-boats. The 4.10pm back from Rothesay was timed to be just before these 'big boys' started to return, and the 5pm from Dunoon was a popular timing, especially as the Cowal did not leave until half-an-hour later. Putting it another way, every segment of both runs was included in the 'Principal Services' summarised on page one of the timetable. There were few wet days that summer and the Argyll ran up record complements. Never again while on the Clyde did she have to turn away passengers so often from the gangway.

The redeeming feature was Saturday. A boat which could handle over a thousand was needed for that day on 'our' run, and Waverley usually stepped in. In return we took over the Arrochar run which was quieter on Saturdays than midweek. Unlike the Waverley we had to do a first run at 10am to Kilcreggan and Dunoon and back before setting off on our cruise at 11.45am; sometimes the passengers hurt our feelings a little, complaining that they had expected something grander. Admittedly, it was stretching it a bit — the timetable did say: By P.S. Waverley (or other steamer)! Retrieving the cutlery off the deck at lunchtime seldom improved the mood. At least they could look forward to a peaceful high tea on the Maid of the Loch if they survived the hike from Arrochar to Tarbet. Timetables for 1955 indicated that privately owned buses run between these points. Could Willie have taken to running his round from Inversnaid? God forbid!

Although I enjoyed every minute of the regular run, as the summer passed I longed for a bit of variety. None was forthcoming. It seemed we were too essential where we were. At the end of each week it was the custom for the office to send out a list of alterations or amendments for the following week. It generated much excitement on every vessel. Small groups of the crew hung about outside the purser's office while the envelope was opened, much as the crews of warships did in wartime, wondering which convoy they were going to join — was it Murmansk or the Med? For the Argyll it was Rothesay and more ruddy Rothesay. We did not once figure in the amended weekday rosters. I later learned that the skipper who had captained bigger and more prestigious craft, rather liked the Maid because of evenings at home or in the allotment and the office were made well aware of this. Donald Crawford would take her in to Craigendoran at 5.50pm in his anonymous overcoat and was up the stern gangway for the train to Dumbarton long before the passengers had started to struggle up the main one.

Excitement came with the Sunday rosters. The Maid of Argyll had no scheduled sailings on Sundays. The only Maid which had a regular commitment was the Cumbrae which was billed Rothesay and Largs to Loch Long (Ardentinny). The full trip cost six shillings. There was no service to the Holy Loch for the Ashton, so three little maids had to compete for the overtime to be earned on the Largs to Millport run which entailed seven round trips back and forth. In those days there was no car ferry from Largs to 'Tattie Pier' on Cumbrae and day-trippers to Millport had the fun of the half-hour sail past Keppel and through the Eilans into the old pier. For the two Maids which were still unemployed, it could be a day off, a charter — usually from Bridge Wharf, or occasionally a tender to a visiting liner. Lying alongside one of these gave one a whole new perspective on relative size. The Maids were popular for this task, with uncluttered decks and good handling. The masters of huge liners did not take kindly to having their immaculate topsides scraped and dented by tenders. Those who disembarked on the Argyll often made very disparaging remarks about it being only one better than going ashore in a rowing boat.

The Millport run was an easy if boring day. Nearly all the tickets sold were straight singles at two shillings a time. John and I did 'run' about. The one 'off-duty' had illicit excursions ashore at Millport till the Argyll returned. The Garrison Cafe was a favourite venue — the uniform could, combined with a few judicious words about 'deep-sea', turn a few pretty heads. On wet Sundays when Millport hardly pulsates with life, it was better to retire below with the *News of the World.*

On my first day on the Argyll, I began to learn by heart the announcements I would make time and time again over the loudspeaker 'Steamer for Gourock, Dunoon, Innellan and Rothesay'. 'The steamer is now approaching Innellan Pier, Passengers for Innellan please prepare to disembark from the upper gangway. All tickets ready please'. 'Passengers on the Cafe Cruise must not, repeat NOT, disembark at Rothesay'[1]. I had the opportunity to make the announcements on Waverley as she approached Rothesay on one of the few sunny days during her 1993 season. It came out as if 40 years had never happened. To prove that nothing had changed, we still left the pier with six passengers 'who forgot to

---

[1] *Memories play strange tricks. The Argyll did not have a loudspeaker system until the 1970s. It must have been the Jupiter or the Jeanie Deans.*

get off'. I can still do the lot in my sleep and still wake up sweating as to whether the 'fans' (by that time boards slotted into a frame) are correct. If you got it wrong it was much more serious than on Loch Lomond .We had enough confused passengers, even when the boards were right without adding to it unintentionally. The geography of the Clyde estuary is complicated even with the map available in the timetable. One can sympathise with the civil servant who wrote from London suggesting that in the winter, money should be saved by putting a bus on the service to Millport and Brodick. He was invited to inaugurate the new service himself!

On the Clyde I met a new kind of animal — the pilot. On Loch Lomond the mate handled the wheel going into or out of piers, while the skipper twirled the telegraphs. On the Clyde, it was the pilot — the leading seaman who shouldered that difficult and skilled task. Many a captain was saved by the pilot from the error of his ways. They could seldom explain how they did the job — being born to the sea and the feel of boats was, I suppose, the secret. In later years I was to try my hand at it. As a vessel loses way it becomes increasingly hard to steer at all, particularly if a paddle-steamer. She has to be 'set up right' for wind and tide well before the pier is reached. The pilot and the skipper in concert with the chief engineer at the 'movements' down below formed a vital team. Any one of them could have easily landed us up the beach. These were frequently delicate, sometimes fraught relationships. Not so on the Argyll. The pilot (under the nominal control of the assistant purser!) supervised gangways and cargo and was like the bo'sun or coxswain in the Merchant and Royal Navy, the leading NCO. Put it this way, he had as much power as a school jannie which in my experience is frequently more than that of a headmaster. It was wise to be on good terms with the pilot.

The mate, particularly if inexperienced, relied heavily on the pilot, to mitigate the worst effects of his miscalculations, particularly if the master, having entrusted to them the approach to a pier, was resting below. Nothing brought him faster from his cabin, than the crunch of ships' belting on the delicate piles of a pier. The belting is a collar of heavy wooden beams with metal facings which is attached to the most vulnerable parts of the hull, a few feet above the waterline. It could absorb a lot of punishment, but there were limits. Likewise the huge piles of the pier face could give a bit but not enough for a really heavy meeting of irresistible forces.

The third member of the triumvirate was the chief engineer Johnny Tait. He was one of the most delightful men I have ever been privileged to meet — 'one of nature's chentlemen' as Para Handy would have said. He was small, inclined to tubbiness with a round cherubic face, perched on top of which was a battered cap, never with a white top, and always askew. The badge had slipped round to nestle adjacent to and just above his left ear. He always wore grubby once-white dungarees, except at mealtimes . He had the smile of an innocent child and a child's delight in his engines. They seldom let him down — if they did he was reputed to castigate them by hurling that battered cap at them. The fact that these same engines were pounding away in the Aegean Sea over 30 years later must be due in no small measure to his early ministrations. He had always time for the banal questions which passengers persist in asking; others of his ilk retreated below the grating at the engine-room door when they saw the aficionados of the Steamer Club hoving into view. John stood his ground with an affable grin. A bachelor who was believed to live with his mother in Greenock, he seemed reluctant to leave on his day off and was back on board and down below long before his relief had left.

I never witnessed even one of those tense little post mortems between Captain Crawford and Johnny Tait which were so common elsewhere when blame was being apportioned for redesigning (a) the pier and (b) the sponson or the bow. I spent many a happy hour with Johnny on the Arrochar run, learning about how he acquired certificates in both steam and diesel. Like so many officers on the Clyde steamers, he had vast deep sea experience.

I soon learned about Sandy. He was the seaman who handled the waist rope and the after gangway. The waist rope is the one which goes ashore last at the pier when the vessel is virtually alongside. The reason for having bow and stern ropes is obvious enough. The best seamen at throwing a line were detailed to these. They had a great skill, taking a heaving line, separating it into two coils, one in each hand, and tossing it great distances, often 'up hill' to the pier for good measure. When the wind was offshore their role was critical — one miscast and we could be blown 50 yards sideways. On the Clyde, they did not have a ball of plaited rope at the end of the line to add weight and to clout the unwary bystander. That was MacBrayne's practice, and is now Caledonian MacBrayne's, I notice! Many were the curses if the line heavers were let down by less than agile pier staff who let a line slip over their arm, or fouled it round an obstruction. Nowadays with bow-thruster units, and Voith-Schneider propellers, a boat can be put and held against the pier virtually without ropes. Not in the 1950s.

Sandy was not your Olympic ropethrower. When we were virtually alongside he handed the waist rope ashore and then tensioned it expertly so that the Argyll came to rest with no bollards obstructing the gangways; once at rest, she stayed in one place to prevent gangways being slewed sideways with folks attached. He seemed to me to be ancient. He was from Gigha. He had a round moon-like face, expressionless and cunning, curious yellow 'whites' to his eyes and teeth to match. He wore a seaman's cap so constantly that I never found out whether he had hair beneath. I suspect not. His black jersey with C.S.P.Co. emblazoned across the chest was stained with the remains of many a meal. He chewed 'baccy' and seated on the capstan at the stern, could propel the resultant disgusting expectoration 20 feet downwind and over the side without a drop touching the deck. Mind you he had a vested interest — he had to wash down that bit of the deck daily. He seldom spoke, preferring Gaelic to English when he did.

His customer relations were non-existent. When we were busy, he had to put on a light gangway at the stern to help out. I could not make any headway in insisting that he should collect tickets or count passengers. He accepted only those tickets pressed into his hand, including those issued on buses and in cloakrooms and often dropped the lot over the side. He seldom remembered to mention any cargo which was handed aboard. As a result, I would fail to enter it on the manifest and make sure that he put it ashore. I was forever sidling up to assistant pursers on other boats going back to where we had been, begging them to slip a package or a trunk ashore, without giving the game away. If he missed Arrochar on a Saturday, it was Tuesday before my mates on the Waverley could bale us out. It was almost invariably fresh fish and game for the Arrochar Hotel, or emergency whisky supplies for the local bar.

Everybody else on the crew must have been reasonably sane, as I can remember little about them. The food was good, although more cafeteria than à la carte and cuppas between piers were ad lib. You will have noticed that my navigation on the Loch Lomond and the Clyde centred around landmarks which meant food. On the Argyll it was the 'Perch', that curious red and white stone pillar which marks the rocks of Sandy Beach near Innellan where as an infant I had paddled with Rory, the Cowal chauffeur. When I could see it from the ticket window I had just time to eat before Rothesay. Even today I feel hungry when I see it!

On the main deck forward was an 'observation saloon' with bus-type seats. Its main disadvantage was that owing to the sheer of the bow, you could not see forward, and if seated you could not see sideways either. After the Prince Edward, it was quite a decline in standards. Below the saloon — hidden away as so often on the Clyde, as if Victorian designers were still at work and thought it disrespectful, was the bar. You really had seriously to want a drink to go down there at all. After a few days of the train journey, I persuaded the steward (he did not rate a 'chief') to let me sleep down there. It was the only boudoir I have known where you could go to sleep sober and wake up intoxicated after a night's sleep. You could reach out and touch the smell of beer. Every morning I took up my bed and walked to Johnny Tait's cabin where I was allowed to store my bed roll. Only twice did I have to run semi-naked along the main deck to the mystification of male passengers, and (I fondly imagined) the delectation of the ladies. Both incidents followed particularly heavy imbibing even before reaching the bar the previous evening. It made a great difference to stay aboard and be part of the nightlife on board. In effect I joined the family which the passengers never see.

In the middle of the main deck were engine casings with passage ways alongside with a little alcove before you entered the cafeteria or 'refreshment room' which was the full width of the ship towards the stern. The best seats for viewing were here and there was much competition for them amongst regular passengers. There was a narrow stairway to the top deck which led up to a wooden hatch, such as you might find on a luxury yacht. It was a curious feature. The lid could be slid back on good days. If it was closed to keep the rain out you had literally to crawl onto the deck on your hands and knees. Assistant pursers often helped the ladies to cope.

In the cafeteria food was served self-service from a counter at the rear behind which was the galley. Apart from Saturdays, only crew got meals and envious passengers would pine after the galley-boys as they conveyed steaming plates to the crews' quarters. Above the galley was a chimney which seemed higher than the real funnel, and just as smoky. The galley had passages alongside, open to the skies, and the lads peeling the spuds used to sit on the doorstep, giving each spud a flat end; it was claimed to keep them from rolling off the plates when we were rattling along at full speed.

They tossed the peelings to the gulls, which tended to reject them as beneath their dignity. Every steamer had its quota of gulls. It was rumoured that they mustered every morning on Ailsa Craig and were detailed for each boat according to their place in the pecking order and the quality of the catering. Heaven help those that drew the Jupiter when I was on her!

While passengers could walk aft above the galley, that was as far as they could go. The main deck to the stern was open, giving the appearance that a bit had been missed off in the design stage. The story was that the only way the Maids had been sanctioned by 'them' was that they could be quickly converted to minesweepers in the event of war. Undo a few nuts, whip off the galley, and hey presto, an open deck for sweeping gear and depth charges. I believe the story although I wonder what they would have done without the galley! Presumably the secret will be out soon when official documents are opened to public scrutiny. It will be very disappointing if it turns out not to be true.

The bonus of this design was a delightful, fairly private little deck for the crew to sun themselves and yarn. The drawbacks were the close proximity to the wake and the vibration from the twin screws. Add to that the judder from the twin-spade rudders when manoeuvring, and it could rattle the wallies right out of yer mouth. Even so, I have the happiest memories of sitting there, going up the Kyles or turning into Loch

Goil past that lovely bay so inappropriately called 'Swine's Hole' which in later years was the favourite anchorage for my Contessa 26, Charisma.

Only sitting in this little haven at the stern, and if you could dodge the spittle, could you get Sandy to unwind and speak of Gigha, his childhood, and of the perils of the small ferry to Tayinloan. Of course I ended up 'ghosting' letters to his family too on pay days. There was nothing tender about these ones. In return Sandy sometimes collected a few tickets to humour me and would hazard a rough guess as to how many passengers had come and gone at his gangway. By mistake he once got a ticket for the Irish Sweep but we didn't win. No wonder, it was out of date, like most of the tickets he accepted.

There was one night of the week when Donald Crawford did not get home early. That was Wednesday. Evening cruises were the province of the Maids. The big boys returned too late — or perhaps it was beneath their dignity. At the height of the season the Maid of Argyll was advertised to cruise to the Kyles of Bute, leaving Craigendoran at 6.10pm and calling at Gourock, Hunter's Quay and Dunoon, leaving the last named at 7.15pm returning there at 9.30pm and ending up at Craigendoran an hour later. Evening cruises were popular in the fifties. Few boarding houses had TV sets and the shows at the resorts took up only one night of the holiday — Harry Kemp's Cosy Corner and such like. Another reason might have been the midges — only on the water were you safe. They put a damper and still do on romantic assignations in Morag's Fairy

Donald Crawford. CRSC

Glen. Of all Harry Lauder's ditties, the one about 'roamin' in the gloamin',' is the most unconvincing. He must have had a secret formula to drive those vindictive mini-mosquitos away.

On a good evening the Maid could reach her full complement of 627. They were packed on the deck like sardines; the tearoom and bar doing record business. If you wanted a seat, it was the busseats down below and no view. Someone should have sued us.

These cruises gave a welcome opportunity for Margaret to come aboard. Our romance was somewhat circumscribed by her location at Toward Point and mine of an evening in Craigendoran. On Wednesdays after the tickets were sold at Dunoon, and the purser had retired to his cabin, the purser's office was ours, with the shutters up over the window.

All went well with this arrangement until the Glasgow Fair. On the first Wednesday Margaret got on at Dunoon, but only just. We turned away more than 200 unfortunate would-be cruisers. Next week she took the precaution of going along to Hunter's Quay to beat the queues. We left Gourock only 20 short of our complement. To my consternation I saw a queue at Hunter's Quay which stretched right up the pier and along the road towards Kirn. My beloved was about 55th. As we approached, decks almost awash, the mood grew ugly. I resigned myself to a quiet and lonely evening bereft of solace and comfort. We took aboard the few we could manage. A remote and affectionate look was all I could afford to the lass languishing halfway up the pier. Suddenly there was Donald Crawford. He ambled casually up the pier, hooked his arm in hers, smiled winsomely and conspiratorially at the throng which parted magically before him and handed her gallantly aboard. We missed out Dunoon completely, passing 50 yards offshore of the frustrated hordes. On the return, Margaret missed the last bus by the time she got back to Dunoon from Hunter's Quay and had walked as far as Innellan before the local bobby gave her a lift.

One of the great ironies was that Hunter's Quay, despite being the only pier on the Cowal shore which boats could berth at in the worst of gales, had been closed in 1952, allegedly because of lack of business. It had been reopened in 1953 because the Maid of Ashton was small and economical. By 1955 it could generate hundreds for a cruise. It was closed again in the next round of cutbacks, only to be reprieved yet again when in the early seventies it became the headquarters of Western Ferries.

Donald Crawford judged to a nicety how far up the Kyles we reached in each cruise. His train was the deciding factor. Many passengers imagined that the cruise would take them to the Narrows at least. On one occasion we hardly got past Port Bannatyne. Colintraive was considered a good night. It was my job to explain to those who complained, as best I could, that the Kyles covered a wider area than perhaps they envisaged. I had the same problem later on runs which said things like Brodick and thence cruise — 'thence cruise' are words of great elasticity encompassing factors such as weather, tardiness, captain's temper, state of the bunkers and engineer's disposition — or lack of it. Do not say that you have not been warned — that giveaway phrase or its equivalent is current from the Clyde to the Swiss Lakes via Windermere and the Bristol Channel.

My admiration for the skipper grew as the season progressed and I spent as much time as I could on the bridge. It's wings were large for a

*Donald Crawford ably demonstrating his tremendous skill in 'kissing' the
Maid of Argyll against the pier at Rothesay during a gale in 1955.*
GRIMSHAW COLLECTION

small vessel. The master stood on a raised grating, his hands on the
telegraphs, the wheelhouse door open to permit a word with the pilot at
the wheel. With her twin screws, the Maid was highly manoeuvrable, but
even so, it was a joy to watch the judgment of distance, speed and drift
in the wind. We seldom did more than kiss the pier even on the stormi-
est day. Robin Hutchison learned rapidly and as a result we wasted little
time at piers. I used to stand on the bridgewing until the last possible
moment before dashing the 15 yards to the gangway. I was honour-
bound to handle them smartly and hustle the passengers on and off,
under the approving eye of the great man. He seldom failed to wait for
stragglers and even went back if he could, with those who had missed
their pier. On such occasions he would lay her alongside without ropes,
a quick move with our own light gangway, and off.

He encouraged me to learn the mysteries of the waist rope from
Sandy, until on his day off I could cope. Crawford played a scurvy trick
when he learned that I had been practising heaving a line with the
bowman. He invited me to heave the bow-line ashore at Innellan,
which I did with some panache, distinction even. He had fixed things
so that it was not attached to the eye of the mooring rope; it flew
ashore on its own, was deftly caught by Mr Sinclair the geriatric piermaster and returned before I had time to blink! With a withering look,
the master himself then hurled one that was firmly attached to the
mooring rope with a power which was talked about in awed tones in
the fo'csle for weeks.

Why was this man master of one of the smallest units in the fleet?
I set out to solve the mystery. Needless to say I got no assistance from
the man himself. He hailed from Minard on Loch Fyne and in his early

childhood must have seen the Lord of the Isles and the Columba in full flow, along with a host of lesser craft. At that time there were as many as seven piers in use on Loch Fyne and ferries as well. Para Handy claimed to have served as a deckhand on MacBrayne's Inveraray Castle and I wonder if a little bit of something magical was transferred from fictional puffer skipper to the young Crawford. There was the same b. 🟤 e assurance, the pride in 'the smartest vessel in the tred'. His father had been a skipper before him in the Gem Line, and following in his footsteps Donald signed on as a boy, seeing service in the Baltic and the Med and then under the Canadian Pacific flag acquiring his mate's and then his master's tickets. No wonder he enjoyed himself when the Argyll acted as tender to the great Canadian Pacific Empresses as they called en route from Liverpool to Canada.

As so often with Clyde steamer officers, the appeal of a 'home job' found him as mate of Williamson Buchanan's Kylemore in the early thirties. Talent shone forth and when an opening came with the LNER fleet, he took it and in 1932 joined the Lucy Ashton in the Gareloch — an infinitely smaller world than he had been used to. After rising to his first command, albeit temporarily, of the Kenilworth, he spent a year on the Forth on the Burntisland/Granton crossing in the shadow of the Forth Bridge — an experience for a Clyde master shared only, I think, with the skipper of the Jeanie Deans, Charles Maclean. He went back to spend the war years there — not a happy period in his life, he confessed in a rare revelation. In 1946, he was back on the Clyde as master of the Talisman where he remained until the Maid of Argyll was launched. He had also enjoyed a spell on the brand new Waverley, so it was something of a surprise to find him on such a humble vessel. Was it the homelife — the Talisman was now based at Millport? Was it his cavalier manner? Had his LNER loyalties irked the powers in Gourock? It was a forbidden topic on the Argyll where he remained for no less than ten years, as skilled with twin screws as he had been with paddles. Probably he simply wanted to get home early at night!

The bridge suited him; it was surprisingly spacious with no more in it than wheel, telegraphs, rudder indicator and compass. Initially there was no VHF or radar — this came a few years later. At the back of the bridge, running the full length was a huge chest, containing lifejackets and flares etc. On this he perched between piers when on duty, his legs dangling, paying court to an endless succession of visitors, which never included his wife. They apparently had an amicable pact. He preferred to have the two loves of his life completely cut off from each other.

Once he had trained a new mate to his satisfaction, he would retire from time to time to his cabin between the bridge and the purser's office. If he intended to sleep he would bang on the adjoining bulkhead to warn John and myself to work quietly or risk a lurid fate infinitely worse than death. Sometimes he would retreat to study form and pass out his bet for the one-legged bookie's 'runner' who acted as go-between with the firm of Bonacorrsi in Rothesay. The runner was a well kent figure on Rothesay Pier, making his way on crutches to boats on their outward run to pick up the half-crowns wrapped in scraps of paper on which were scribbled the names of the horses, and hobbling back with the winnings, if there were any, on the return trip. It was all quite illegal, but never was a runner better disguised. Now and then after his approach, a seaman or a stoker would leap and shout, arms in the air, to the complete mystification of the onlookers. The more sensible exercised due discretion. A big win could soon evaporate in the sawdust-strewn floors of the bars of the Main Street in Helensburgh.

Whatever had led Crawford to the Argyll rather than to more senior command, he ended up in the right place. He skippered the Jeanie Deans with great distinction in her final two seasons. I used to sail with him there just to watch the master at work, and of course to have my leg pulled. He then spent five years as skipper of the Caledonia when she was transferred to Craigendoran. Many feared that this heavy handful of a steamer, built in the thirties by the Caledonian Company with no thought of the difficulties posed by Craigendoran, might prove a disaster in her new role. Not a bit of it. Crawford saw her out through her vintage years and his, spent a few last months on the Waverley and retired in 1970 to his beloved home and family. Like all great men, he knew how good he was, but he did not like to be reminded of it. He was seldom seen on the Clyde in his retirement years.

The skipper enjoyed the Arrochar run. Curiously he showed no interest in the Loch Lomond end of the tour. He claimed never to have sailed on the Loch or to know any of the characters there. Once the tourists were ashore at Arrochar his job was over. But he enjoyed the cruise up Loch Long and in to Lochgoilhead which was still virtually cut off by road in the fifties; the single-track road being tortuous and difficult. Loch Long can be a gloomy, fjord-like place and as yachtsmen will testify it can have bewildering and savage wind shifts — the notorious 'williwaws' which can take a yacht aback in a trice. I saw one such at Lochgoilhead lift a heavy dayboat resting in a cradle ashore up in the air to deposit several tons of instant matchwood 30 yards along the beach. I was to return there on the Jupiter, probably the most awkward of all the paddlers to handle, on such a day.

For me the memories of Arrochar are of persuading passengers to carry notes to my erstwhile mates on the Maid of the Loch, and of the sheer beauty of the loch in the perfect weather of that summer, witnessed from the bridge wing, or sitting on the capstan with Sandy at the stern. On one of these days, Margaret, who had set off on a bus tour of

Scotland with her maiden aunt was waiting to greet us. Apparently the whole itinerary had been bent by a compliant driver to turn up at Arrochar pier at precisely 3pm. It cost me an afternoon tea for three at the hotel at the pierhead and a bung for the driver.

All too soon the season was over. The new mate had laid his first born on the chest on the bridge to be admired by the family of pursers, cooks and stewards, engineers and seamen. The assistant purser had 'procured' a First Class carpet for the purser's office and could cancel tickets in his sleep. A record number of passengers had been carried, very few of whom had any inkling of what life aboard was really like. I doubt if any realised that the boat was 'home' as well as work place to many of us.

On the Monday of the Glasgow September weekend, as we passed Toward Point for the last time, Donald Crawford dipped the triangular Caley pennant at the masthead in Margaret's honour and this was followed by the three farewell blasts on the siren which were normally reserved for departing Cunarders. Next day, the mate went back 'deep sea', John returned to the booking office at Stirling Station and I set off for the new academic year. Unlike the cruise boats, the Argyll would sail on as a winter boat, with only a brief spell in dock for overhaul and painting. Whether I would rejoin her in the following spring was uncertain. There was a conflict between pride in her and a desire to move on and see more.

The winter set the pattern for those to come; as little work as would ensure obtaining class-tickets — 'duly-performeds' as they were known — passing degree exams and as much time as possible haunting the Albert Harbour where boats were laid up for the winter. I had saved up a few Privilege Tickets which I used for the train journeys to Greenock and the occasional sail on the winter services. After what seemed like an eternity it was almost time for the next letter from the office in Gourock. I had been promised that there would be one.

Piers, Places, People and Paddlers

The fifties was the last stand of the towns and piers of the Clyde. Both have since declined, the towns in prosperity and popularity, the piers in numbers. Although the warning signs were there, life went on much as it had in the thirties. But all the ingredients were there in changing holiday patterns, in road improvements and in harsh economic realities.

The Clyde resorts had by then had a long innings. The coming of the steamboat in the early 19th century had made it possible to predict when ships would arrive at their destinations; timetables became a reality. Before then and for a time after when reliability was still a factor, they tended to be no more than boards with messages like 'Vessel such and such will leave at 8 o'clock or thereby from Greenock, and will call at various piers'. No arrival times were ventured. Once the railways reached the coast — the first was the Glasgow and Greenock Railway to Cathcart Street Station with a walk to the Quay, a new discipline appeared and in the second half of the 19th century, combined steamer and rail services were fast and efficient. Not only were daytrips possible but the first commuters began to appear. The most affluent were the whisky, tobacco and shipping merchants of Glasgow who built grand houses at places such as Kilcreggan, Innellan and Rothesay, as well as at mainland villages like Kilmacolm, on the route to the Clyde coast.

The tiny village of Dunoon was transformed after the Provost of Glasgow built a villa above where the pier now stands. A small wooden jetty was built in 1835 and by 1897 there was a two-berth pier complete with Tudor-style waiting rooms and a signalling tower to handle — among the other traffic — the flood of daily travellers to Greenock and Glasgow. Dunoon was by then a resort which attracted visitors from far afield. It was the first pier to have a loudspeaker and music system in 1934 and three years later came the famous promenade where I was to watch the cavalcade of many vessels in the forties. In the thirties you had to pay extra to get up there. Significantly, as Dunoon declined the promenade fell into disrepair, was roped off and ultimately dismantled. Who would want to pay good money to watch a car ferry unloading?

Dunoon and Rothesay, which had grown prosperous in a similar manner but with the edge in the affections of Glaswegians, were busy in the fifties but the local worthies would, at the drop of a hat, lament the end of the real heyday. Still, there were no vacant shops on the main streets; even wet days brought thousands on the ferries and the cruise boats, and the Cowal and Bute Games were occasions for a build up to weeks of excitement. The former required the services of half the Clyde fleet, queueing up to disgorge myriads in the morning, largely sober, and take them back, in various stages of disrepair long into the night.

Rothesay would soon feel the draught of the withdrawal of naval custom, but submarine depot ships, like mother hens with their chicks gathered about them, still lay in the bay and pinnaces dodged amongst the steamers and the 'oary-boats' as they berthed behind the pier. Their antics were the object of amused derision from the seamen on the steamers. It was fun watching a petty officer and ten sailors taking all of 15 minutes to come alongside with a vessel a fifth of the size of a paddler which could berth in a minute with half the number of men on deck. The comments were fairly ribald when they got it really wrong. I remember standing at the head of the gangway on the Argyll on one occasion, watching a pinnace fail to go astern in time and belt into the pier with an expensive sounding thud. A row of matelots drawn up on deck fell over like dominoes, desperately clutching at each other as they fell. Gratifyingly the officer at the end fell overboard. In the confusion, it was Sandy who, with a turn of speed I had never even suspected he possessed, vaulted the stern rail of the Argyll, ran across and fished him out with the boathook which had lain unused at the pier end for years. The Merchant Navy man's contempt for the nautical skills of the Royal Navy fanned in many a convoy incident in the Battle of the Atlantic was enhanced as the news passed round the Clyde fleet as they berthed at Rothesay. Sandy refused steadfastly to be photographed let alone interviewed by the Buteman. In a fine gesture, the captain of Adamant sent a bottle (or was it two?) of Johnnie Walker Black Label, which was unobtainable on the mainland then, to Donald Crawford when next we called. Naturally, he shared it all out amongst the crew.

Some would say that the real decline of Rothesay began as early as 1936 when the open 'toast-rack' trams were taken off the tracks to Port Bannatyne and Ettrick Bay. The conductor would swing spectacularly along the outside as he checked the tickets. It reminds me of the way it's still done on the cable-cars in San Francisco which must be today's equivalent 'hurl'. Fortunately the pace was sedate — no more than 12mph on the private tracks surrounded by yellow gorse and whinbushes on the last stage of the run.

I went there by bus in the fifties. It was less fun, with only the tram-

The Jupiter at Rothesay Pier in the mid-fifties. CRSC

rails at Ettrick Bay on the 'Atlantic' side of Bute as clues to what had been a great tradition. I never dreamed then that even the Glasgow trams would be gone less than a decade later. Rothesay in the eighties had a deserted, neglected look, with distance lending enchantment — it looked better from sweet Rothesay Bay. Now thanks to the concerted efforts of its townsfolk, it is beginning to recover some of its former grace. Sadly the beaches remain bereft of bathers and rowing boats.

Only a hardy handful commute to the mainland on today's leisurely timetable. Sadly few if any ferries arrive with capacity crowds. Better to holiday in lands without wet days, than to risk the vagaries of 'Scotland's Madeira' as it was bravely billed in the guide books. Even on the best days now the beach is deserted, the rowing boats few, the bay empty. In the fifties the beach was black with people. What was it that made sturdy Glasgow matrons take to paddling, splashing and giggling, their skirts tucked up to reveal to public view their ample thighs in a way that would have been unthinkable at home in their own close-mouths? Their menfolk meanwhile would retreat to the deck chairs (sixpence a day) and doze, knotted handkerchief on head, bottle of ale propped up in the sand.

· The buildings on the pier at Rothesay have been whittled away to the starkly utilitarian, without even a tearoom, and the full three-berth length is no longer there with its lengthy crocodile queues; one for the turbine and Campbeltown, one for Wemyss Bay on the paddler Jupiter and the far end for the diminutive Maid of Argyll.

Dunoon too is but a shadow. Many of the great hotels are gone or converted into homes for the aged. Argyll Street is some way short of its former glory and the man-made attractions are few in number. There is a modest revival with at times a positively festive air in the new open air concert-stand near the pier, but the Dunoon of the past is gone, the bustle replaced by somnolence. Some brave souls commute still, but not the small army which in the sixties as a teacher I joined in the summer months. It was 'led' by Geoffrey Grimshaw, a civil servant in Greenock some of whose photographs adorn these pages, and who was the only person to have a ticket which entitled him to travel between any piers on the Clyde on any day of the year. He was a steamer buff of a different order from the rest; he could balance romance with reality and was reputedly consulted by 'management' in Gourock about their plans for new vessels and new routes.

He was known to all who worked on the boats as 'Stormy Weather'. It was believed by some that he was the harbinger of gales and tempest. Others, including myself, subscribed to the view that it was due to his windswept appearance and the fact that he walked along the West Bay for the boat each day permanently leaning into the wind, even on the calmest of days. He spent every spare moment sailing on the steamers, summer and winter and could work the timetables to be on the greatest number of boats in one day — sometimes 20 plus. Today, without a car, his maximum number per day would be one or two if he sprinted between piers.

It was Geoffrey who enlightened me about the signal stations which were still a feature of Clyde piers in the fifties. In the 1870s when there were many rival companies vying for custom, racing for piers became so dangerous and collisions or near collisions so numerous, that it was decided to put a stop to it. The Clyde Navigation Act of 1887 gave power to the piermaster rather than the skipper to decide which steamer had precedence. Two years after the Act each pier had a triangular box erected at a height where it was clearly visible. One point faced the water with the two adjoining sides visible to vessels coming from either direction. On each side were three discs which were normally black. These were signals to as many as three steamers approaching from either side. The inshore disc was for the steamer nearest to the shore, the middle for the middle steamer, and the outer for the furthest steamer from the shore. The piermaster changed the disc to white for the steamer which had the right to berth first and the others had to give way. Red and white lanterns were used at night.

The system worked well and skippers who ignored a signal were liable to prosecution. In the twenties and thirties the signals were often needed, in the fifties only every now and then at the busiest of times. Nowadays it would be almost a miracle if even two vessels approached a pier at the same time. Where these towers still stand today they are relics of an age of excitement and rivalry on the water long since gone. The tower at Dunoon has a blank face where the discs used to be.

Largs has survived rather better by dint of being on the mainland. It has had the advantage of being a cross between a resort and a railhead terminal, which it still is for Cumbrae. In the fifties vast crowds awaited every cruise vessel, coming by car, excursion bus, and train. The rivalry between the Moorings at the end of the pier and Nardinis further up the prom was at its height. Both were fine examples of thirties architecture — glorified cafes indeed, but cafes with style nonetheless. They would have been more like continental cafes were it not for the stern licensing laws and the Scottish weather. It was soft drinks and knickerbocker glories of gargantuan dimensions that featured on the menu, together with a mouth-watering range of cakes and ice-creams. Folks made their way all the way from Glasgow to sit in the basket chairs at the much sought-after glass-topped tables in the windows of the Moorings and sample an eclair and with great daring, perhaps Russian Tea. In the winter, with the sea-facing doors closed to the elements and entry gained only through the sweety shop on the corner where the counter, an island in the middle, was packed with boilings and bon-bons, it was a haven of warmth for those who waited to join the Talisman for Millport. Something of that feel still remains in Nardinis to this day which carries on the West of Scotland 'Tallie's' tradition: the best ice-cream is still made by those of Italian extraction. It is well worth a visit. Sadly the Moorings is no more, with its porthole shaped windows and its balconies. The flats which have replaced it echo the appearance but not the splendour of a Scottish institution whose queues in the 'fair' used to be as long as the ones down the pier for the Duchess of Montrose.

That pier has incidentally remained much the same as it was in the 1830s when it was built. It is L-shaped, open and bare, and, has a forbidding stone front. It is more a quay than a pier, and was treated with respect then as now by every captain who berthed there. Its construction is unyielding and unforgiving. Wooden piers give and spring back. Largs Pier redesigned the delicate parts of many a steamer as I was to witness. In the fifties, there was always a small motor vessel along the side of the pier beside the Moorings for the shuttle-service to Millport — the one which the Maid of Argyll, being bigger, took over with her sisters on Sundays.

Millport was prosperous in the fifties and a frequent ferry service was carried out by the Ashton and the Leven. These were small glorified launches, 60ft long, which had been built by Denny's in 1938 specifically to give visitors to the great Empire Exhibition in Bellahouston Park a view of the Clyde and the shipyards — the 'Clutha' cruises they were nicknamed after the cross-river passenger ferries in the City. They spent the war tendering to convoys at the Tail o' the Bank and ended up together on the Millport run with the Leven replacing another well known launch The Wee Cumbrae in 1947 and the Ashton coming later. The Ashton, when retired in 1965, was bought by Ritchies of Gourock and renamed Gourockian. Curiously she was then chartered back to her former owners from time to time when they were short of a boat. The Leven

The three-funnelled Saint Columba at Innellan Pier, viewed from the steps of the Royal Hotel, 1950. ANDREW NAIRN

ended her days at Paignton in Devon where she was known as Pride of the Bay.

If life was lively on the Argyll on a brisk day, it was positively exhilarating on the Ashton and the Leven, especially round Farland Point where they had to turn across the prevailing swell to enter Millport Bay. Rows of green faces would line the rails on a breezy day, their owners longing for a quick end to their misery.

Every day paddlers called at Millport on ferry services and cruises. The turbines which could not easily reach the main pier called at Keppel Pier opposite Fairlie Pier where there were frequent trains to Glasgow. It was also the winter base for the Arran boat. Keppel Pier was built partly because Millport can be a difficult place to get in and out of — even in a yacht and partly because as Millport's villas grew in number in the late 19th century the walk to the Old Pier got longer and longer. It was opened in 1888, with a single berth like so many small Clyde piers. In the twenties a bus service to the town was started.

Cumbrae was one of the first places to feel the impact of a new philosophy which car ferries, improved roads and cuts in costs were to bring. The aim now is to find the shortest distance between two points, put on a ferry which can do the maximum number of short trips per day and leave the rest to the roads. In 1972, a ferry slip was built straight across from Largs at the old 'Tattie Pier' where puffers had called for many years for farm produce and at which the Sunday papers were unloaded. Once the new service was introduced, Keppel Pier was gone in a year and the Old Pier has struggled ever since, losing its ferry service to Largs, being closed and eventually rebuilt for calls by the Waverley and smaller cruise vessels. A sturdy campaign by the townsfolk was needed to achieve the re-opening. The magic returns when Waverley calls. I recall one day in the summer of 1993, when the whole town seemed to turn out for her call en route to Arran. Millport looks and feels like a place that has had a 'heart-transplant' with a pier far removed from its centre and dependent on cars, buses and taxis. There is little elegant now about a trip to Cumbrae. Fortunately its other charms are enduring.

The fate which almost befell Millport was part of a process which has inexorably eliminated the lesser piers of the Clyde leaving for example only one real pier on each of the other islands — Rothesay in Bute, and Brodick in Arran. The statistics tell the tale. In the late 19th century there were more than 120 piers and ferries in the Clyde estuary. By the 1930s these had been reduced to 53. The ferry at Corrie was discontinued in 1939 when no boatman could be found, and the last regular call was at Pirnmill on 16 March 1940. By 1955 there were only 32 piers left. That still left a lot of scope and interest but many of the places they served were no longer dependent on the steamer as their only link. Today with the full impact of the ferry system, there are only six main piers in use serving Cowal, Bute and Arran and slips for smaller ferries at Colintraive/Rhubodach, Lochranza and Claonaig in Kintyre, and at Portavadie to Tarbert, (the last two are summer only). Western Ferries rival service to Cowal has created a new pier at McInroy's Point near Cloch and revived an old one at Hunter's Quay. The only small piers which remain are at Tighnabruaich, Kilcreggan, and Helensburgh. One of the enthralling things to do when touring the Clyde is to look for clues as to where piers once were. The wooden piles and deck decay and collapse. It is usually the stonework which gives it away. Grand gateways leading to a sharp drop onto the beach give the best clue.

The closure of Craigendoran Pier in 1972 left the north bank of the Clyde bereft of direct links with Cowal and the lower firth. Perhaps it might have been different if Craigendoran had not been in such an isolated spot, over a mile from the middle of Helensburgh. In the 1870s the good people of that town were more attracted by keeping a railway line away from the seafront than they were in having a new pier where bigger steamers could call. Perhaps they were right. In 1955 as I made my way on foot to Helensburgh after a hard day on the Argyll, or later the Jeanie Deans, I came to question that judgment quite severely. On the other hand Craigendoran was the most pleasant and most intimate of all the mainland terminals. When the pier closed I managed to acquire the board which had once been used to indicate the berth occupied by Jeanie Deans. It can be seen today in the collection of mementoes maintained in the Sidings Restaurant, owned by Bob Gemmell, which lies beside the east coast railway line north of York. Ironically Helensburgh pier is still in use today.

Of the smaller piers still open in the fifties and which added so much to the pleasure of passengers and to the colour of the Clyde, I had my favourites. Blairmore has a beautiful setting with the joys of Loch Long and Loch Goil still to come. I never knew who owned it — perhaps no-one did. I did more leaping ashore there to catch our own ropes than at all the other piers combined. Innellan, where you can still see the outline of the first pier and the extension out to the second, was a nice contrast to the big busy piers closer by. On the end of it there was a massive bell for fog-warning, which I have often heard tolled as we groped our way in, unseeing in the haar.

The high point of Innellan's day was the call of MacBrayne's remaining vessel on the Clyde, the magnificent Saint Columba with her three funnels, a perfect miniature of the Cunard Queen Mary. She had started life as the Queen Alexandra in 1912, a turbine steamer with two funnels and was distinguished as the only Clyde steamer to have rammed a U-boat during the First World War. She was taken over by MacBrayne's in 1935 and emerged from a major refit with a larger top deck to accommodate the third funnel and an extra mast. The new funnel was a dummy — you could see through the windows below it from one side to the other. The three red funnels with black tops were also nicely stepped. After the war the Saint Columba no longer started from Bridge Wharf but every day in the summer she ghosted down from Greenock where she lay overnight to the railway pier at Gourock, and thence to Dunoon, Innellan, Rothesay and on to Tighnabruaach, Tarbert and Ardrishaig. She carried proudly the Royal Mail pennant and was a magnificent sight at full speed in the Kyles of Bute and round Ardlamont Point. Although a rival to the Caledonian boats, she was respected and accepted — after all the Royal Route, graced by Queen Victoria, had been going for a century with every ship on the route a famous one, not least her illustrious predecessor, the magnificent paddle-steamer Columba which had served the route from 1878.

The Columba was probably the most famous of all the Clyde steamers with two huge funnels, her curved bows cleaving the waters of Loch Fyne at a magnificent 19 knots. She was the largest steamer ever to sail on the Clyde at a foot over three hundred. Saint Columba was a worthy successor — the longest turbine and MacBrayne's first; one of the fastest and the first Clyde vessel to be converted to oil burning as early as 1937 some 20 years before the rest. If she could not outpace the Hamilton and the Montrose — and this was hotly disputed — she could certainly outlast them. As their stokers cursed and sweated when the call came for more steam, the engineer on the 'Saint' would sit on a deck chair down below and twiddle a knob to increase the flow of oil to the burners.

Tighnabruaich and Tarbert were other favourites of mine. I never reached Tarbert as a purser, but during the winter a sail on the Loch Fyne which undertook this route all the year round when Saint Columba was safely laid up for the winter, was a special treat. The road to Tarbert was long and arduous and most passengers for Islay came by boat and then crossed the isthmus to West Loch Tarbert to join the MacBrayne's boat for Port Ellen, Port Askaig or Sandy's home island of Gigha.

Tarbert bustled summer and winter with mail vans, lorries, passengers lugging suitcases and livestock on the hoof or in crates. It was all far more fun than watching container lorries which board the ferry at Kennacraig today. Their coming signalled the end for MacBraynes and the Royal Route. Loch Fyne took over all the year round after Saint Columba was scrapped in 1958 and lasted on the route until 1969.

Thereafter the Maid of Argyll and the Maid of Skermorlie kept things going for one winter— what an awesome responsibility for the Maids to sail in such an illustrious wake. I hope that they had by then mastered the knack of keeping the knives and forks on the tables as they rounded Ardlamont in the winter. On 29 May 1970 a huge chapter in the history of the Clyde came to an end. For well over 100 years a steamer had called every day except Sunday at Tarbert pier, and at Ardrishaig in the summer months. Ardrishaig is now used mainly by vessels waiting to enter the sea-lock of the Crinan Canal.

Tighnabruaich was a treat in the fifties. The new road, magnificent in its way, bringing fresh and glorious views of the Kyles, had not yet opened. By land, it was down the single track road which is still much the same from Strachur on the east side of Loch Fyne, via Strathlachlan and Otter Ferry, up to Kilfinan and over to Kames. It was a long, wearying journey. It gave Tighnabruaich a gloriously remote air and a pier which really was the core of its life and being. The Royal Mail Ship Saint Columba brought the mails on her outward run and picked them up on her return. Most of the things the town needed came on her or on puffers. George Olding, the piermaster presided over the very heart of an empire. Industrious, laconic, given to ribbing assistant pursers, he was

Tighnabruich Pier on a Saturday afternoon, 1957

one of the few who could handle a full gangway unaided on the pier, heaving it up with prodigious strength. He did this many times a day in the fifties, although there were no longer the 20 calls a day which the pier had seen at its peak. Today the Waverley calls occasionally, together with the lesser vessels like Clyde Rose (the former Keppel) and the Second Snark (once Denny's tender to convey dignitaries out to new vessels during their trials). 1993 saw the welcome return of the 'Jupiter' class vessels, in that year bringing 32,000 visitors.

In the thirties a steamer lay overnight at Kames and called early in the morning at Auchenlochan before Tighnabruaich — three piers which were hardly a three minute walk apart! On occasions another vessel lay at Ormidale round on Loch Ridden to augment the early morning dash for Wemyss Bay and the trains.

In the fifties, there was the daily call and lie-over of the Queen Mary from Glasgow, turbines en route for Inveraray or Arran via the Kyles, and the Jeanie Deans at 4.10pm on her trip round Bute. In addition on Tuesdays, the Ayr excursion steamer Caledonia called with the Maids and the diminutive Countess of Breadalbane berthed from time to time.

Tighnabruaich had the most cosmopolitan of the passengers who came to the Clyde. 'All-the-way' folks from Glasgow mingled with foreign tourists to whom The Kyles (and Loch Lomond) were a must, and rather upper class yachting types who left their boats there — not yet glassfibre bathtubs but elegant varnished yachts and dayboats such as Dragons and Loch Longs. They rubbed shoulders alongside farmers delivering chickens to neighbours in Bute and Cowal as they packed their wives off to shop in Glasgow. I particularly remember one visitor from Belgium who read the sign at the pier which proclaimed that the local hotel was 'fully licensed'. He came back, tongue hanging out of his mouth half an hour later shaking his head in mystification at the British and their odd use of language. After all, it was Sunday!

If Corrie had had a pier, I'd have loved it; save that it was Lochranza and Whiting Bay which attracted me most. Brodick was and is a dull sort of a pier, lacking intimacy and warmth. Lochranza was the back door to Arran — as in a sense it still is with its ferry to Kintyre. It came to life twice a day when the Duchess of Hamilton called on the Campbeltown run. At 12.15pm and 4.35pm the sleepy somnolence was disturbed and the ubiquitous Ribbecks' buses appeared. There was just time to undertake Tour 10B — round Arran by coach, tea at Lagg and back aboard. The alternative was to return from Brodick to Ardrossan having sampled the exquisite apple tart and the less appealing historic treasures of Brodick Castle. Alas, the apple tart is no longer on the menu.

There were assistant pursers who claimed that on their days off they had cycled right round the island and been back in time for the steamer. Later when I did that I wisely allocated three days, stayed in the youth hostel and took in the dance at Lochranza village hall where the last waltz was always *He'll Have To Go* by Jim Reeves. Every time I hear it, even to this day, I am transported back to a magic night and a holiday romance with Helen, a nurse who would have graced the pages of a Mills and Boon novel.

Whiting Bay was the longest pier on the Clyde. In the days before the 'shortest distance' ethos, Arran steamers called there and at Lamlash, some sailing directly to the mainland. In the mid-fifties, before the car ferry Glen Sannox appeared, two steamers were required to maintain the Arran service.

When the letter from Gourock came in the spring of 1957, it said that the summer allocation of pursers had not yet been made, but would I care to come and spend the Easter period on the Caledonia assisting on the Arran run, mainly from Whiting Bay. This was my first real steamer, with a cabin to myself, and 'deep sea' to boot. When I joined her at Ardrossan, I found that the captain was none other than the legendary character 'Fergie' Murdoch. His summer command was the Duchess of Hamilton with which he will be forever associated. He was the Donald Crawford of the former Caley fleet. Rotund and portly, with a gleam in his eye, he had such a positive delight in handling vessels that it was a joy to sail with him. Long after he might have gone to the Queen Mary II as the senior command, he stayed loyal to his Duchess.

It was as well he was in command that Easter, because apart from a sunny spell lying at Whiting Bay, when he sat in the lee of the wheelhouse telling us of his experiences, it was wind and gale all the way — after all, it was a Glasgow holiday weekend.

There was no risk of the Caledonia foundering — she had been built by Denny's at a time when the London Midland and Scottish Railways were entering a period of ordering heavy sturdy boats — two sets of sisters, Caledonia and Mercury in 1934 to be followed by Jupiter and Juno

PS Caledonia arriving at Whiting Bay in 1957. Grimshaw Collection

in 1937. In both cases the second-named was lost on war service. The Caledonia, renamed Goatfell for war service, was bombed several times but bagged two enemy aircraft to add to the Saint Columba's U-boat.

Caledonia and her near identical sister looked quite unlike any previous paddler. Their paddle-boxes were concealed, that is to say there was no fan-shaped paddle cover. Instead the paddle-boxes were white like the hull, with a run of windows right round them. The ones in front of and behind the paddles were genuine windows — they illuminated the ladies and gents loos! Those in the middle, four in all, were fakes without glass. Behind them were the paddles — huge heavy affairs with steel floats instead of the more usual wooden ones. They emitted a solid, heavy beat which made these boats distinctive at a great distance. When the paddles were reversing, water flew out through the 'windows'. At times, those not in the know must have imagined they were sinking. Caledonia had one immense elliptical funnel — the widest on any of the boats and a very high bridge with wings which, in the modern fashion, protruded beyond the hull. She was just high enough never to suffer the indignity of having them wiped off by a pier at low tide!

The sisters set new standards for paddler accommodation. They could carry 1750 passengers with ease. They had elegant glass-enclosed deckhouses, inside which a double width stairway swept below to the dining saloon on the main deck forward in the fashion of the turbine steamers. Windows were big making the view for diners panoramic. There were long upper decks with plenty of space for passengers, especially on the front of the bridge and beneath it — in fact, in the position where most paddlers actually had their bridge. They were solid, well built, comfortable and therefore not flyers — 17 knots on trials was respectable, no more. Caledonia seldom reached that speed again.

The overall effect of this novel design was to make her look like a turbine from the side. Newspaper articles questioned this apparent attempt to hoodwink the Scottish public. Perhaps turbines were being seen to be all the rage and paddlers considered old-fashioned. With no worries about shallow water piers like Craigendoran, the sisters had a generous draught and were good seaboats. That Easter the Caledonia had to be. In strong winds and high seas we made it into Ardrossan and no more, thanks to Fergie, and at Whiting Bay we virtually had to carry the passengers and their luggage on and off. We brought two cars over but did not even try to put the planks out. By now I had found my sea-legs and was never to be queasy again until, that is, I cruised on larger ships, the 'school ships' Nevasa and Uganda. The big ones still get me every time.

As I stood on the main deck beside the Caledonia's three massive pistons pounding and punching us through the waves, I witnessed one of these little vignettes one can savour but is powerless to prevent. An elegant elderly lady, with a black feathered hat and a dead fox draped around her neck made her way to the toilets in the paddle box — but the wrong ones. Without a glance at the notice above the door, she walked in. I had 30 seconds to imagine the scene within. Then came a high falsetto scream, audible above the pistons and the sea, the door burst open and she emerged in haste. With masterly composure she collected herself and slowly walked off as if nothing had happened. Only the businessman I witnessed walking straight through the ornamental pond along the front at Glasgow Airport, complete with bowler hat, briefcase and rolled umbrella has matched that enviable sang froid. He left a watery trail all the way to his Mercedes, with not one single backward glance.

For four days I really enjoyed the luxury of the officers' accommodation below decks forward of the engine room — there was a cabin with twin berths for two assistants in the summer and they were made up by the stewards in that peculiar way that tradition dictated. I never cracked how you were meant to sleep in them. The sheets and blankets were so arranged that there seemed no way in between them, and once you did get in, no way out. Probably Drake or Nelson had set the fashion.

The Caledonia was by now the summer Ayr excursion steamer. Although she was awkward and heavy, and with that high bridge likely to be caught on the wind, she did well despite the narrow entrances there and at Troon. She did better than the first Ayr steamer — the Bonnie Doon, which was so unreliable and had to be towed back so frequently that she was known in auld Ayr as 'Bonnie Breakdoon'. The Caledonia did have a contretemps with the harbour wall at Ayr when returning in a gale from Campbeltown, but her gunwales, belting and stern plates were quickly repaired. No passengers were injured, thus preserving the remarkable safety record of the Clyde fleet. There were collisions in fog, inevitable groundings near piers but the safest place in the world in the fifties and since, must have been, and still is, on a Clyde vessel.

That said, I can recall later in the season, when passing through the narrows at the Kyles of Bute in the Jeanie Deans, seeing Caledonia aground in the trickier 'crooked channel' at that odd angle which always grips the heart when seeing a vessel in distress. No-one who saw the Waverley later and more publicly stranded on the Gantocks at Dunoon can ever forget such a sight. The Caledonia had just been given a new boiler and converted to oil burning. The grounding, the cause of which was never explained, altered the water level in the boiler and damaged the new gear, leading to her limping to Greenock after she refloated on the tide, and a period out of service. It was a clear sunny day with a stiff breeze. Perhaps not for the first time, a paddler had simply refused to answer the helm.

Caledonia served Ayr well until 1964 and was a great favourite cruising to all the resorts in the upper firth as well as to Arran and Campbeltown. Evening cruises to Brodick Bay, Pladda, and Holy Isle (but not specifically round it!) were a sheer delight of a summer's evening. Ayr is sadly lacking as a resort since the withdrawal of all services in 1964. I went to live there in 1965 and felt very deprived indeed.

Caledonia was then adapted to the even more unlikely waters of Craigendoran. It was a sad day when Donald Crawford rang 'finished with engines' on the telegraphs for the very last time in October 1969. She had topped her versatile career with a few days as the last paddler ever on the Royal Route to Tarbert. She was soon off to a new life on the Thames. Flying the flag of Bass Charrington the brewers and renamed Old Caledonia she ended on the Thames as a floating pub. I enjoyed many a pint on her wide top-deck of a summer's evening, imagining Fergie Murdoch there beside me reminiscing, but feeling distinctly homesick. A fire in 1980 so badly damaged her, that she had to be scrapped. It was a sad end to a great lady.

The Talisman — Anything But!

It was in May of 1956 that I learned where the summer would be spent. My hints that I wanted to sample life aboard a 'real' thirties Clyde steamer were partly answered. The diesel electric paddle vessel DEPV Talisman fulfilled some of the qualifications, but fell markedly short on the little matter of motive power. A quick look at the records kept turning up the words 'first' and 'only'. This is seldom a good combination. She was an experiment no-one dared repeat. When the only LNER vessel to follow her — Waverley in 1947 — was being planned, shudders of horror ran through the limbs of the Marine Superintendent at the prospect of another Talisman. He went for steam. And yet, the Talisman, like the Lucy Ashton, returned more times from the grave than did Lazarus.

You could belittle the Talisman, you could not ignore her. She saw off most of her contemporaries, staggering off to the knackers yard in Dalmuir as late as 1967. She gave so much trouble in the years between her building by, inevitably A&J Inglis in 1935, and 1939, that she was laid up in mid-season, with rumours rife about scrapping, or taking the steam engines out of another paddler, the old Waverley for a transplant. One by-product of this was a reprieve for another survivor the Lucy Ashton which had been condemned for the first time even before the First World War. It had hardly been decided between LNER, the builders, and the machinery suppliers English Electric to have one last go at sorting her out when the Admiralty took her and with that rare humour for which they are famous, renamed her Aristocrat. She did surprisingly well and was involved in the Dieppe and the Normandy landings.

After the Second World War, her trial speed of 17 knots was reduced to a plodding 14 by modifications to her deckhouses which sunk her lower in the water and by traditional wooden floats in place of steel ones on her paddles. She developed a whole new set of problems, which invariably came in mid-season or when there was no back-up vessel available. The engines were not the only problem. Her handling left much to be desired and at times she simply decided to ignore the telegraphs with results which I was soon to witness. No pier was safe from the intimate attentions of this lady. In 1953 they laid her up again to rust and fade in the Albert Harbour. What little embellishments there were in her spartan interior, tended to 'walk' as they frequently do from all condemned ships. Then fate intervened, with the result that when I reported to the Captain David McCormick and purser Jimmy Carter in the first week of June 1956, there she was, on the 'Millport Station' as it was traditionally known.

I joined her at Wemyss Bay. She looked conventional enough from the head of the pier. She was around 220ft long, a little shorter than Waverley and could carry 1252 passengers. She had conventional paddle boxes — nothing concealed about these, which were white and unembellished, apart from a black curved nameboard with her name picked out in gold. Her one funnel, rather upright, gave nothing away — indeed more smoke could come out of it than from a coal burner. I was later to witness her party piece. When she was really warmed up, lying alongside at Millport or Wemyss Bay, a huge cloud of black smoke would erupt from the funnel. Sometimes this was accompanied by a sheet of flame as excess lubricating oil caught fire. By the time calm was restored, frightened bystanders had sometimes summoned the fire brigade!

Her hull had a fairly straight, sharp stem and a cruiser stern, fashionable in the thirties. It was rather severe, and to my eyes graceless. One could somehow guess that she had been built to a price, and it was almost as if, in the excitement surrounding her revolutionary engines, insufficient attention had been given to the aesthetics. She was, to put it bluntly, no oil-painting. As I walked down the pier, I heard a familiar cacophony. She rattled, she shook, in fact the decibels exceeded all four Maids in unison. By contrast at the next berth lay Jupiter, silent apart from a slight hiss of escaping steam, and a lovely soft whine from somewhere down below. My heart sank; the morale of the crew was visibly on the low side. The master was no bundle of extrovert fun himself. On the positive side, Jimmy Carter was equable, experienced and sympathetic. By God, he had to be. The mate was so anonymous, I've forgotten his name. The pilot was Archie Stewart a man of great talent, which was just as well.

I had never been to Millport but several trips a day soon put that right. The Talisman had a run which had much to commend it and a nice mix of essential connections, cargo and goods and an 'afternoon cruise'. We backed out of Wemyss Bay, turned to starboard and headed down the firth bound for Largs. I did not grasp the significance of that seemingly simple and successful manoeuvre. For whatever reason the Talisman would not necessarily swing her bows as the helmsman wanted. A strong wind across the bows and she would only go the way she wanted. If that was to port, then the only way back was to carve a large circle upstream. Inconvenient in the open firth, this could be decidedly embarrassing in

Talisman at Wemyss Bay. The flags denote a charter. GRIMSHAW COLLECTION

more enclosed waters. I got used to dealing with passengers who, not unnaturally, thought they must have got on the Dunoon steamer by mistake when she headed off directly away from Largs. I remembered Donald Crawford reminiscing about his days on her and the need to compromise without loss of cool or dignity. Theories abounded — were the paddles just too far aft to balance her? Did she have too little draught at the bow? Speculation was endless; the crack of the crew tended to blame the rudder. In common with those of many Craigendoran steamers it was on the small side. Even today the Waverley shows signs of a similar affliction, with a turning circle of quite vast dimensions — at least a quarter of a mile.

My first memories of down below in the officer's quarters were of how the black hole of Calcutta must have been. Talisman rated only one assistant purser. The cabin was tiny, dark, with a porthole just on the waterline. My predecessors had clearly not seen fit to visit a first class railway compartment for a carpet! Still, it was home — 'a small thing but mine own' — albeit down some very precipitous steps. I dumped my week's supply of white shirts on the bunk, set the cap at a jaunty angle (or so I fondly imagined) and went to explore.

As I remarked Talisman had been built to a price. The LNER was short of money in 1935, and, compared to her contemporaries it showed. The best bit was the dining room which was on the main deck forward just as in the turbines. Paddlers tended to have them aft as there was no vibration at the stern. It would not have mattered where it had been sited on Talisman — we were back to the jumping cutlery syndrome. The dining room could seat 92 (in addition to the officers' table which lay behind a curtain) and was nicely panelled in polished walnut. The windows were

105

large and the view excellent. Behind it on the starboard side was the galley. It had an Aga range, but was otherwise all-electric. This was not good news for the cook; fuses could blow, as well as tempers, at the drop of a hat. The lounge and smokeroom/bar at the stern which originally had been Third Class were pretty plain and uninspiring. Most of the original upholstered chairs and settees had gone. One of them now lay across the bottom of the stair from the boat deck into the saloon — presumably to make sure that no-one escaped that way without paying. As well as a rather nice balustrade stairway up to the promenade deck at the front, and a more curved one aft, there were two narrow and steep stairs, one each side of the funnel casing. They would have taken you straight into the engine room on any other paddler, but not on this one.

The main diesel engines, four in number, were situated below the main deck and at that level, all that could be seen was a large glass enclosure in which was a mysterious gleaming circular contraption, bearing the legend English Electric and, if my memory serves me well, blue in colour. This was the revolutionary direct drive system attached to the paddle-shafts and which could turn them at up to 50rpm. The directors of the railway in 1935 had been proud of their new technology and keen to put it on display — a visit to the engines having wider connotations than mere mechanical interest. Watching this thing whirring round was better than watching paint dry, only in so far as it was close to the bar and a reliable source of fortification. Unfortunately the steps up and over the paddle-shaft were steeper and higher than on any other vessel I ever saw, and on the way back from the bar, were a potent source of trouble for the pleasantly inebriated. The full set was to fall down the stairs beside the funnel and then trip over the paddle-shafts on the way to the loos. It was frequently achieved by any engineer unwise enough to go on deck — the alarm bells about which I was soon to learn — could bring them rushing in a panic from the most unlikely and revealing places.

After a first call at Largs Pier, which we hit with a thump that shook the passengers but apparently not the crew, I set off to explore the upper deck. The deck houses had been altered after the war and looked similar to ones added then to Jeanie Deans and fitted to Waverley when she was built. The forward one had some nice Lloyd loom chairs, the after one wooden seats. On the front of this one, facing the stairs down, was the purser's office, which had been converted from the former sweetie stall and the deck chair store. It was surprisingly comfortable; a couple of deck chairs had been thoughtfully retained for sunny days. Where it had once been situated, closer to the single tall elliptical funnel, was now a space for the conveyance of cars. The destination 'fans' were up above and I had to shin up a ladder to change them. There were no railings, and on a dirty day it could be a bit of an ordeal.

On this first run for me, we reached Millport at 9.55am and I realised what a treat was in store. Millport is perhaps the most interesting of all the Clyde piers to approach. From Largs the steamer sails down river with Hunterston, now sadly disfigured by the redundant steel terminal to port and the island of Cumbrae to starboard. Once past Keppel, it is hard to starboard round Farland Point — a tousy spot when the tides are meeting there and round into Millport Bay The passage to the pier is through a narrowish gap between rocks to port and the outer and inner Eilans to starboard. After the inner, a sharp turn to port is required to come alongside the face of the pier. There are shallows all around and at the pier at low tide, little to spare. As at Rothesay and the West Bay at Dunoon, there were always rowing boats full of suicidal Glaswegians to negotiate as well.

The pier buildings were simple — low huts and the signal tower — and in those days always packed with people, trolleys, piles of cargo and livestock. At the head of the pier lies the Royal George hotel, the town stretching round the bay to the right. In the fifties Millport was popular with holidaymakers, golfers, and day-trippers, many of whom hired a bike to cycle round the island. A couple of Bedford buses owned by Millport Motors took the less energetic round and also ferried passengers to Keppel Pier to meet the Hamilton and the Montrose. We lay here overnight and there was clearly much to do and see. There were dances and ceilidhs to which I felt sure the uniform would provide a flying entry and I knew that for a spell the Turnbulls, one of the more charming branches of my family clan would have a house in Millport for the Paisley fair.

It was the custom for the Clyde working vessels to start the day early and finish early. We would be tucked up at the Old Pier by 7.15pm every evening, while the night was young. Years later only the competition from Western Ferries and public demand would change a situation which left Dunoon, Rothesay, Millport and Brodick cut off by early or mid-evening. That in turn would force a shift system for the crews, unheard of in the fifties. The idea, commonplace today, of two crews and two captains with intense on and off rosters was long into the future. Unlike Loch Lomond, there were at least days off for the crew, although never at weekends. The lower ranks covered for each other as best they might. As they tended to live aboard, a day off could simply mean sailing around with a daunder ashore wherever we happened to be. For officers, excluding assistant pursers, a relief appeared and thus the closed community of the crew was enriched by the regular appearance of a group of nomads, often having to hitch lifts on one boat in their attempts to reach another. Like bees collecting pollen, they brought the news of what was going on throughout the fleet.

It paid to learn their ways. While some were content to fall in with the practices they found, others would insist on having it their way for one day a week. The reputations of relief masters were shared around assistant pursers — were they easy going, uniform martinets, or punctuality fiends? Were they subject to last minute changes of tactic which laid the boat alongside with the wrong side in, with seamen and pursers left high and dry with the wrong rails down for the gangway? This could be no laughing matter. With safety paramount, taking out the centre support of the double gates and swinging them back took time; often they were ill-fitting and rusty. A space had to be jealously guarded round the hessian mat which protected the deck, so that gangways could come aboard. Passengers seemed to love pressing forward, eager to be first off, seemingly even if it meant the amputation of a foot or at least a toe. This was where paddle-steamers scored. There were chains across the steps at the back of the paddle box and across the wings of the sponsons on either side which could restrain the reckless and the feckless until we were ready to turn them loose.

Another pet-hate was mates who could not decide which deck to have the gangway on, according to the state of the tide, causing last minute dashes through the throng either up or down. The wiser ones left it to us. In the interests of survival, you quickly learned to make the right judgment when still several hundred yards from the pier. To make matters worse some piers were high like Gourock and Dunoon and others low, especially Rothesay, where at high tide, the assembled throngs could give the impression that they were walking on water; there was a real risk there of berthing on top of the pier rather than alongside it.

On the Talisman, we longed for the relief skipper. Our own was going through a difficult patch. He was later to serve with cautious distinction for many years as master of Queen Mary II, but he was in 1956 new to the Talisman and just beginning to grapple with her ways. These could take years to master. He was a huge man with lugubrious features with, at that time, a strong tendency to the morose. He appeared to be constantly preoccupied with the impending horrors of taking the next pier. He was not given to small talk at the breakfast table, especially not with assistant pursers, whom he held comprehensively in low esteem. His sustenance consisted solely of two boiled eggs and I still have a vivid picture of this vast man with a rim etched across his forehead where his cap had been, hunched over and dwarfing an egg cup with a company crest; one egg getting the treatment, a spare in the saucer. Conversation withered when he appeared. In time it came about that he dined when others did not; mates, engineers and pursers seemed to find urgent things to delay their arrival until he had gone. Even the gregarious Jimmy Carter could not guarantee to bridge the social gap. The stewards were simply terrified; me too!

On only my second day, the purser had suggested in the boiling heat of the day that we adopt the common practice of appearing on deck with caps, black ties, and white shirts buttoned at the wrists, but without jackets. As I mounted the steps to the paddle-box as we neared Largs, a deep bellow, drowning the noise from the funnel, instructed me publicly and embarrassingly on the niceties of naval sartorial etiquette. I cringed, went scarlet behind the ears and fled into the office for my battledress jacket. I wore it even in my cabin for weeks after that in case he might appear. The next day, his relief humorously upbraided me for wearing a jacket in the stifling heat. His simpler rule was easier to live with — never jacketless at table.

I have to admit over the years to having growing sympathy for the strict approach. One thing which mars the otherwise impressive performance of CalMac today is the slackness of the approach to uniform. Passengers expect to see better than a man with a pullover, no tie and no cap on the bridge of a 3000-ton ferry. Insignia and rank badges inform and reassure. Discipline at the top sets the example for all those with whom the public come into contact — seamen in denims and stewards in motley garb give a poor impression. Former colleagues in education in Strathclyde and Suffolk who read this will smile as they blame Captain McCormick for my insistence in later years that a jacket must be worn by officers attending any major local government meeting. In a moment of pure déjà vu, I once saw the aristocratic chairman of Suffolk County Council, heat wave or no, blistering the hapless chairman of the education committee for disrobing in public! The real lesson for both that council chairman and the captain of the Talisman is that you should never humiliate people in public. The quiet word maintains respect and protects people's feelings.

Impeccably attired, I began to get into the swing of things. Monday mornings started with the Cumbrae version of the 'deathboat'. We cast off at 6.35am for the first run to Wemyss Bay. There were few doting wives in evidence to see off husbands going back to Glasgow to work, while leaving the family in Millport for a longer break. On a fine morning it seemed no hardship to be roused by the steward before 6am and climb sleepily on deck. The sights that greeted one were various and unpredictable. I did not expect to come upon a mature bull tied to the railings by his nose ring, exercising an irascibility presumably associated with the temporary withdrawal of what the wee steward from Govan would call his 'conjugial rights'. Whole sections of the rails shook and vile liquids cascaded onto the deck so recently hosed down. The bull soon had a whole paddle-wing to himself and not a living soul dared wander downwind of him.

There could be crates of chickens, assorted goats and sheep, and our speciality — calves in bags. The freight rate for them was considerably less than when ambulant, presumably because they took ashore with them in the sack what the bull so profligately left behind. It was my job

The Talisman aground at Arrochar, 1952. ORR, POLLOCK & CO. LTD., GREENOCK

to enter these on the cargo manifest and work out the charges with the ready reckoner. There must be something about farmers; there were inevitably disputes and appeals based on various combinations of poverty and the bad luck imposed upon them by the Cumbrae weather. The trait is in evidence today in their counterparts in Cumbria.

Much of the cargo came aboard on trolleys of the sort there used to be on every railway station in the days when porters could still be found. They were humphed aboard over the planks by the sweating seamen at all stages of the tide and packed between the funnel and the purser's office, where at least they were handy for checking. There were cases and hampers — Passengers' Luggage in Advance — and a bewildering array of sacks, boxes, cartons, milk churns and odd bits of machinery for farms and fishing boats. It was fascinating to see the whole support system for an island pass across the decks of one vessel. Soon the car ferries would make two or three cargo trips a week loaded with lorries and vans and the glamour would go. However, for the time being it went on as it had done for a hundred years and more.

The early run out from Millport at 7.20am for the rest of the week and the next one at 10.15am were heaviest. There was no alternative to entering the cargo on the manifest on the open deck, cowering against the funnel casing in the worst weather, cap held on by the chin strap in case the skipper passed by en route to his assignation with his eggs. At Wemyss Bay the trolleys for the return trip were parked under that lovely glass arcade which swept so grandly down from the station and which has recently been restored. We had, mercifully, at least 45 minutes alongside on the first run, so the game was to get up there and negotiate with the porters to leave the trolleys just long enough to allow the manifest to be completed in sheltered comfort. There was a doodlebug on the pier, so the trolleys tended to leave linked up as a train with myself running after the last one, pencil in hand, if time was tight. A seaman had to be 'ordered' to man the gangway while all this was going on. Helping to haul trolleys over the planks was the price I had to pay — these things had a life of their own, with the towing handle attached to swivelling front wheels of small diameter. In later life I have had little trouble with supermarket trolleys as a result of this exacting apprenticeship.

By 12.45pm (there was no truck with continental 24 hour timetables then) we had completed two round trips calling at Largs each time, except Saturday lunchtime when we could be full leaving 'the Bay'. We had supplied Millport with essentials and perishables, including ironically fish, and brought trippers galore. We were ready for our cruise. This was grandly billed as the 'Cumbrae Circle Cruise' — or more accurately as one of them. The Jupiter sailed round in the opposite direction.

Leaving Millport at 1.15pm and calling for the crowds at Largs, we arrived at Rothesay at 2.45pm where we lay until 4pm. While the passengers were ashore there was time for the kind of nap that the Argyll's roster had never afforded. She was usually just arriving as we left. We turned round to sail past Craigmore, its pier long closed but its tearoom yet open, and round the beautiful coast of Bute. The Talisman had called until as recently as 1955 at Kilchattan Bay Pier and was still advertised to sail round the bay before making for Millport, approaching from the other direction than that of her normal route. In time the pretence was dropped completely and we could make Millport comfortably for what was in effect the last up run at 5.05pm to Wemyss Bay. It was a cruise composed of segments, all of which were separately advertised as service runs. It made good financial sense and it was popular, especially as it gave a Rothesay outing to folks staying at Millport and Largs. Trippers could join at Rothesay and complete the full circle by changing at Wemyss Bay. Our last run back to Millport was quiet except on Fridays when the fathers returned. With their families safely on the pier at Millport awaiting their homecoming, they needed no encouragement to make for the bar with no need to pretend that they were going to see the engines.

On Saturdays, there was no cruise; instead there was an extra 'bus-run' to Wemyss Bay. Sunday more than made up. We had a long lie before sailing off at 2pm for a cruise to Kyles of Bute (with time ashore) which cost six shillings from Millport and Largs, four shillings from Rothesay. We reached Tighnabruaich at 4pm allowing, on a good day, 40 minutes ashore. We arrived as Queen Mary II left and fielded the usual crop of latecomers. After the Talisman left you were virtually marooned. The Kyles was for me real cruising and I enjoyed it immensely. The passage through the narrows never failed to excite me. You could guarantee pretty well every passenger would be on deck as we slid between the black and red buoys, the water seemingly sucked out from the rocky eilans as we passed, almost touching them with the paddle boxes. On Sundays we relaxed visibly as a crew.

The darker side of the Talisman's nature unfolded as the weeks rolled by. There were numerous manifestations. One was the frequency with which we tended to hit piers, or take unpredictable sweeps which left my heart in my mouth. One can only surmise at the effect on those manning the bridge. There was neither opportunity or inclination to pop up and see at first hand. The captain grew more twitchy by the day. He could not blame the engineers. Uniquely in the fleet, at that time, the Talisman had 'bridge control'; in other words when the captain moved the telegraphs, they were directly connected to the engines. Alibis were out. On the other hand, to be fair, there was a history of the Talisman wilfully ignoring commands. The telegraphs operated two small motor-driven, and at times unpredictable, generators called 'exciters'. It was an apt description.

Exciting moments on record had included running aground at Kilcreggan in 1948 when there was no response to 'half ahead'; she was soon high and dry 400 yards from the pier. All the passengers were taken safely ashore and tugs pulled her off next day. She contrived a similar feat at Arrochar in 1952. Passengers were ferried ashore in the lifeboats. Five hundred of them were on the Three Lochs Tour, so the Prince Edward must have had a long wait at Tarbet. A year later she had surprised everyone waiting at Dunoon Pier by sailing past at full ahead and circling for 45 minutes at full speed before they could stop her. After that, of course, they couldn't start her and she had to drop anchor while things were sorted out. One can imagine the apprehension any skipper must have felt approaching a pier. After this Donald Crawford must have enjoyed the Maid of Argyll if only for her sheer predictability. His successor Colin McKay, later to be associated with the Waverley, had developed a novel technique for coping at Millport. When coming out astern, when she was at her most unpredictable, he would lower the anchor, which would hold the bow in place while she went out, dragging the anchor along the sandy bottom.

Largs seemed even more of a problem for Captain McCormick. A good thud on the concrete was routine. One sunny breezy morning on the first run of the day to Wemyss Bay, we struck it so hard that expensive noises came from the paddle box and great dents could be seen in its protective belting. The captain could hardly come down to inspect the damage. He affected a casual nonchalance which he maintained until Wemyss Bay where he came down ever so slowly from the bridge and made his way ashore, as if for a casual stroll. Every eye was on him. As he passed the offending paddle-box, the nameplate with TALISMAN in gold letters, as if

The DEPV Talisman. GRIMSHAW COLLECTION

in silent reproach, fell off, bounced on the belting and plopped into the sea. He continued on his way up the pier without changing pace, or even succumbing to what must have been an overpowering urge to glance backwards. When he returned half an hour later the board had been retrieved, running repairs to the box effected and the nameplate was back in place. Not a word was ever uttered about the incident. Of course, it turned out to be just the precursor to all sorts of incidents. On another occasion, by way of a change, we were so far out from Largs Pier and for so long, attached solely by a single rope that a wag on the pier shouted to the bridge 'Just wait there and we'll extend the pier to reach you!'

By this time I was as curious as anyone might be as to why this ill-fated craft had been 'saved' in 1953. A string of coincidences turned out to be the answer. In 1953 the Duchess of Fife, then in her jubilee year was withdrawn from the Millport run, full of years and honour, a victim of the modernisation programme. It was decided to replace her with the Marchioness of Lorne, which had been built pre-war for the Holy Loch run and looked rather like a smaller version of the Caledonia without the flying bridge, but with one squat funnel and concealed paddle-boxes. With plans to close the Holy Loch piers well advanced and in the end reversed only by public pressure and the coming of the Maid of Ashton, the Marchioness was available for Millport. She was notoriously slow managing less than 12 knots; she had barely made 12 on her trials even with coal brought in specially by Fairfields who built her. On the Holy Loch run, she survived; on the longer passages of the Millport run she could not. There were complaints from the public, and her master, Colin McKay, a stickler for timekeeping, if not disgruntled was certainly far from gruntled. What was to be done? An unlikely solution presented itself.

In spite of her eccentricities, the Talisman had virtues. She was economical, using a fraction of the fuel a paddle-steamer would use; she

113

could be warmed up in minutes and would be a good winter stand-by boat. Her root problem over nearly 20 years had not been the unique electric motor in the glass case wrapped round the paddle shaft, it had been the four diesel engines which generated the electricity to make it turn. If it had not been for the fact that she could sail on any two of them, she'd have hardly sailed at all. But, wait a minute, were not all these new British Polar engines doing great things in the 'Maids' and just beginning to do so in the car ferries? Was it worth the gamble of completely new diesels? British Polar had four 'on offer' from a broken contract. A deal was struck, the ship breaker's contract was cancelled and off she went in the spring of 1954 to D&W Henderson for a transplant. On 17 June of that year she ran trials, managed 15 knots, one more than her best after war service and a week later it was the Marchioness of Lorne instead which went off to the breakers and the Talisman which took over at Rothesay one afternoon halfway round the Cumbrae Circle. The story, as you have seen, did not have an entirely happy ending. The diesel engines were satisfactory, the systems and the hoodoo remained.

Captain McKay found her faster but less predictable. On one occasion, as she passed through the Eilans and prepared to swing into Millport Pier the steering failed completely. Some very speedy work by engineers got things going again, but it was a heart-stopping moment. After that, not one, not two, but three failsafe systems were fitted to ensure that whatever happened, the electric power for steering would not fail. In addition, alarm klaxons were fitted to go off if there were any serious problems with the engines. By the time I served on her, these went off quite indiscriminately, almost always as false alarms. Hardly a meal passed without an alarm; stewards routinely took back half-eaten meals to keep them warm while engineers sprinted below. It was decidedly nerve-racking.

And then it happened. As we passed the selfsame spot where the steering had gone in 1954, it happened again. In theory it was impossible; in practice all three systems failed, which they had never once done in test drills. The skipper rang for full astern and, by God, he got it! You will recall that going astern was not Talisman's strong point, but this time, miraculously, she flew straight back out, retracing her own wake, missing every rock and island. The steering worked perfectly minutes later. It was much longer before we plucked up courage to approach the pier. Ned Higgins, the chief engineer and the captain were a bit introspective for a while after that. They could not simulate what had happened, no matter what they tried.

There were other incidents in the years that followed. On one occasion while lying serenely at Tighnabruaich she took it into her head to move off on her own, with no-one at the helm or the bridge telegraph. She was just beginning to rearrange the topography to the west of the pier with that infamous bow when an engineer — breaking all known records even for the Talisman — legged it below and threw the requisite emergency switch. There is no record of the conversation at table after that one. It is perhaps just as well. They had pulled her off by attaching a new stern rope and letting her heave herself off. With her luck she might well have gone right round the pier and ended up with her stern on the beach! It was all great fun and not lacking in excitement. In spite of it all, many Millport folks developed a great affection for this flighty matron.

The night life in Millport was to my taste. In the long summer evenings, I managed twice to play a full round of golf before darkness, rushing off before the passengers, up the pier with clubs clanking merrily, much to the annoyance of the skipper. I saw little of Margaret, even from a distance, as we passed Toward only once a day Monday to Friday. But thanks to 'free' connecting trips arranged by other student pursers, we managed the odd assignation. Donald Crawford still gave her a wave from the Argyll, passing close in as was his wont, near to the inner buoy. The more circumspect, especially the turbines went round the outer one, far offshore except at high tide, as the shallows over the reef could rattle every plate and cup in the saloons.

I was soon to be in a position to pass Toward no less than 14 times on Saturdays. The Jupiter was short of an assistant purser in mid-season, and Captain McCormick with suspicious alacrity offered my services to Hector Connell. Was it something I said, I wondered? I needed no second bidding and transferred my kit to the Jupiter at 9am next morning at Wemyss Bay. A real steamer at last!

The Talisman grew to be a happier ship, her erstwhile captain moved on in time to the Queen Mary II, where life was predictable and the regal lady's manners impeccable. In later years I came rather to like the Talisman. On winter Sundays she did a remarkable round trip linking all the main piers from Gourock to Millport. She became a Mecca for the nostalgic, the hardy and some would say the foolhardy. I remember on one bitterly cold day, her saloon heaters suffered a fault. Exhibiting all the acute symptoms of hypothermia, I repaired with Geoffrey Grimshaw, Wilf Gellatly and other worthies of the Clyde River Steamer Club to the Royal George in Millport for warmth and sustenance. It took a lot of willpower to go back when the trumpet on the funnel blew for the return trip.

Jupiter

The Jupiter had style. She was built in 1937 on the same slip as her sister-ship Juno, which was lost during the war. Fairfields were used to building big ships which was presumably why they had room for two Clyde steamers bow to stern. Their hulls were virtually identical in dimensions to that of Caledonia and they shared the feature of concealed paddle-boxes. There the similarity ended. Jupiter and Juno had two elegant funnels; in the modern way, both were in front of the paddle-boxes. In the old style like the first Glen Sannox, Columba and Iona, one funnel was behind the paddles, one in front, giving a powerful but old-fashioned look.

Jupiter was intended more for ferry services than cruising and was heavily built to face up to winter gales and rain. There was no boat or upper deck for passengers and no observation saloon forward, merely a deck shelter. Her bridge was lower and more graceful than Caledonia's, with the captain's cabin behind. The space between the funnels was open for cars and cargo. Behind the first funnel was a little book and fruit stall which was so exposed that only the boldest passengers braved the deck to get there on stormy days. The girl who ran it had a fair chance of succumbing to hypothermia. Above the deck-shelter and purser's office were the destination fans close by the after funnel. They were reached from a ladder at the back which I was to shin up in all weathers, hanging on to my cap and my dignity as I ascended. At least on Saturdays when we went back and forward all day between Wemyss Bay and Rothesay, the destination boards could be left alone. I found that the funnel made a back-drop against which Margaret could see me from her house at Toward Point. She could see the white-top of my cap as I waved it to and fro while I could just make out her towel as she stood on the wall which adjoined the shore. It was not long before caps were waved from the bridge too. The captain, Hector McKenzie was a kindly if quiet soul and the relief mate was none other than Robin Hutchison, my old shipmate from the Argyll. It was like a home from home; the purser was John Brewster from Stirling.

In marked contrast to Talisman, Jupiter was well furnished below decks. Her engines were the most impressive of all the paddlers — big, powerful, gleaming. There was always that evocative aroma of steam and lubricating oil which today's railway buffs savour when steam specials come over the Settle to Carlisle railway line and into Appleby where I now live. I walk up to the station just to sniff the air and memories of the Jupiter come flooding back.

Forward of the engines was a lounge which, although it had been third class when she was built, was rich in red Serayah wood panelling, and had red flooring tiles polished until they shone. One deck down was the dining saloon, a small one for a mere 30 and with only portholes to provide light. It was gloomy and so was the food! The steward and the cook were the most casual I came across. The same raw materials the other vessels received came aboard, but these two could make the end-product completely tasteless and usually cold, except for the salads which were lukewarm. On occasions when more diners were expected, as on the Sunday cruise, the tables were taken up to the lounge above. Raising the level at which meals were served sadly did not have a corresponding effect on the food. The officers resorted to private supplies secreted in their cabins to augment the official fare, like boys at a public school with their tuck-boxes.

One of the stewardesses was known throughout the fleet as 'Timber Aggie'. Apparently, she had been a fearsome axe wielder during wartime service in the Women's Forestry Corps at Benmore. She was huge, brash, and tough. She could swear like a trooper and sink a pint faster than any man. She was reputed to have a heart of gold. If so it was well concealed behind her more than ample bosom. Assistant pursers were low in her social reckoning. Each unspeakable course she served at table landed before me with a thud which indicated how fortunate I was that she was serving me, and that if the Caledonian Steam Packet Company had not taken leave of their senses, I would have been assigned to more appropriate duties in the galley, instead of lording it at the Captain's table.

In the days when Jupiter had undertaken many busy evening cruises, Aggie had been employed as a barmaid. She could pull pints simultaneously with both hands, while pouring a gin and tonic with her teeth. It was vouched for beyond dispute that when called short with a full and drouthie horde at the bar, she would pull a company-crested chamber pot from beneath the counter, conceal it beneath her skirt and lodge it between her thighs. She could have served as a model for the barman in Jeff Torrington's *Swing, Hammer, Swing!* — in order to enable him to protect the till at all times he was reputed to have run a catheter up the inside of his leg!

I made my way aft on this first day, blissfully unaware of all this, through the first class smokeroom, and down a deck to the officers' accommodation. It was splendid — a cabin for two shared with Norman Roxburgh, later to be Junior Purser on the Countess of Breadalbane. The woodwork and decor was to the same standard as the public rooms. Apart from the captain with his eyrie behind the bridge, all the officers had cabins here and they were, with a couple of exceptions, a cheery lot.

To the best of my knowledge Jupiter had a unique feature. There were officers' 'usual offices' at the after-end of the port paddle-box. These contained a bath which was steam-heated. The method was to fill it with cold water and then open a steam valve. Within a few minutes it was piping hot. I found the same principle later in the glorious brass and copper 'Windermere Kettle' of my steam launch, Galatea. Fill it with water, turn a valve, and 30 seconds later instant coffee or afternoon tea.

There was a problem with this luxurious feature though and it related to Archie Paton, second engineer. The bath was his obsession. He washed and polished it twice daily and regarded its use by others as an unnecessary undoing of his sterling work with Ajax and scourer. As the door lay straight across from the engine-room he had a prime viewing position to watch anyone approaching with a towel and sponge. Archie could assume a ferocious scowl calculated to deter all but the most determined or the positively unhygienic. At times he would complain about the profligate use of steam, hinting darkly that a late arrival at our destination could be pinned at the door of a hapless bather. I very much doubt if this was critical to her performance, but it has to be said that Jupiter, capable of 17 knots in her heyday, now needed all the help she could get from any source, be it steam, tide, wind, or act of God. When laden she tended to dig her bows in as she tried to gain speed. The result was 13 knots at best. The boiler was ailing and the tubes were leaking. Both Archie and the chief, whose name appropriately was Hope, were non-competitive by nature. The latter was known as 'Abandon' — his reputation for reducing to a crawl the speed of any steamer on which he served was well deserved. If the skipper rang down for more speed for a 'race' they put the regulator back a notch instead. Archie conserved the company's coal supplies as jealously as he guarded the bath. We became used to sneers and ridicule from all the boats that roared past us. I still have a mental picture of the Saint Columba passing us in the Kyles so swiftly that I could swear we were going astern. We still loved Jupiter.

In spite of the food and Archie, this was a happy ship provided that people took care only to have a bath on Archie's day off. Undoubtedly the crew hung together because this lovely steamer was under threat. The main ferry routes were now the province of the car ferries, which could all cope with cars and cargo with hydraulic ramps and turntables in place of the planks; lesser cruises now were cheaper for the Maids to carry out. Jupiter was almost a spare boat, ideal when big crowds were about at the fair, or the Cowal Games. She could shift 1509 passengers and disembark them in minutes. Her paddle-boxes, were so expansive that no less than eight gangways could be used at one time, four on top and two on each sponson. As the crowds poured off at Wemyss Bay for the train, she would heel over and slowly right herself as they left. Passengers had to be kept off the paddle-box wings until she was berthed, or the paddle nearest the pier would dig-in with the heeling, and choke itself with water while the other was virtually high and dry. This did not help the handling. The rudder was too small to cope and even hard over Jupiter had a tendency to embark on an unscheduled circular cruise!

Jupiter could accommodate up to six cars on her decks. In those days, before things became computerised, you could tell where these cars came from. An 'S' meant it was Scottish (as it still does). SB was Argyll, HS Renfrewshire, VS Greenock, and XS Paisley. Postmarks on letters have gone the same way sadly. Greenock letters are postmarked Paisley, and Cumbria seems to have crossed the Border to become part of Dumfries and Galloway.

On weekdays, life was leisurely and we spent much of each morning lying at Wemyss Bay, watching car ferries, the Talisman and cruise ships come and go. We had ample time to do the balances, and check the ticket stocks while watching others toil. The seamen had three tasks which were vital to the daily routine. First they had to see to their area of deck — the ship was apportioned to them in sections. Each day the brasses had to be done, the bell, the telegraphs, the door-handles and the ends of the rails, where there were gates and the wood was brass-trimmed. Each seaman jealously hoarded his rags, his steel wool and his Brasso for these tasks. Ship shape is the word to describe the end-product. Later after coaling, the decks would be washed with hoses and scrubbed down until they shone.

Highland seamen were highly dangerous with a hose in their hands. Leave a window open a quarter of an inch and they would home in on it. No-one could be sure that the hose would not wander their way if they gave the slightest pretext. This was their pure Gaelic phase each day and the mischief was upon them.

Coaling was laborious and messy, the stokers wheeling barrows down the planks from a rail-truck on the pier and shovelling it below. Their language was earthy and Lallans. Jimmy, a weedy wraith of a man, who seemed too insubstantial to survive in such a demanding job, would accompany the coaling with what we eventually concluded was his idiosyncratic version of the songs of Harry Lauder; but he was severely glottally challenged and it was difficult to be sure. The dirge was also too tuneless to add much to the available evidence.

Jimmy's wife was one of a number who came aboard for direct receipt of the wage packet from the purser's window of a Friday. A small crocodile of women, assorted weans dangling about their persons, prams left at the gangway, was a sure sign of payday. The wives opened the envelopes and their men folk docilely accepted their allowance, before the crocodile once more reclaimed dry land. It was a hard life for many folks then, and keeping the men from the drink a constant burden. These were, in the old Scots word, really 'trauchled' women. There was no equality then; the women carried the burden of responsibility and family and had no thought to a job of their own while the weans were about their feet.

At lunchtime each day we set off for Rothesay, where we prepared for the Cumbrae Circle, in the opposite direction to the Talisman. We left Rothesay at 2.45pm as the Talisman arrived, calling at Wemyss Bay and Largs before going round Cumbrae and calling at Millport at 4.30pm. On the last lap we would pass Talisman en route from Rothesay. After all that we did just one round trip to Wemyss Bay to lie up for the night. It was not taxing and I sensed that it was not likely to last. Although rather profligately converted at the end of the season to oil-burning, but with the boiler still suspect, Jupiter was soon withdrawn. She sailed only 20 weeks as an oil-burner, at a conversion cost of £30,000 — a lot of money in the fifties.

Back and forth between 'the Bay' and Rothesay made Saturday a busy day. Amongst the passengers were the odd celebrities. Richard Todd the film star had connections in Bute, and Colin Clark and Grace Murray were regulars at the Winter Gardens — their double-act on the bridge on the way over was an impromptu rehearsal of their act. Sunday was a complete contrast. We sailed light to Bridge Wharf in the morning, canted laboriously round with the aid of ropes strung across the river, and prepared for the afternoon cruise to Dunoon and Lochgoilhead, leaving at 2.15pm and returning at 9.40pm. The whole trip was a delight and the short stop at Lochgoilhead allowed legs to be stretched. This cruise sadly was never well patronised and survived only as long as the Jupiter herself — one more season. By the time we reached Glasgow towards the end of the season it was almost dark; the sunset could be beautiful and stark, the cranes and gantries of the idle yards silhouetted against the sky. Then there was another 'light trip' down river — how pleasant boats are at sea without passengers. It's just as true of schools without pupils and hospitals without patients.

For me it was an easy day — hours between piers and every opportunity to take the wheel, assess the talent and develop meaningful relationships. Captain Connel did not share my keen anticipation of the Sabbath. His face fell visibly as the roster confirmed on Friday that we were to be Lochgoilhead bound. He was no lily-livered weakling but strong men buckled at the knees at the thought of getting Jupiter in and out of Lochgoilhead, with its shallow water and scarcely enough room to

A sunny afternoon at Lochgoilhead on board the Jupiter. GRIMSHAW COLLECTION

back out in a half-circle to head back down. But then, no pier was easy with the Jupiter.

We who loved her were loathe to admit it but she was a complete brute at slow speed, not unpredictable like the Talisman, just liable to wallow around at the mercy of events until something happened. At Rothesay where there is a sharpish turn to come alongside, many's the time we simply ended up too far out parallel to the pier, but beyond the range of the heaving line. We then had to paddle back and forward along the full length of the pier until some freak of wind or tide blew us close enough to get a rope ashore. The piermaster, a soul of tact, was careful not to signal which berth was ours until we were actually alongside.

The uncertainty as to whether we were coming or going made us particularly prone to the apocryphal but true tale of the man who rushed down the pier, hesitated, and leapt like an Olympic longjumper onto the paddle-box to lie gasping but triumphant. There was a variety of ways of breaking the news that we were in fact coming-in!

Throughout her career Jupiter had attracted harsh words — she was 'somewhat decried' as a pre-war newspaper spoke of her. Words like 'clumsy' we could take, but 'barge' and 'scow' hurt to the quick. Admittedly, Jupiter had her moments in the jousts with Largs Pier when the wind caught her. One of her exploits was at Hunter's Quay where she veered off course and demolished some rather posh yachts moored at the fashionable racing HQ of the Clyde. She can hardly be blamed for missing Brodick in a thick fog and rearranging the foreshore but the excuse rates a mention. It seems that a horse had been loaded backwards at Ardrossan — at least as bad an omen for mariners as killing an alba-

Jupiter alongside the Empress of Scotland in 1952. GRIMSHAW COLLECTION

tross. Oddly when P&A Campbell ordered their Cardiff Queen from Fairfields in 1947, the same design was accepted, although she was made 15ft longer in an effort to lessen the tendency to nose-dive. Like Jupiter she became much loved in spite of her drawbacks.

I must admit that in my spell aboard, we had a lot of fun. Sometimes we would lie at anchor in Rothesay Bay when not required and raising the anchor was always pure pantomine. There was no absolute guarantee that she would go astern to pull it off the bottom. If there was anything — an old cable or other debris left by the Royal Navy — to foul we could manage it. The Jupiter had always been expected to go anywhere as required and it was no surprise when we found ourselves on the Arran run for a few days. She acquitted herself nobly in a severe storm. Unlike the Caledonia with its high bridge and superstructure, Jupiter heeled little and adhered to the timetable.

Flushed with success we went back to the Cumbrae Circle and failed to stop in time at Millport at low tide. We were aground, unable to land passengers until the tide rose and we floated off. A certain mate's career which had started on the Maid of Argyll, nearly ended that day. There is nothing worse for a navigating officer than to be aground for 40 minutes with the bridge at exactly the same level as the wags on the pierhead. The best the mate could manage was that it was deliberately done to clean the weed off the bottom on the sand! Talisman had a near monopoly on this excuse. I later found out that Jupiter had been aground for half an hour at the same place earlier in the year, 'cleaning' the hull on the way to Arran. On the way back she damaged her paddle-box on the piles of the pier, just for good measure.

Inevitably Jupiter was heavily involved in the Cowal Games, carrying the hordes over to Dunoon in the morning and back in the evening. Jupiter always did the last run which was well after 10pm and in the dark. As we approached the pier was awash with pipe bands in various states of disarray. Cups and trophies full of McEwans and Tennants best

122

were brandished as bottles clinked beneath kilts and the wailing of a hundred pipers was like a thousand cats on the tiles on a bad night. We herded, we cajoled, we even carried them aboard — and then it happened. One lurched, lost his footing and plunged into the murky depths. In the inky black, the belting was crashing against the pier in a way that would crush anyone trapped there to certain death. For once the seamen, usually quick to act, hesitated, calculating the odds. They drew back. Out of the corner of my eye, I saw the relief purser, the quietest and gentlest of men, stripping off. They put a rope round his waist and in he plunged. He was instantly lost to view in the waves, the spray, and the backwash from the slimy green piles of the pier. Time stood still. After what seemed like an eternity, he reappeared, a sodden unconscious kiltie clasped in his arms. Gentle arms pulled them onto the sponson and thence onto the deck. I remembered the life-saving drill I had learned for my course at Gorbals Baths and we brought the piper round. I was half-cut with the impact of his returning breath! The purser was selling tickets ten minutes later and he refused to speak to the press or to be a hero. That is why I do not name him even today. I later learned that he was a wartime hero, with decorations to testify to his bravery. I have since observed again and again that really courageous men are almost always amongst the least assuming and most modest. Hollywood got it wrong and still does.

The records show that in 1893 at Rothesay, a man and a young child fell into the water when the Mercury was casting off. A young man, Joseph McGuire, stripped to the waist, jumped from the pier to the paddle-box, grabbed and held the man until willing hands pulled him aboard. Down he went again to rescue the child. As they were re-united on deck he vanished into the crowd on the pier. Only a label on his jacket left on the pier enabled him to be traced. Not every story has such a happy ending. On a winter visit I saw a man die in Greenock in the Albert Harbour before he could be fished out. Two minutes was all it took, the strength visibly draining from him, before a rope or lifebelt could be found.

A week or two before the season ended, I was transferred yet again, this time to Queen Mary II where the assistant purser was plagued by re-sits. It was to be an interesting introduction to life on the busiest vessel in the fleet, to which I returned a couple of years later. In truth by that stage Jupiter hardly justified one purser let alone two. I had tears in my eyes as I stood at Wemyss Bay watching Jupiter cast off and make for Rothesay, while I boarded the train for Glasgow. She was the most elegant, of steamers, warts and all. If one were to be given the privilege of sampling today the magic of the Clyde and its great steamers of yore, one could do no better than savour Wemyss Bay to Rothesay on this fine vessel. I vowed to rejoin her next year without fail.

She lasted one more season, a little speedier with her oil-burning gear. The coal-holes in the deck were no longer needed, the manhole covers bolted down. She was withdrawn in the autumn of 1957 and for three years lay rusting and neglected. Hopes of a reprieve were raised each spring as her name continued to be listed in the fleet shown in the summer timetable. But her paddles had turned for the last time. Never again would she raise steam to drive them nor to heat Archie Paton's bath. A 'Save Jupiter' campaign failed and she was towed off to Dublin, there to be broken up. She was the last steamer, the last paddler, the last two-funnelled ship ever built for the Caledonian Company while under LMS control. As HMS Scawfell, she had brought down three enemy aircraft, and claimed three more as probables. She in turn was done for by the coming of the purpose-built car ferry.

A Flyer at Last — Jeanie Deans

I had rather expected to return to the Jupiter for the 1957 season. Without a railway background, I felt that I had done rather well to get so far up the ladder and that only those with real influence could aspire to one of the Duchesses. Just as in the thirties, one paddle-steamer rivalled them for glamour, reputation and speed. Jeanie Deans was one of the hallowed names, the biggest and best paddler built by the LNER company, with a string of firsts to her name. She was the first with the modern two-funnel style — both ahead of the paddle-box; the first to have triple expansion three-crank steam engines — in other words there were three great pistons to watch with their conrods swinging up and round, sheer power in every stroke. All the more recent Clyde paddlers followed her example.

I had fallen in love with her during my stint on the Maid of Argyll at Craigendoran, where she too was based and much preferred her to the Waverley, which at first glance looked like a smaller sister ship. What I had not known was that while I had been appraising her with favour, her master, Captain Charles MacLean, had been doing the same with me! Apparently my skills at the gangway and in cajoling seamen to co-operate had been noted. There was now a vacancy on his ship and after checking with Jupiter's skipper to see how well I had coped with Saturdays on the Wemyss Bay, Rothesay run (on one of these we had transported, fed and watered 12,000 souls) he asked for my

The Jeanie Deans at Arrochar in the early thirties. Note the lack of deckhouses. ROBERT GRAHAM

The Broomielaw, c1880. Fifty years later, the Jeanie Deans was relatively well appointed compared to the paddle-steamers in this etching

appointment to Jeanie Deans. It was my first experience of being 'head-hunted'.

And so on the Glasgow Spring Holiday weekend, I joined with a deal of pride, not down-river but at Bridge Wharf in Glasgow. Jeanie was one of no less than seven vessels which carried out charters from there on 25 May. What a scene of bustle and life. It must have been like this a century before when up to a dozen paddlers left daily for the Firth of Clyde. It was, unlike most Glasgow holidays, a glorious day and with only a call at Rothesay and no tickets to collect, an ideal way to get to know my new home and its inhabitants.

Jeanie Deans was a happy ship with a settled crew, still strongly 'North British' even after nine years of rule from Gourock. They had only just had to face up to the Caley house-flag at the masthead for the first time, and my arrival with my non-regulation issue LNER cap badge went down well. Captain Charles MacLean was a gentleman in every sense — quiet, polite with a hint of humour. He hailed from Silloth in what is now Cumbria and spoke feelingly of his youth in that remote but gracious resort. He had served at Craigendoran since 1931; as master of the Jeanie from 1945. He was to retire from her in 1962.

The chief engineer was also Charles MacLean which caused a certain amount of good-natured confusion. The latter lived in Innellan and often appeared from the bowels of the engine as we approached the pier there. He was tall and spare, enjoyed a laugh which caused his cap to settle even more precariously than when he set it at his own unique angle. His cap was a giveaway in any crowd. We have lost something since the fashion changed to being bareheaded. Hats maketh the man — and the woman!

Both MacLeans were intensely proud of the Jeanie and worked as a team to keep her in fine fettle. The only real criticism one could make was that they were by nature more protective than competitive and to my intense frustration would invariably turn down the chance of a race with another steamer. There were no unseemly wrangles between them about what went wrong at piers, which was probably because nothing ever did. They knew their jobs and the Jeanie lived up to her reputation as a lady with impeccable manners. She was the only one of the thirties steamers to have a really well designed rudder which must have been a factor in her ability to go where she was pointed. The Jupiter and Talisman could clout more piers in a year than she did in a lifetime. An argument with King George V in 1934 off Cumbrae, in which she came off worst with a twisted bow; a few minutes aground in the crooked channel in the Kyles in 1955, and breaking six windows at Arrochar when a relief skipper tried a fancy approach which came unstuck, was the sum total of untoward incidents recorded in her whole career on the Clyde. In 1957 we had a moment or two at Innellan of which more later.

In Neil Nicholson the Jeanie had the best pilot in the fleet. He was a quiet West Highlander, handsome in the eyes of the ladies and with natural leadership qualities. He could place the Jeanie where he wanted her to an inch in a full gale against the tide. It was no surprise when later he transferred to Loch Lomond to become captain of the Maid of the Loch. He made an effortless switch from the focsle to the elegant dining tables and handled the Maid with ease — no mean feat as we shall learn.

Neil had 'brought up' a succession of assistant pursers, with a timely word and quiet advice. If there was trouble at the gangways he seemed capable of flying from the bridge-wing straight to the deck — he was reassuringly beside you before you even realised that there was a problem. Belligerent passengers were no match for the smile and the charm. When Neil was finished with them they could scarcely remember what their problem had been, never mind caring whether it had been dealt with. Neil enjoyed a pint or two — never more — of McEwan's Heavy in a hostelry in Helensburgh which had sawdust on the floor and a rail to lean on like a wild west saloon bar. Two pints was stretching it for a callow youth like me and he would supervise the resultant return stagger to Craigendoran with great discretion, even to the point of ushering me through the door of the cabin which I shared with a fellow student whose name, alas, I have forgotten. This fellow was excellent company, but rather inclined to melancholy after the degree exam results came out. He would retreat below to his books on the long trips round Bute each day, swotting for the September resits.

Two seamen became my firm friends — 'Dolly' Macsween, and

The port paddle-box. GRIMSHAW COLLECTION

Roddy — they were a delightful pair, reserved but mischievous with the hose and given to 'having on' the innocent and gullible. Dolly returned to the fishing after a season or two, but Roddy stayed with the company for years serving on most of the fleet. I was to enjoy unsolicited free trips, car included, for years to come!

They were with me on the night of the local Conservative and Unionist party dance at the Queen's Hotel, on which we happened by chance on our way back from the pub in Helensburgh, the blue-rinsed ladies with their heaving bosoms and picture-hats not being our customary social scene. Then, as now, the Tories seemed to have been short of funds. I had hardly entered when I was virtually compelled to buy six raffle tickets, my protests brushed brusquely aside. Later in the evening, when they were beginning to work out that the three of us made an odd little grouping, compared to the faithful that is, there was a roll of drums and the draw commenced. I won all six major prizes — all bottles, all spirits. It transpired that the proceedings had been rigged but that the selected tickets had fallen into the wrong hands. There was consternation, palpable and ill-concealed. Thoughts of demanding a recount or a dope-test receded when Dolly and Roddy rose to their full height, their manly chests and sinewy arms contrasting markedly with the weedy worthies of the committee men. We retreated gracefully, guarding our flanks and our booty and were soon in the cool night air with more booze in our arms than any of us had ever possessed.

Our arrival on board the darkened vessel did not pass unnoticed with the result that the foscle and stoker's quarters became very lively indeed. Six bottles among a baker's dozen can induce a state of euphoria in the shortest of order. My reputation was made; it was assumed that I had rigged the raffle for their benefit. As we drank ourselves daft a great storm blew up which made the Jeanie lurch and bang against the pier. I rolled to my bunk, every stagger coinciding providentially with a lurch of the boat in the opposite direction. I lay in my bunk, my head spinning in perfect unison with the paddler's gyrations and slept like a top. Thank God we were not on the early run the next day!

There have to be drawbacks to everything. On the Jeanie Deans it was the purser — the only one I sailed with who was a regular pain. Willie was old, soured, wizened and tiny. In short a crabbit nyaff. He walked in tiny half-steps, his cap perched exactly at regulation angle. He instinctively disliked assistant pursers and showed it. He did his books laboriously, licking his pencil, muttering aloud sums which he invariably got wrong, but determined not to seek help from the fancy-pants from varsity whom he believed were too clever for their own good. He need not have worried too much about my arithmetic, which is suspect to this day. Those who know me will realise the state he was in, when it transpired that even I could correct his calculations. It was wise not to annoy him when the ink-balance was due and we were certainly asking for it if we tried to bring girlfriends into the office when he was in the throes of it. Oddly enough, he seldom made mistakes when selling tickets and giving change to passengers.

He was not, to put it mildly, an ambassador for the company. An American who unwisely asked him if the Jeanie Deans sailed to 'Lake Lomond' was treated to a geography lesson which was graphic, succinct and heavy on expletives. His type does not appear in any Saatchi and Saatchi management portfolio. In Willie's book, the customer was never right and coming on the Jeanie at all was an invasion of his privacy. Happily we caught him redhanded in an illicit little scam with persons unknown and thereafter held the whiphand. He even let us do his sums for him after that. Captain MacLean remarked that he seemed a changed man. We did not tell him that the evidence was locked away at the back of a lifejacket cupboard.

1957 was a particularly good year to serve on the Jeanie Deans. Along with Queen Mary II, Jupiter and Waverley, she had been converted to oil-burning and this had given her a new lease of life after a spell when her performance had been worthy rather than exciting. On trial in April of that year she had managed 18 knots — a remarkable speed for a paddler, all the more so as it was fractionally more than she had managed when built by Fairfields in 1931. As constructed, she had but one small deckhouse, oddly small funnels, and weighed only 635 tons. After the war she had been given new elliptical funnels, deckhouses fore and aft with a passenger deck above the aft one and a covered bridge. Now she weighed 840 tons and was all of four inches lower in the water.

It was the deckhouses that made her look like Waverley. In reality

Waverley, built soon after the alterations to the Jeanie, was smaller with a sloping bow and a modern cruiser stern. In the thirties the Jeanie Deans had been the sole LNER all day cruise vessel, challenging the turbines as far away as Girvan and Ailsa Craig, and sometimes out-pacing her archrival the Duchess of Montrose. She countered her superior speed as she was handier at piers and able to gather speed more quickly.

Now she was back in form, her indifferent years behind her. Her hull was slim and graceful, a straight stem cleaving the waters like a knife and an elegant counter stern giving her a period yacht-like grace, enhanced by her great length — at over 250ft the largest paddler of her era. As I have said, the two Charlie MacLeans were not keen on racing, feeling that they and the Jeanie had nothing to prove. However, on two occasions in that season they had days off at the same time. The relief skipper was one Duncan Maclachlan, in his seventies and pulled out of retirement from his delightful sandstone house, Travancore at Sandbank, to help out. He belonged to the racing era, his moustache positively bristled when a challenge was offered. Deep-set eyes twinkled, pipe poured forth thick black smoke, and the old-time yachting style cap was pulled tighter over the eyes. The relief engineer found the extra-notch which was reputedly cut on the regulator by an engineer in the thirties of whom it was said 'he would race with the seagulls', and we were off. In short order we saw off the Queen Mary II, the Waverley (what tension that caused at Craigendoran) and most significantly the Duchess of Montrose. After all these years of losing gracefully to all and sundry, I fear that I could not resist extravagant waves of the hat and other less courtly gestures to pursers on those hapless vessels.

At that time the Jeanie seemed in much better condition than the Waverley which had been built only ten years before. Her hull was sound, albeit with a decided ripple in it which one could see clearly when standing on the starboard paddle-box. This was the result of a near-miss by a bomb during war-service on the Thames which had tested her Clyde-built frames to the full. Waverley by contrast seemed to have been built of poor post-war quality materials when steel was scarce and wood-work utilitarian. Rust appeared on her as soon as the crew stopped painting her and she was in constant need of running repairs. If one had been asked to bet on which would still be around in the 1990s, nine out of ten would have said the Jeanie. It is a great testimony to those who now lavish care and attention on the Waverley, that the last seagoing paddle-steamer is still with us. She's in better condition now than she was in the fifties.

I was transferred during the season to the Waverley for a week to help out when both student pursers 'took ill'. This coincided with a rail-strike which left Waverley without oil-fuel. Strikes were commonplace in the sixties and as a result we were often without the oil-tankers which

A superb view of the Jeanie Deans on her 'Round Bute' cruise

had only just replaced the coal-wagons formerly brought to the pier by a wheezing tank engine. As I lay sunning myself on the deck contemplating a period of delicious indolence, Captain McKay indicated politely but firmly, that as things were, three days chipping and painting would do Waverley no end of good and would have similarly beneficial effects on myself. I was suspended under the bow on a bosun's chair, and scraped and painted all of 20 feet of her hull, including the raised metal letters of her name. The Maid of Argyll was kept in service as she used less fuel and every time she called at Craigendoran I was the unwilling recipient of quite uncalled for advice from Donald Crawford.

The Jeanie's roster was an easy one. On weekdays she carried out the enormously popular 'Round Bute' cruise. Leaving Craigendoran at 12.35pm meant that there was just time for bus parties to arrive to have lunch at an extra sitting while we were still alongside. In those days buses from Fife and Edinburgh would have taken hours to go through Glasgow and reach Gourock. There was no motorway, no Clyde Tunnel, and only the chain ferries clanking across at Renfrew and Erskine. The ferries at Govan, Whiteinch and Finnieston involved too many cobbles and tramlines to be an alternative option. Therefore a terminus on the north bank was ideal and as many as 20 Alexander's Bluebirds would disgorge their loads of trippers and pensioners to swarm aboard even before the boat-train arrived, after which we were often up to our full complement. We could take 1480 passengers, and at times left without room for even one more at Gourock where on a number of occasions several hundred were left disappointed. If possible they were diverted onto the Queen Mary II which had come down from Glasgow and which should have left for the Kyles five minutes before we did. When one sees

Gourock Pier desolate and deserted today with weeds growing through the planks, it's hard to remember that around 9.00am and at lunchtime every day vast crowds thronged the pier. The Caley's answer to public relations, Eddie Baker, a bald-headed eccentric with flapping arms and a loudhailer would rush about dementedly trying to form queues for each vessel. He could have created chaos in a well run monastery, never mind a pier full of bewildered passengers, many of whom had only the haziest notion of where they were going. I used to stand on the Jeanie's bridge wing as we approached, people dashing madly hither and thither as his voice emanating from the megaphone rose to a high falsetto shriek. The pier staff who could have sorted things out without Eddie's intervention would simply retreat to their bothy for a quick brew until everything had calmed down. Sometimes we even had to go ashore and reform the queues ourselves. Even then we had to reshuffle occasional refugees between the Jeanie and the Queen Mary at both Dunoon and Rothesay.

Eddie was an enthusiast. Marketing and publicity were in their infancy but he did his best work in the winter, producing brochures and posters for travel bureaux around the UK. In the sixties when real problems began to emerge as passenger numbers declined, an efficient marketing machine was built up which has done much over the years to publicise the attractions of the West Coast. By then, Eddie's day was past. He was one of the last great amateurs. His pièce de résistance was virtually to dare anyone to go on the Saint Columba in the morning. MacBrayne was the 'enemy' and he was not above sending folks off to quite different destinations from the ones they wanted to go to, as long as it was on a Caley Steamer. On one occasion he all but got the marine superintendent of MacBraynes onto the Hamilton before the hapless soul got in a word to explain who he was. One of the great joys of the Cowal Games was to think that while he was organising the crowds at Gourock, the formidable Joe Beattie was knocking hell out of them as they arrived at Dunoon. The pipe bands must have marched up Argyll Street filled with relief at having escaped these two. Their own pipe-majors could hold no terrors for them by comparison. It was rumoured that Eddie once went over with his megaphone to 'help out' at Dunoon...!

After the Gourock call the rest of the day was comparatively calm. We called at Dunoon and Innellan and then Rothesay where we disembarked lots of day-trippers, and normally picked up several hundred for a cruise which lasted three hours and involved going round Bute clockwise, calling at Tighnabruaich at 4.10pm to field those left behind by the Queen Mary, and back to Rothesay for 5.10pm. Retracing our steps, we reached Craigendoran at 6.45pm where the hordes were soon back on the waiting buses and aboard the boat-train which lay steaming gently in the platform which had been extended to the pier from the main Helensburgh line. The dining saloon had been in constant use with several sittings of fixed price luncheons, at 6/6d, followed by high teas at a shilling less. It was good sturdy fare, served by stewards in waistcoats; soup, roast beef or salad and scotch trifle for lunch; cold meat or fish for high tea, augmented by buttered bread, scones, and cakes. Passengers and crew ate well on the Jeanie Deans and there were few complaints. The officers mess was curtained off from the saloon, but this was normally drawn back so that we could join in the fun. A la carte menus and dish of the day specials were undreamed of then. There wasn't a bottle of wine in sight. The dining room was for eating, the bar for drinking. There was admittedly a new-fangled cafeteria which was the first sign of the self-service revolution to come. We did not realise then that set meals would soon be but a memory.

The cruise round Bute was a purser's dream — nearly two hours without a pier. My fellow-student swotted, I assessed the talent, or increased my proficiency at the wheel, having a regular 'trick' past Ettrick Bay and Inchmarnock and still had time to sleep off any excesses from the night before. Willie we never saw. On really good days Dolly, Roddy, Neil and I sat at the stern beside the emergency steering wheel and the capstans, lolling on coils of rope and feeding the gulls. It was idyllic. It is one of the prettiest sails in the Clyde, with both east and west Kyles full of colour and interest. In those days dolphins and basking sharks were a common sight. Frankly, I'd have paid for the privilege of doing the job.

Innellan was a feature of this roster. The Royal Hotel, now no more, but then frequented by the gentry stood on the hill above the pier with the air of the great Scottish hydros like Kilmacolm, Peebles and Pitlochry. Each day the car would bring down a few posh folk to join us. Mr Sinclair, the piermaster would duly fuss about them, soliciting his tuppence in pier dues.

A regular amongst them was the 'Duchess'. I knew her by no other name. She seemed old to me and was probably therefore in her forties. She was exquisitely dressed with furs and furbelows, flowing dresses, Ascot style hats and sheer stockings. The car brought her to the gangway, pier dues were waived, and I would gallantly hand her aboard. She would lean on my arm helplessly, eyelashes a quiver, as we traversed the gangway. With a devastating smile, a wave and a waft of perfume she was gone to the bridge as a path opened up for her through the assembled throngs on the deck. On our return the ceremony would be enacted in reverse. As she reached the end of the gangway she would press half-a-crown into my hand, the car door would open and close, and she was whisked off. Years later the illusion was shattered. I learned that in reality she was a high-class prostitute catering exclusively for the needs of the officer classes and the relief master, who shall not be named, was her main customer, but not her only one. Years later I was to lunch with a real Duchess, a Lady in Waiting to the Queen. She was poised, gracious and

MV Glen Sannox after conversion to stern loading. CALEDONIAN MACBRAYNE LTD

elegant, but not half so convincing as the Duchess of Innellan.

There were two variations to our mid-week routine. Sometimes we stood in for the Maid of Cumbrae which did a run at 8.40am to Dunoon and Rothesay, conveying to Dunoon those who wished to join the Waverley there for the run to Arrochar and the Three Lochs Tour. We were back at Craigendoran at 11.40am, having called at the tiny pier at Kilcreggan, just in time for the bus parties to come aboard. We didn't much care for this trip, normally having all morning to cancel tickets, strike balances, bank the takings and replenish our stocks of small change.

The other break in routine was the occasional tender to a liner anchored at the Tail o' the Bank, calling in from Liverpool en route to Canada. There were small Cunarders — Saxonia, Carinthia and Ivernia, I think, and Canadian Pacific Empresses, huge vessels with white hulls and yellow funnels. One of them, the Empress of Scotland, if my memory serves me well, had three enormous funnels. She had been Empress of Japan before Pearl Harbour! She towered above the Jeanie as we came alongside. The paddle-box would be piled high with luggage; the decks full of emigrants, many in tears, having their last look at home. It was a poignant experience. You must remember that most of those who left did not expect to return for years. Cheap transatlantic flights were well in the future and so Canada and a new life were a long way away. Emigration then had more in common with what the Pilgrim Fathers had once endured.

The ambition of everyone on board the Jeanie was to get aboard the Empress. One reason was to gaze in wonder at the splendour of the great public rooms and to savour a world beyond our reach. The purser's office alone was about as big as the Jeanie, with a staff of 30. The other reason was duty free tobacco and spirits. Customs men guarded the doors and access was forbidden. But nothing is impossible and the crews of the liners were sympathetic. I managed more than one guided tour. A relief purser once came back with a suitcase packed with Capstan and Senior Service. As it lay in the office, the senior customs man used it as a desk to sign the ship's clearance papers!

As we drew away from the liners, salutes on their great steam whistles would drown out our replies, and rows of faces on the top-deck would reveal tears and a longing to hang on to our homely presence. Before long anchors would be weighed, and off they went. Customs House Quay in Greenock was where we lifted and dropped passengers. We would take out relatives to greet the homeward bound and, of course, joy was unconfined on these occasions.

Once after tender duty, we made for Gourock and lay there for several hours. In the next berth lay the brand new car ferry, Glen Sannox, awaiting her maiden voyage with VIP's. The same length as the Jeanie Deans but half as broad again, she had a huge superstructure by the standards of the day — like a block of flats, the local paper said. Her car-deck was immense; above it there was covered passenger accommodation far in advance of anything seen until then on the Clyde. The floors in the foyer were inlaid with the company crest. Only the dining room looked small and inadequate. Impressive, and very different, she was the shape of things to come. She would take over the Arran run from the Marchioness of Graham — from planks to ramps in one simple move — she could take 55 cars to the turbine's six and 1269 passengers. At least she was fast. Her great Sulzer Diesels could drive her along at 18 knots, which no ship in the present fleet can remotely match, although the Isle of Lewis, a grand new ship for the Ullapool-Stornaway, run can reach 18 knots and cuts almost an hour off the time of the crossing.

What I did not know then was that the Glen Sannox was another character in the making. In her many years on the Clyde and later in the Western Isles too, she was to become as well loved as any of the old steamers and a worthy successor to the paddle and the turbine Glen Sannox. When she was sold in 1989 to serve in the Red Sea, her passing was as much lamented as any. I wonder if the same will be true of her present day successor, the Caledonian Isles which at 308ft is the longest vessel ever to sail on the Clyde — only the legendary paddler Columba before her exceeded 300ft — just. Many feel that Glen Sannox would have been a more fitting name for this giant which can carry 129 cars and 1000 passengers.

On that day, I climbed back onto the paddle-box of the Jeanie with a heavy heart. As we made for Craigendoran, I knew that future generations would miss that unmistakable beat of paddle-wheels; for some reason in the Jeanie, every eighth one louder than the rest.

Saturdays were heavy days, as they had been on the Talisman and the Jupiter. The five-day-week was coming in and most holidaymakers now changed over on Saturdays. With the Maid of Argyll off to Arrochar, we made a trip to Dunoon at 10.05am calling at Kilcreggan and Kirn, loaded with those off for a week or a fortnight and piled high with luggage. It was the custom of Dolly and Roddy to make these piles as high and precarious as they could, as a challenge for me as I laboured with the manifest. On one glorious sunny Saturday I was only a quarter way through the heap when glancing up I saw Kirn pier less than a mile away. Panic set in, together with the sure knowledge that Willie's retribution would come upon us. But the Lord was kind. It was Clyde Regatta week and the entire fleet of yachts lay becalmed across our path — elegant Dragons, Loch Longs and 'twelve metre' yachts. The gallant Captain MacLean gave way and stopped engines. We lay for 40 minutes 'as idle as a painted ship upon a painted ocean'. At last there was a breath of wind, the armada came to life and moved on with every trunk and suitcase by then accounted for in the manifest.

Saturday afternoons meant a trip to the Kyles of Bute with almost an hour at Tighnabruaich, and home by 8pm. Billed as a cruise, it was more of a holidaymakers' return trip. We did no lunches, and very few high teas. Folks had spent all their money and were so skint that a cup of tea was their stretch. The stewards made up for it on Sundays. We left at our usual time of 12.35pm but called only at Dunoon and Rothesay before a three hour cruise round Cumbrae and Bute, or to Skipness in Kintyre (where the car ferry from Lochranza now plies).

Sunday was the day to have friends aboard. Favours granted in the past were returned by the chief steward in the form of free meals for aged parents and even octogenarian grand-parents. This was a better life than the Gourock-Dunoon run all day on a car ferry. The Jeanie sped smoothly and effortlessly through the sparkling waters of the Clyde, the band played, the decks were full of smiling faces. It was bliss to be alive.

The season passed like a flash. Early in September we got a fright when a paddle-rod broke as we were approaching Innellan Pier. We were helpless, and drifted slowly towards the rocks to the north of the pier. No other vessel was near, and so we prepared to drop anchor and pray. Charlie MacLean, the engineer, was too busy to notice that the way we were headed we could end up in his front garden. We prepared for drama; the lifeboats were swung out. At the very last moment Charlie appeared covered in oil, seaweed and water, waved the all-clear to the bridge, and we limped slowly out to sea. Ten minutes later we were sufficiently restored to make our way back to Craigendoran.

It turned out to be an early warning. In 1964 the Jeanie and her old rival the Duchess of Montrose were withdrawn, as cruising collapsed in the face of cars and package-tours and as maintenance costs soared. The Jeanie was bought to revive paddle-steamer sailings on the Thames with the new name of Queen of the South. Sadly her boiler was weak and those paddles worn out. The Thames had too many pieces of debris to foul and damage wooden floats. She missed more days than she sailed and made an undignified exit to the breakers in Antwerp in December 1967. A sad end to a grand old lady, a happy and a lucky ship.

Maid of the Loch — Haste Ye Back

The welcome back to Loch Lomond was warm. The Maid of the Loch was in her prime. Now five years old and with the Prince Edward gone, she carried out all the sailings herself and traffic was more than enough for her to pay her way. As the largest ship by far on Loch Lomond — indeed on any inland water in Great Britain, she was expensive to run. She had a crew of 35 to support and steam engines, however glamorous, are costly to fuel and to maintain. It was surprising that she was built as a paddle-steamer at all. She was, I suppose, a delightful anachronism and not surprisingly the last ever paddle-steamer built in Europe.

The Maid was a beautiful vessel, from the passenger point of view the most luxurious of any. The engines were on the main deck — twin cranks, not three as was now the fashion on the Clyde. The engines built by Rankin and Blackmore in Greenock were as beautiful as the vessel herself and fully open to view. At the stern was a glorious observation lounge with big windows right round the stern — a feature which was possible only on inland waters for safety reasons. It was panelled and furnished with modern Danish-style tables and leather upholstered chairs. Towards the bow was a light wood panelled dining saloon — bright, airy and beautifully appointed. All the silverware which had graced the loch steamers for 100 years was used to great effect, in the service of the traditional lunch and high tea. The Maid was destined to be the last vessel in Scottish waters to have sittings and set meals. The fish course for high tea was 'Scotch Salmon' and it was highly popular, except with the crew who grew tired of what was in those days a luxury food. The galley was between the engine-room and the saloon, with doors on both sides which resulted in small groups of passengers watching every move. It was a favourite roosting spot for crew in the evening — the galley fires were still hot enough to allow sausages to be fried for alfresco snacks to be consumed on the little open platform on the front of the paddle-box. The cook was Gordon, the doughty footballer from the Prince Edward.

Access to and from the promenade deck was by curved companion

Maid of the Loch at Balloch Pier in the late fifties. CALEDONIAN MACBRAYNE LTD

ways on the paddle-sponsons, both before and behind the paddles. Their rails were adorned with attractive and colourful heraldic shields. On the promenade deck were two observation lounges with high windows. There was a cocktail bar in the one at the stern. It was as if all the Victorian inhibitions had been cast aside at last. No longer was the bar hidden in the bowels of the ship. You could drink and admire the beauty of the scenery — even stroll on deck glass in hand. The barmaid was positively comely; the 'Timber Aggie' era was over with a vengeance. Above the deck-saloons was a top deck which swept right up to the funnel and the bridge. Needless to say the bridge was in front of the funnel now, and no longer open to the elements. The view from the bridge was uninterrupted and superb — no need for the helmsman to jump from side to side to see round the funnel, half-blinded by smoke and soot.

The funnel was yellow but without the customary black top which had been tried in her first year and looked too 'heavy'. As a result there was always a soot stain round the funnel top which grew more visible as the season progressed. Later I had the same problem with my steam yacht Galatea, but it was somewhat easier to reach up and clean it with a paraffin rag. The Maid's elegant hull was white, with green at the waterline. White Loch Lomond style paddle-boxes with horizontal slats, a name plate and Celtic decorations added to the effect making the Maid look like a rather splendid private yacht. Later when her costs were attracting the attention of Dr Beeching, she was inevitably nicknamed 'the white elephant'.

The atmosphere was as friendly as ever on the loch, but had changed in one respect. The bohemian devil-may-care days were over. The Maid was too big, too expensive, too magnificent to take liberties with. Donald MacDonald the skipper was a lovely man, but a cautious one. Apparently he had been quite a lad in his youth on the Princess May and the Prince Edward but he was now weighed down with the responsibility of his new charge. And well he might be. In order to reach Luss Pier, in a shallow part of the Loch, she had been designed with a draft of only four feet seven inches. Even the Maids on the Clyde with a fraction of her superstructure drew nine. Everything above the main deck was made of aluminium to save weight. The deckhouses, the funnel and the bridge behaved like great sails, blowing her bodily sideways in cross winds. She just did not have 'sufficient grip on the water'. Once when we cast off at Inversnaid, she was half-way across the loch sideways before we made any headway up the loch at all. On calm days, her behaviour was impeccable. It was ironic that on an inland loch, with waves seldom a problem for a vessel of more than 550 tons in weight and nearly 200ft in length, sailings should be cancelled because of winds which were of insufficient strength to disrupt services on the Clyde. This sort of thing had never happened with the Prince Edward and Donald felt it keenly on the days when he decided it was not prudent to leave Balloch. He felt that it might be seen almost as cowardice and imagined 'them in Gourock' cursing as they had to retain the Three Lochs Tour passengers on the Waverley at Arrochar and put up the cancellation boards in Queen Street Station. His feelings were not helped by the mate, the deposed skipper of Prince Edward, who would hint darkly that if it were only up to him...! The boldest people are invariably those who are one safe step away from the crunch decision.

Still, it was a clear indication that the Maid of the Loch might have been better designed. Voices were heard speculating as to how much cheaper and more exciting it might have been to put new engines and boiler in the Prince Edward in 1953, rather than build the Maid. It is true to say that hulls can last indefinitely in fresh water, even if engines do not. The Ullswater steamers Lady of the Lake and Raven were built in 1877 and 1889 by Seath's of Rutherglen who built the Lucy Ashton around the same time and are still going strong albeit with diesel engines. Likewise the elegant Tern with her unique canoe bow still sails happily on Windermere to this day. Built in 1911, Prince Edward was a mere stripling by their standards. These thoughts were distant in 1958. We did not then know that the Maid's life was to be one long struggle for survival which is still not yet concluded.

Donald MacDonald skippered a happy crew. While most of my old shipmates had gone — Bob Swann to full-time catering in Glasgow — a few faces were familiar in the dining saloon and on deck where the Highland voices were predominant and the Skye accent the most frequently heard. Donald looked what he was, a deckhand in an officer's uniform. While his ability was not in doubt, he looked ill-at-ease with the stripes and the gold braid. His uniform jacket never quite fitted. His ears were curiously flat on top as if nature had shaped them perfectly to support a cap at the very least two sizes too big for him. The hands on the telegraphs were horny from years of handling the ropes and gangways.

The Gaelic was a problem — for me that is. It was often used on the steamers as a means of excluding outsiders from a conversation and for talking about officers not so much behind their backs as right in front of their noses. It was also useful when they casually took up their innocent-looking position on the paddle-wing below the gangway. In those pre-miniskirt days there were perspectives to be gained from that angle which were denied to the conventional observer. Descriptions of such sightings in Gaelic escaped censure. Expressed in English there would have been instant dismissals and outraged ladies.

With memories of the frustrations on the Edward, I had prepared my secret weapon, Over the winter I spent spare moments with a copy of *Teach Yourself Gaelic* unearthed in a book shop beside the Columba Hotel in Oban. After several months my knowledge of that beautiful melancholy language was less than perfect, but I could more or less follow a conversation. My grandfather, the slate quarryman from Toberonochy would have been impressed at this rebirth of the culture in me. He probably knew all of the swear words which I was at pains particularly to master. Soon after my return to the Maid, the opportunity came. The men were clustered at the gangway, criticising the boarding passengers, admiring a finely turned leg or two when I slipped in a helpful and relevant sentence. They continued as if nothing had happened for a full minute much as the villain in a Western walks on for a pace or two with a bullet through his heart before slumping to the ground. When it dawned on them, consternation ensued. They were speechless in two languages. I took full advantage and dressed them down, lucidly, colourfully, some might even say vulgarly. This one performance absorbed my entire Gaelic vocabulary. Sadly, thereafter, I seldom had need to practice my new-found skills. We found that we could all converse in English after all. But I earned the highest accolade a student purser could have — full access of an evening to the focsle for a dram or a mug of char and a camaraderie I recall with total affection to this day. These were real men, proud and resourceful. The news spread round the fleet, with my knowledge of Gaelic being gratifyingly exaggerated in the telling. When I returned to the Clyde, my reputation amongst the seamen had preceded me and I might just as well have won a gold medal at the Mod!

The new purser was Hamish Horne who hailed from Caithness or Sutherland, I forget which, and who was in time to transfer to the Clyde and become a member of the permanent staff. He did not take long to find his feet, which was just as well, because the Maid had an exacting timetable, which was the result of amalgamating what had been for 30 years and more a two-ship roster. On Mondays, Wednesdays and Fridays, it was one trip a day rather like the Prince Edward's Friday run of 1954. The stop at Ardlui was just as welcome, with the football matches as keen as ever, and walks by the lochside enlivened again on the warmer days by a bathe at the mouth of the river. But the Ardlui Hotel now had no side-door visitors — the world and the personalities had changed and something had been lost in the process. It was not just on the Clyde and Loch Lomond that things were changing; life was being taken more seriously, the accountants were taking over. Perhaps the camaraderie and the sense of proportion brought on by the war was fading too.

On the other weekdays, the Maid undertook two round-trips with the first 'up-trip' and the last 'down' entailing calls at every pier. The intermediate runs omitted piers to allow the shortcut straight down the loch through the beautiful narrows at Luss. Being bigger, and with a more cautious captain, the Maid no longer dashed through at full speed. This was less exciting but it did give more time to savour those gorgeous wooded passages between Inchtavannach and the bonnie banks, and the stunning views of Rossdhu House, the home of the Colquhouns of Luss. A world-class golf course is now being finished nearby and will surely prove to be one of the most beautiful anywhere.

Even cutting corners, we did not reach Balloch in the evenings until 8.40pm. The last hour could be very beautiful, particularly as the season progressed, and it was in the gloaming that we approached Balloch. It was the closest we came to an evening cruise. An Evening Circular Tour was advertised from Glasgow and Dumbarton. Passengers left Glasgow at 3pm on Thursday, took the train up the West Highland line to Ardlui and joined us after an hour or so to explore the attractions. Ardlui station, which was one of the classic 'Swiss chalet' stations set in an island platform on the West Highland Line, was a fascinating place as the steam trains stopped to exchange the tablets which allowed access to the next stretch of single-track line. The signalmen were only too willing to allow me at times to hand up the little leather wallet with the huge loop handle for the driver to grab as he passed. At times this was done at a speed which defeated the eye, but not on that famous occasion during the Glasgow Fair in 1953 when two trains were due to pass at Ardlui. With all the crowds they had extra carriages and were both too long for the loop. The 'up' train had a coach sticking back onto the single line. Much shunting and cursing filled the next 40 minutes or so, with helpful advice from the Edward's crew who came up to see the fun. In those days most of the trains were drawn up by 'K4's' like Loch Long and the Great Marquess. Occasionally they were double-headed by Reid's legendary 'Glens' — Glen Falloch, Glen Luss or Glen Douglas.

There was an unlit buoy off the pier at Balloch which had to be left to port and which helped the skipper to line up on the pier. In late August and September it was virtually dark when we neared Balloch. Donald MacDonald's son would row out to the buoy with an oil lantern to guide us safely in. Once it was trimmed to his satisfaction, he would fish contentedly with the painter of his boat attached to the buoy until we came into sight, when he would hold the lamp aloft. As we passed we could just see the glow from his cigarette. By the time we had berthed and put out the extra ropes to secure the Maid overnight, he would be ashore, lantern in one hand, the night's catch in the other. With the boat train gone and the boiler damped down, it was a dark and gloomy vessel he boarded to pick up his father. As in all the steam boats, there was only a noisy little generator to provide the power for a few light-bulbs at strategic places. You had to know your way around with your eyes shut.

The Maid had one feature, not available in any Clyde ship at this time. Most had public address systems, but only the Maid had a gramophone. In those days, the technology did not allow for 78s to be played on a turntable, unless it was completely upright at all times. If there were waves, there could be no music. It was only just possible on the loch except on really windy day, provided it was accepted that the needle would jump every now and then. The turntable was in the purser's office, together with an odd collection of records. There were certain traditions. Every trip had at least two renditions of *Loch Lomond* by Robert Wilson or Kenneth McKellar. Jimmy Shand figured prominently too. If the weather was abysmal, it was time for *Island In The Sun* sung by Harry Belafonte. It cheered up the sodden passengers no end. They would shake their fists at us in appreciation. Invariably the last record of the day was *Haste Ye Back* sung by Calum Kennedy. I still know the words off by heart, call again you're welcome here. Passengers and crew would join in and there was hardly a dry eye in the house. Hearing it now, or the B side *The Road to Dundee* is guaranteed to bring the memories flooding back — may your days be long and happy, may your friends be ever near.

There was one record in our collection which we knew to have a predictable and gratifying effect. It was *How Much Is That Doggie In The Window?* The chief steward, Alan Rennie could not bear even one bar of it. On a good day it took him 17 seconds from the opening note to sprint from his office on the main deck near the rear stairs on the paddle-box and fling open the door of the purser's office, storm in, swear volubly, and threaten withdrawal of all supplies of food and drink, unless the offending record was removed forthwith. He smashed three copies in that season, but it was well worth using the petty cash to get another one in Alexandria.

Alan was a superb chief steward. Standards were of the highest. The dining room and the cafeteria below were sparkling and clean, the meals served were impeccable and the food in the best of shape. He apparent-

The dining saloon of the Maid of the Loch still serving lunches and high teas in the early seventies. DUMBARTON DISTRICT LIBRARIES

ly ruled by fear, but his staff revered him and a lunch or high tea on the Maid was a real treat. An increasing number of American tourists were 'doing' Scotland at this time, and the loch was a must. From the cocktail bar with the only cocktails available in the fleet, to the Scotch salmon, these visitors savoured it all. Alan was of course a wheeler dealer, his office the hub of intrigue. But passengers and crew got the best that he could manage. On Sundays when we sailed to all piers at 2.30pm the sittings for high tea were often fully booked even before we left Balloch. In penance for playing 'that' record, I would help out at busy times between piers — this could entail silver service one minute and gangways the next. At least there were tips to be earned in the dining saloon. Sadly, Alan died a few years later and the catering, while adequate, was no longer exceptional.

I will always remember the scene before we sailed each day. Alan would supervise the transfer of stores from his supply-room in the station; Sammy would be bringing the fish, the baker's van from Gourock would be there too. As the passengers were alighting from the train, lads would dash amongst them, with trays of rolls on their heads, for all the world like African women in the films. It was organised confusion. Alan had to know the exact complement even before the skipper did, both to set his plans and to settle the daily wager. You had to be closest by less than 20 to win. No winner meant doubling the kitty for the following day! At 9am purser and steward had to nominate the passenger-load for the first run. Alan won much more than he lost.

The Americans were something apart from the normal visitor. Most noticeably they had cameras, which few Scottish trippers had. They fired off with a recklessness we found truly astonishing. They could go through film worth my weekly wage of £2.10/- in a matter of minutes. Their main aim was to spot and photograph red deer. In the summer few of these wary beasts are to be seen on the hillsides of Loch Lomond; they have better things to do. On one trip, after being pestered beyond reason by one large, loud Texan passenger bedecked in check trousers and a tartan jacket, topped by a Stetson, I confess to pointing at the vacant heather in the heights above Inversnaid and shouting 'There — dozens of them!' To my surprise and delight, he shot off three films, and expressed himself totally satisfied. It became the practice to help all our transatlantic cousins in this way — a manifestation of our Scottish reluctance to let a good, paying guest down! An indiscreet yank had told us that they never developed the films until they got home, which was probably just as well. It's great what you can imagine when you suspend belief.

Even more intriguing were the Americans who seemed to have a list of things to 'do' and to tick off. They would come aboard, make for the bar from which they emerged only when we were playing *Haste Ye Back*. They had 'done' Loch Lomond and were destined to bore their friends to death about something which they never actually saw. It was one of these whom Hamish rashly tried to coach into saying 'loch' rather than 'lock'. He eventually mastered the liquid sibilance only too well and his top set of teeth promptly flew out, clattering down on the counter inside the window. Hamish casually retrieved them with a spotless handkerchief, gave them a quick polish and handed them back with a flourish, demurring 'Yours Sir, I think?'

Hamish grew more nervous as July approached. His wife was due to give birth to their first child in Raigmore Hospital in Inverness. He longed to be with her as soon as the baby arrived, but of course there were no 'days off' on the loch and Hamish was too new, too keen to remain a purser to ask Gourock for leave. When the glad tidings came, he was in a dreadful state — joy jostled with frustration. Donald Macdonald called me to the bridge. 'Can you cope without giving the game away'? Could I cope! This was a dream come true — full command of ticket-tubes, the dating machine and the cash-drawer! Hamish was wracked with conflicting loyalties when offered the prospect of an illicit dash North. The stakes were high — what if 'they' found out? He probably also dreaded that he might come back to find that we were £100 adrift. In the end, he went for just two days. We managed fine. The seamen coped with the tickets and the daily passenger log as never before; the captain fussed over me like a mother hen. Alan Rennie sent up special treats to sustain me. When Hamish got back, radiant but apprehensive, the balance was accurate to the penny, the tickets in immaculate condition, and his assistant purser proud but exhausted. As usual, no-one in Gourock had paid any attention to us. I never met Hamish's wife, but she sent me a note the contents of which I still treasure. In these days of generous paid leave, even paternity leave and public holidays, it is worth remembering how cruelly restricted people's lives sometimes were 40 years ago.

I thoroughly enjoyed that season and part of the next on the Maid, when I broke in yet another new purser who suffered from the handicap of being unable to count and calculate. We spent many hours trying to trace the discrepancies which resulted from his mental arithmetic. Once we had got him into the way of doing every sum on paper with the ready reckoner, things improved. He lasted only a season — a man born too soon. He would have been utterly competent today when the computer and the calculator do all the thinking for you.

There were sad moments too. One of the pier porters who handled the heavy gangways at Balloch was so small and light, he was always at risk of injury. He should not have been there, but he needed the money. To our horror, one day as the gangways were being lifted off, it swung round with him attached: he lost his footing and fell between the pier and the paddle-box. It was some days before his body was recovered. We had a sense of shared guilt, although what could we have done? While we were mourning him we had another blow. A blind hiker came aboard at Inversnaid and told us he was intent on walking the treacherous and busy road from Tarbet to Inverbeg for the Rowardennan foot-ferry alone. Nothing could shake his belief that he could manage this. Efforts to change his mind delayed us 20 minutes at the pier, and involved skipper, pursers and chief steward. We read of his death in the local paper that weekend.

These later years of the fifties were the last golden ages on Loch Lomond. The crowds still came, even on wet days. I would stand on the pier looking up the platform as the train puffed in and the single-compartment doors swung open. There were never less than 300 or so and often many more. I would be conscious of Alan Rennie's eyes on the back of my neck, his face pressed against his window below on the main deck, expecting the first estimate of how many. The spud-peelers were poised at the galley, the bar and tearooms on stand-by and Hamish ready for the flood of tickets for the first lunch sitting. This one had to be complete by Tarbet so that the Three Lochs Tour contingent could depart duly fed and watered. These morning runs were a nice mix of tourists, walkers and foreign visitors. Later in the day, there were more locals. It was seldom Pa, Ma and the weans out for the day, except for Vale of Leven folk. Glasgow families more often made for the Clyde.

The patent lack of interest in the loch boat from the managers in Gourock seemed welcome then. It was better to be left in peace. Things went on much as they had for a century and more, but it was to prove a mixed blessing. The sixties brought decline in numbers of passengers both on the Clyde and the loch. The Beeching philosophy was introduced. Ships, like branch lines on the railways were seen as individual cost centres. Dubious accountancy often failed to take account of the wider business brought by their mere existence. While the concept of railways as a public service prevailed, there was a move against frills and frivolity. To the dessicated mind the Maid was just a red line in a balance sheet. Appeals to see the Loch and the Maid as the central jewel in the tourist crown fell on deaf ears. While other countries preserved their assets as working museum pieces if nothing more, there was no real sentiment at the top in British Railways. The figures were trivial when the Maid began to lose money and based simply on raw receipts with no recognition of the benefit to the tourist infrastructure, the local economy and quality of life in the area of Loch Lomond. The accountants descended and the Maid was earmarked for the chop.

And so the struggle began. The Maid only just escaped the axe in 1963 and the new electric train service — still known today as the 'blue trains' although they are now painted the ghastly Strathclyde Regional Council orange — was almost terminated at Balloch town station, a mile short of the pier. It too was saved, but sadly not Ardlui Pier. The piers were hardly big earners for their owners and needed repairs. Ardlui Hotel gained little from the steamer calls, certainly a lot less than from the burgeoning passing trade on the road, and so the pier at the head of the loch closed and with it the evening train connection. Although the Maid still did a 'thence cruise' beyond Inversnaid, the narrowest and arguably most beautiful part of the Loch was hardly visited. This is particularly unfortunate as it is best seen from the water — a bit like the non-existent deer!

For the first time the Maid was heavily promoted to boost business; the pursing staff was augmented by a hostess imaginatively billed as — wait for it — 'The Maid of the Loch'. The ancient gramophone and the 78s were updated to a tape-deck. The little succinct commentaries which I devised and read out live to keep passengers aware of the landmarks were replaced by an extended recorded commentary. It drove the crew up the wall and also any passenger looking for a bit of quiet contemplation. Progress be damned!

The closure of Balmaha Pier in 1971 left a big hole in the timetable, and when Tarbet, once thronged with 'Three Lochers' followed in 1975, there was hardly anywhere left to call and the Maid began to look no more than competition for Lynn's small cruisers from the river Leven at Balloch. Her great size and crew of 35 made the competition unequal at best.

1974 was a bad year with many sailings lost through a combination of boiler trouble and bad weather; only 75,000 passengers came up the gangway. By this time there was growing concern locally to save her and renewed publicity, revamped rosters and a lot of hard work kept her

The Countess Fiona, formerly Countess of Breadalbane, leaving the pier at Tarbet in 1990

going. In 1978 she lost the rear of her two masts, because of wood-rot — shades of her predecessors which never seemed to have enough masts to go round!

In 1980 Luss Pier was reopened. At last there was justification for having built a paddle-steamer in 1953 to cope with shallow waters. Luss is a popular place, easy to reach by the improved lochside roads; it is, of course, the Glendarroch of Scottish Television's soap *The High Road*. With a subsidy from Strathclyde Regional Council and growing passenger numbers, things were beginning to look good. In 1981 there were no less than 114,000 passengers, the net loss a mere £73,000. But we were now in an era when government, remote in London, knew the price of everything and the value of nothing. The Maid was withdrawn at the season's end. She has lain at Balloch ever since, a rusting monument to lack of vision, neglect and the dashing of the extravagant hopes of a succession of owners. Only very recently have the PSPS given her a cosmetic repaint but it is unlikely she will sail again. However, she might be preserved as a static feature which would enhance Balloch Bay and give youngsters an inkling of the loch in its glory days.

One of her sadder functions has been to act as go-between for passengers from Balloch Pier to a much smaller vessel Countess Fiona, registered in Alloa by her brewery owners which took up sailings in 1982. We last heard of this vessel when as Countess of Breadalbane she was accidentally used for target practice by the Royal Naval torpedo testers at Arrochar. How she got to Loch Lomond to sail for seven seasons before, in turn, being laid up makes a fascinating tale. She had started life in 1936 as the railway cruise boat on Loch Awe, had been transported to the Clyde in 1952, had sailed in the Western Isles and was now back once again on inland water.

This tiny vessel — about 90ft long and about a quarter the overall size of the Clyde Maids was built by Denny's of Dumbarton and like Maid of the Loch and the Sir Walter Scott on Loch Katrine, dismantled and rebuilt on the lochside. Loch Awe had been served by a number of small steamers rather like Loch Lomond, carrying cargo and passengers to isolated communities. As the loch is deep they had been screw vessels, and the Countess was the biggest and best with twin screws, Gleniffer diesel engines and a speed of about 10 knots. She had pleasant lines, deckhouses which were miniatures of those on the Clyde boats of that period, and a tiny dining saloon. Sadly she had no funnel, but rather heavy exhausts at water level just like those of her 'big sisters' Swan and Teal on Windermere. To make matters worse, the galley chimney was where the funnel ought to have been. She was laid up during the war and sailed again with train connections from 1948 to 1951. But Loch Awe was too remote, and what was to happen later on the Clyde and Loch Lomond happened much earlier there. The service was discontinued. As it turned out she was not left to rot for long on the slipway near Lochawe Station.

At that time the Marchioness of Lorne was due to leave the Holy Loch run for the Millport service. The Ashton and the Leven were too small to replace her — there were howls of protest. The solution was to haul the Countess up the steep slope on to the Oban to Glasgow road, and haul her behind huge tractors via strengthened bridges over the top to Loch Fyne, to be put into salt water near Inveraray. A lot of trees suffered in the process. She was refitted by Denny's and soon on the Holy Loch run. It transpired that she was not much more popular than the even smaller boats. Posters at Kirn and Hunter's Quay proclaimed: 'Cheap, for immediate disposal, for quick sale, the desirable vessel Countess of Breadalbane complete with oars, guaranteed safe in calm water.' Soon the Maid of Ashton took over and the protests diminished.

The Countess turned out to be highly suitable for charters, feeder runs to serve cruise-boats, and late night Friday runs to places like Tighnabruaich. She was a familiar sight on the Clyde, ploughing sedately on, overtaken by everything in sight. Re-engined in 1957 she could now manage 12 knots. She gave 'Cafe Cruises' to the Holy Loch from Gourock, and afternoon cruises to the same destination from Largs and Dunoon. Her purser was a student, rated as 'Junior Purser' and her skipper was a promoted pilot. She was often laughed at, but with affection, not malice.

In 1971 she was sold to Roy Ritchie, the Gourock ferryman whose converted fishing boat Granny Kempock was a familiar sight in the fifties. Ritchie used the Countess — now Countess of Kempock on services to Blairmore, Kilcreggan and Helensburgh, sometimes chartering her back to her former owners. After Roy Ritchie's death, she plied the exposed waters off the west coast of Mull, cruising to Staffa and Iona — quite a feat for a boat designed for tranquil inland waters.

In 1982, she undertook the second overland journey of her career. She was hoisted out in Glasgow by the huge Finnieston Crane. The 'Finnie Crane' as it is affectionately known was built to load steam locomotives from the great engine builders of Glasgow for export to railways in China and throughout the Empire. It holds a particular place in the affections of my family. My father was a distinguished headmaster of the local junior secondary school, and the crane was adopted as the school badge. It has probably lifted nothing since 1982 with the exception of George Wylie's marvellous straw locomotive a couple of years ago, but it stands high as a landmark of the past, the surrounding sheds and warehouses having long since disappeared.

In two parts, hull and superstructure, the Countess made a slow journey to Balloch, causing traffic chaos on the A82 as the pieces trundled along. She was launched again, stuck fast in the sand, and had to be pushed out in a most undignified manner by the grab of a JCB. At long last she had a funnel, albeit a dummy, and had been tidied up internally. The funnel was too far aft, but it did make her look oddly endearing. Tarbet Pier was reopened in 1984 and the Countess called everywhere except Balmaha and Ardlui. Things were looking up again. In 1989 the Countess Fiona was provided with new full-width deck shelters, furnished to modern standards, a new funnel, red with black top, in just the right place, immediately aft of the wheel house, and two metal masts. She looked trim and graceful, although it had taken 53 years to get her right. Her owners went into liquidation while she was on the slip next winter for overhaul and she has been there ever since, stranded. I feel sure she will sail again — perhaps even in the Forth and Clyde Canal! She is the last surviving example in the West of Scotland of the craftsmanship of Denny's of Dumbarton, a firm which built more than half of the vessels in the Clyde fleet of the fifties, not to mention many cross-Channel steamers for good measure.

The Real Queen Mary

I can recall momentous meetings with Secretaries of State about the future of education in England, lightened only by glimpses over their shoulders of the Queen Mary lying sedately on her berth in the Thames where she is now a floating restaurant. It was more than 30 years since I had served on her as junior purser. In the middle of the 1959 season — my last — a buff envelope from Gourock delivered in the internal mail to the Maid of the Loch at Balloch, tersely informed me that I was to serve out my time as junior purser on Queen Mary II which sailed 'doon the watter' daily from Bridge Wharf in Glasgow. When I had returned to the Maid of the Loch in 1958, it had been agreed that if the opportunity arose, I would go back to the Clyde to what was the position most prized by student pursers, available only on the Queen Mary. Junior purser rated not only a pay increase and greater responsibility, but a narrow band of white with duck-egg blue trim on the cuffs of the jacket. Full pursers had two of these, assistant pursers none.

I had made my first trip on the Queen Mary II in 1939 at the age of three, bound for evacuation to the Cowal Hotel in Dunoon. I had watched her from there many times as she ploughed back and forth throughout the war years between Gourock and Dunoon. In the fifties, in stately progression from Glasgow to Tighnabruaich each day, she was regarded as the flagship of the fleet, her skipper being the Senior Master. Other vessels in the fleet treated her with deference, and gave way when she made for a pier. If the Duchesses were the greyhounds of the fleet, the Mary represented solid respectability and she pulled rank.

I had served on the Queen Mary II for a few weeks before the end of the 1956 season as an assistant purser. I had enjoyed it and went back to greet friends and characters on a ship where life was predictable and ordered. Captain Mick Brophy — an Irishman among Scots, was genial and relaxed, and treated by all with the greatest of respect. Due to retire at the end of the season he was master of his craft, with time to entertain widely on the bridge and to preside at the officers' table. This was, uniquely on the Clyde at that time, in a separate rather grand dining saloon for captain, mate, engineers and pursers. Brophy liked all those not actually engaged in sailing the ship to join him for high tea, a ritual which occurred between Rothesay and Dunoon on the return trip. The mate probably preferred to be on the bridge at this time. He was a tense and taciturn man, not given to small talk, this being widely attributed to his wartime experiences in a Japanese POW camp.

Meals must have been almost as grand at the captain's table on the Cunard's Queen Mary. The silverware there certainly could not have been any more impressive; likewise the food, a feature being a 'special' for the crew to relieve the tedium of the traditional menu which was invariably fish or salad, followed by scones, cakes and lashings of tea. The other Queen Mary, I am reliably informed, tended to serve dinner rather than high tea. Their loss, not ours!

Foremost amongst the bon viveurs at the table was Jimmy Gibson the purser. Along with Jimmy Montgomery, he was senior purser in the fleet. His team of junior and assistant pursers — three to four in number according to the stage of the season — had to cope with a volume of passengers far beyond that of any other vessel. All who came aboard in Glasgow had to purchase tickets. At other mainland termini, many already had combined rail and steamer tickets. Jimmy was equal to the task, a real professional who had seen it all. The eccentricities of passengers he took in his stride. By some quirk of design, the passengers outside the purser's window could not hear asides uttered even a mere foot back from the window. Jimmy excelled in extreme courtesy to the public, interspersed with a scurrilous, libellous, commentary audible only to the other pursers. I can still savour the profuse thanks he used to extract from those whom he had just so roundly and cruelly insulted. It was just as well the sound system was so secure. Nowadays with 'magic windows' that work on both sides, Jimmy would not have lasted a week. He was no slouch at describing the ancestry, mental limitations and physical abnormalities of student pursers who fell below the high standards he set. Amongst these was Richard Orr, later to assume the lofty mantle of Adviser in Classics to the Corporation of Glasgow Education Department, and later to Strathclyde Region. Like many a famous man, his behaviour as a student gave little indication of what lay ahead.

He soon introduced me to the delights of a Calder's Wee Heavy. These came in very small bottles that looked like neat little hand grenades. Their effect on the cerebellum was just as explosive. They had the consistency of tar and two was more than enough. At that time, for reasons best know to himself, Richard affected night shirts and it was thus attired that on one occasion we made our unsteady way along Clyde Street, through St. Enoch Square and into Argyle Street returning by Renfield Street. We dallied at sundry hostelries en route. We were not arrested; some passers-by didn't even appear to notice. By the time we got back to the ship the tide had gone down and, as was normal practice at night, the gangway had been replaced by a ladder. I fell more than 20ft to the deck, hardly touching the ladder at all on the way down. Next morning I found myself miraculously unbruised — an excess of drink can clearly have its benefits! But even in the Tighnabruaich Hut situated within the gloomy buildings of Bridge Wharf I required the assistance of dark glasses and showed a marked preference for passengers with quiet voices. I even tried unsuccessfully to muffle the ticket-machine with a towel.

More seriously, it is worth recalling that such were the throngs at Bridge Wharf in the fifties that in addition to the purser's office on board, there were both Rothesay and Tighnabruaich boxes ashore (I think they had wheels — like old fashioned bathing huts) and in these pre-decimal and pre-calculator days one soon became adept at quite intricate sums involving adult tickets, children's tickets, privilege tickets, dog tickets, deck chair tickets and meal tickets. To make things worse the age for half price travel tickets for children was 14, but 10 for meals. Even now I bow in silent thanksgiving for Miss Nielson's daily mental arithmetic lessons in Shawlands Academy Primary Annexe in Deanston Drive.

Exquisite timing was required to close the hut in time, lug the ticket case and the till back aboard and to hurl ritual abuse at the assistant pursers before we were off, the screws churning the muddy waters of the river. Earlier in the morning we had taken pound notes to the value of £1000 and more to the bank in leather bags — that was the kind of money you drew in a whole day in 1959. I have to confess that for me the main work of the day was now over and time could be found to ensure that all the ladies, or at least the younger ones, enjoyed their cruise to the full; that foreigners from Edinburgh were kept fully enlightened of the far-from-home delights of the Clyde and that the day's gossip was absorbed at Gourock.

The sail down through the shipyards was an experience in itself. Every yard was still in full swing which meant the flash of welding torches and the unforgettable clatter of the massed riveters at work overwhelmed us. There was everything to be seen on the stocks from troopships at Barclay Curle's to dredgers at the Simon Lobnitz yard at Renfrew. Yarrows could be relied upon to have a frigate or two nearing completion. By the time the notorious bend at Bowling was reached, so awkward for the Queen Mary to negotiate in 1935, we could see the tugs being built at Scotts. There was no Erskine Bridge then of course, but the Erskine Ferry ploughed back and forth, constantly on the move. On busy Sundays those returning from the coast could count on an hour or two in the queue which built up there. By that stage in the journey we had managed to negotiate that odd-looking vehicular ferry at Govan whose car deck went up and down with the tide between massive girders, a

The Queen Mary II in her last season in two-funnelled guise, 1956

whole flotilla of passenger ferries — the cluthas — and the chain ferry at Renfrew, whose captain was the butt of many a joke in the Christmas pantomimes at the Citizens' Theatre, ranging from his navigational competence to his coping with storm and pestilence! Today they are all gone with the exception of a passenger ferry at Renfrew which seems to function primarily for the benefit of the patrons of the two pubs situated on either side of it. As a small child I enjoyed Sunday trips on the Renfrew Ferry — from Spiersbridge you could go in the blue tram over the private track to Barrhead, right through Paisley and down to the ferry — all for a 'half penny special'. The return trip on the ferry, eating ice-cream on the top deck, cost the same.

The sail from Bowling to Port Glasgow is the first really beautiful stretch on the river — along the 'Lang Bank', so assiduously dredged over the years to keep the channel open. It was usually half-speed past at least one dredger with its attendant long-funnelled hopper lying alongside to take the spoils out to sea. Talking of spoils, it was usually here that we would meet the Shieldhall and the Dalmarnock, two of the most familiar vessels on the Clyde. Each day they carried the processed sewage from Glasgow to a trench several hundred feet deep which lay in the open sea just beyond the outer ends of Bute and Cumbrae. This still goes on today, although it is not considered as environmentally desirable as it was earlier in the century; presumably it is already under review by the EC. What was a pioneering move in the days of typhoid and dysentery has been overtaken by changed attitudes to health and the environment. The grim joke was that these were the only vessels on the Clyde where the purser did not pilfer the cargo! They were smart, immaculate ships, a credit to their crews and the Corporation of Glasgow. The Shieldhall had passenger accommodation and a dining room for 80, which was used to give the city's pensioners a day's outing and a slap-up feed. It was a very good idea but I suspect that their olfactory senses were no longer what they used to be.

The Shieldhall was new, having been built by Lobnitz of Renfrew in 1955, and had two triple-expansion steam engines. After service in the

Clyde, she carried sewage out to sea for many years in the Southampton area, where she was subsequently preserved. Her new owners who use her for functions and charters describe her coyly as the last working river passenger and cargo steamer! Her bridge and engine-room are well worth a visit — an evocative mixture of brass and steam.

At Port Glasgow there were rows of wooden stumps in the water, close inshore, which mystified many a passenger. They had something to do with the importing of timber, the logs being prevented from floating off with the tide by the uprights which could still be seen. After that we passed the great yards of the lower firth. Scotts and Lithgows built everything from cargo vessels and passenger liners to submarines. We frequently had to tread water while tugs assisted vessels in and out of the docks. Once we were held up for an hour by a delayed launching ceremony, receiving a grandstand view of a mighty tanker held by a mass of clanking chains gliding down the slip to be fielded just in time by its attendant steam tugs. They needed to be slick since the channel is narrow at Greenock, despite the great width of the river. A few seasons later the skipper of the Mary was fined for ignoring the warning flags and sneaking past seconds before a launch took place.

At Gourock, there was the daily meeting with the Jeanie Deans which entailed a lot of waving to old shipmates. We called at Gourock at 1.00pm except on Saturdays, Dunoon at 1.20pm, Rothesay at 2.10pm leaving just before the Jeanie Deans set off to cruise around Bute and finally berthing at Tighnabruaich at 2.55pm. The Mary lay there serenely with additional ropes from permanent anchors in the seabed attached to bow and stern because she dwarfed the pier. My custom was to enjoy a promenade ashore, with mundane duties such as ticket collection and gangways delegated to the assistant pursers. While they toiled there was time for a chinwag with pier staff and an ice-cream from the cafe-cum-grocers at the pierhead.

On one occasion I needed something a bit more potent to still the nerves. We had hove-to off the mouth of Loch Riddon so that an Anglican Bishop could cast upon the waters the ashes of a parishioner whose dying wish this had been. After a moving eulogy, the Bishop opened the casket and to the horror of Norman the seaman in attendance, made his way to the rail on the wrong side — where the wind was blowing from. Too late, the inevitable happened. Not a word was spoken; Norman's offer to help brush him down was courteously rejected. The bereaved widow was not amused, nor was Captain Brophy who had stood the while on the bridge-wing, with his cap doffed in respectful tribute.

The Mary left promptly each day at 3.55pm usually with almost all of those she had put ashore. Those who did not make it would be picked up by the Jeanie Deans 15 minutes later. Departure from Rothesay was at

King George V on a rare visit to the Clyde. She was long associated with the Oban, Iona and Staffa cruise. IAN QUINN

4.45pm — and woe betide any car ferry or 'Maid' which obstructed our passage. Forty minutes and high tea later we called at Dunoon and then it was straight to Bridge Wharf, turning at the entrance to the Queen's Dock and backing the last stretch, steered by a rudder in the bow which was now the stern, if you see what I mean. The fact that she did not call at Gourock on the way back meant that assistant pursers had a lot of announcing and chasing to do before she reached Dunoon, occasionally arranging a train journey from Glasgow Central back to Gourock for those who had been deaf to their pleas to transfer to the car ferry at Dunoon. It was a leisurely day's sail, requiring nothing approaching her original 19 knots, which was just as well, since before she was re-boilered in 1957 her quoted speed was down to 15 knots. Because of her reputation and no doubt because her master was Commodore of the Fleet, in deference the other vessels of the fleet gave way which made her lack of speed less embarrassing. The Saint Columba, from the rival MacBrayne stable, was less respectful but fortunately our paths seldom crossed.

I could easily have gone home each night, as it was only 20 minutes on the tram but it was far more fun to stay aboard. The officer's quarters down below had a grand stairway of their own and were the best in the fleet. Nonetheless on sultry nights Richard and I would take our bedding up to the promenade deck where there was a second purser's office near the stern. It was now used only for cancelling tickets but the twin counters made a good base for our beds. The only snag was that if we left a window open for fresh air and chanced for whatever reason to oversleep, the seamen washing the decks would give us a wholly accidental dousing with the hose. At least I could reply with a well directed stream of Gaelic oaths. Richard's imprecations in Latin and Greek impressed them less.

The Queen Mary had been built in 1933 specifically for the 'all-the-way' sailings. By coincidence a maiden aunt of mine was present at the launch by Lady Colquhoun of Luss and recollects the feelings of those present that even by Denny standards, the Mary was something special. Her maiden trip was from Craigendoran to Loch Long as a thank you gesture to all the workmen who had built her. It must have been quite a sight to see her there with her three great screws trying to grip the shallow water. Even the Maid of Argyll had her moments there. I have stood on the bridge when even the unflappable Captain Donald Crawford speculated as to whether we were all going to end up in the station waiting room, with the engines still going full astern!

Billed at Britain's finest pleasure-steamer she was soon in service, winning a special and permanent place in the hearts of Glaswegians who appreciated her spacious decks, furnishings and lavish equipment. 263ft long, it was her breadth which made her different. The Duchesses of Hamilton and Montrose (of 1932 and 1930), the greyhounds of the fleet, were 10ft longer, but were also three feet less in the beam and that made all the difference. The feeling of space on her decks and in her saloons seemed infinitely greater than the statistics would suggest — whether this was to do with illusion or geometry I cannot say. Her tonnage made her the biggest vessel of her day and she appeared sturdier than any, even portly in some eyes. Appearances can be deceptive; designed for the upper firth, her ribs and frames were lighter than those of the Duchesses. In her heyday, 18 knots was flat-out for a lady who was solid, respectable and regal, and by no stretch of the imagination flighty.

The new era of turbine luxury had been inaugurated with the King George V in 1926. This vessel which was in post-war years to be associated with the famous cruise from Oban to Staffa and Iona, had been the first to have a glazed-in promenade deck with a spacious open deck above. The Duchesses carried on the tradition and the Mary took it much further; her boat-deck went so far aft as to give the tourist class (she was a two class ship) shelter from the elements without having to go below to saloons on the main deck. It gave the little mooring deck aft a great deal of protection from wind and rain. The seamen would foregather there for a chat and a smoke on beautiful days in the Kyles, or in the evening as we sailed up-river. As I would be at the wheel in the Kyles, the whole complement could safely muster to air their Gaelic well out of my earshot. The most memorable of them was Norman, a fixture on the Mary for 20 years or more. Silver-haired and elegant, he was the only suburban seaman I ever came across, departing after we berthed each night for his semi-detached in Muirend. He had a unique ability to get onto every photograph or film ever taken of the Mary — except mine. I was at that time

Britain's finest pleasure steamer 'QUEEN MARY'

Pleasure sailings on the Firth of Clyde
Full details of cruises, fares and party rates from:
Caledonian MacBrayne Limited,
The Pier, GOUROCK, Renfrewshire.
Tel. (0475) 33755.

Caledonian MacBrayne

CalMac's publicity shot for the ship they considered to be their best. When built in 1933, the same publicity catchphrase was used and when this picture was taken she had reverted to her former name.
CALEDONIAN MACBRAYNE LTD

too poor to own a camera still less buy film — a borrowed Box Brownie was my limit in those days.

Unique to the Mary was the broad open stairway in front of the bridge which gave access from the boat-deck to the fore-deck without having to go through the forward saloon. On the other turbines the door at the front of the saloon would allow blasts of wind and rain to assail those in the basket chairs, every time some one went in or out. The Mary had the first ever dining saloon on the fore-part of the ship which still exists in part today, the splendid windows overlooking views of the Festival Hall and the Thames. It was truly magnificent — all stained wood-work, crisp white napery, silver cutlery and teapots and immaculate stewards with bow ties and black waistcoats. There was never any likeli-hood of the Queen Mary's cutlery vibrating off the tables as it had done on the Talisman and the Maid of Argyll.

By the fifties the pattern of set meals was changing ashore — it was then that Reo Stakis was introducing chicken and chips in the Prince's Restaurant at the top of Renfield Street and fast foods were beginning to broaden the menu for Glaswegians. Reid's and Miss Cranston's no longer had it all their own way. The Queen Mary and the Jeanie Deans were the first to have self-service cafeterias in 1954. The sittings for set lunch and high tea continued but cost and convenience marked a slow decline, until in the seventies the Maid of the Loch alone kept the tradition going.

Catering standards declined until only sausage rolls, scones, and beverages in plastic cups were available. Happily in recent years there has been a marked improvement. Vessels such as Claymore, the Lord of the Isles and Isle of Mull have a splendid range on offer from haggis and neaps to onion bahji. In these modern vessels there is not the unhappy blend of traditional woodwork and formica which marred the internal appearance of the Mary and the other steamers in the late fifties, and which still does to an extent in the Waverley today.

Removal in 1950 of the class distinctions on the steamers was a more welcome change. The remnants of the dividing barriers however continued to be useful for ticket collection as we backed slowly up to Bridge Wharf each evening. Gates could be closed beside the engine-room (there was little to be seen there apart from the central control panel on the turbines) which enabled us to drive potential fare-dodgers through into the gents' loo which was the only way on that deck from bow to stern saloons. A stewardess was required to assist by scouring the ladies' loo for ticketless matrons and maidens. There is a curious remnant of class distinction today on InterCity 125s — a little swinging door between first and second class beside the buffet. With class divisions gone the Queen Mary had a wealth of saloons and dining areas which enabled her to cope with vast crowds. She was in great demand for charters and works' outings. On wet days, there was ample room below.

In external appearance, the Queen Mary had a slightly raked stem and a cruiser stern which was to my eye particularly elegant. There were originally two heavily-built funnels — white with black tops, the livery of her original owners Williamson Buchanan who were responsible for the frosted glass windows on the main deck which were etched with mysterious Turkish symbols — the Crescent and the Star. I later learned that this reflected their house flag. In 1935 they gave up business and their steamers, all turbines, were redistributed. The up-river steamers, The Queen Mary and the King Edward went to the Caley fleet, and King George V and Queen Alexandra (soon to be transformed into the Saint Columba) to MacBrayne's.

The Mary's funnels, after the war Caley yellow with black tops, were to be the subject of great debate in the fifties. Her boiler grew increasingly delicate with the passing of the years and the available pressure dropped, as did her speed, to a modest 15 knots — barely enough to see off a car ferry never mind a 'real' steamer.

As part of the wider modernisation process it was decided that she should have a new boiler, just as powerful but half the size of the original. This was single-ended and so one funnel would suffice. For the 1957 season she reappeared transformed to the eye with one large oval funnel. I had been smuggled into the yard — I think Barclay Curle's — for a preview. Many Glaswegians were outraged at what had been done to 'their boat'. To my eyes she was no more or less handsome — just different — perhaps more reminiscent of a cross-channel steamer than a Clyde one. She looked more modern but less traditional. There was now greater space on the boat deck, but no longer were there two warm funnels to huddle against on cold days. What was more damaging to her appearance was the cropping of her masts in 1969 to enable her to pass under the new Kingston Bridge. Sod's law being what it is, she never did pass beneath it. The Glasgow terminal was moved downstream when Bridge Wharf was closed.

In the thirties the Mary sailed from Bridge Wharf at 10am often full to her capacity of 2086, cruising to a different part of the coast of Arran each day. There was so much traffic that the first ever passenger turbine steamer, the Kind Edward of 1901 took the premier sailing at 11am to Tighnabruaich. She survived until 1952 after which there was only one sailing each day. One of her turbines can still be seen in the Kelvingrove Museum in Glasgow, as well it might — it served as a tiny working model for the massive engines soon fitted to blue riband Cunarders. It is amusing to note that her designers made provisions for paddles to be fitted in the event of the turbines failing to deliver, which perhaps epitomises the canny Scottish characteristic of tempering pioneering spirit with prudence.

In 1935, as mentioned in the first chapter, came the change of name so that the Cunarder, Yard Number 534 on the stocks at Clydebank could become Queen Mary. The last Clyde steamer to bear a royal title became Queen Mary II, the Roman numerals being part of her registered name until 1976. In that year her larger sister was retired to static display in America and the 'real Queen Mary' retrieved her name.

Passengers who flaunted their knowledge of history would appear from time to time at the purser's window to point out that there had been only one reigning Queen Mary in English history. In the fifties it was topical to respond that this was the sort of confusion which was leading extremist Scottish Nationalists to blow up pillar boxes bearing the inscription 'EIIR'. The Tudor sisters Mary and Elizabeth may have been Queens of England but held no sway north of the Border. For further enlightenment we would then refer them to the portrait and the brass plaque in the forward saloon expressing the gratitude of the Cunard directors at the willingness of their Caledonian counterparts to accept the change which was a constant source of curiosity to trippers in the years between; every student purser knew the story off by heart, and would probably repeat it in his sleep.

Long after my days on the Queen Mary were over — I left reluctantly on 30 September, 1959 to start my teaching career in Whitehill Secondary School next day, the Queen Mary sailed on. In 1973 the single oval funnel was painted red with a black top, with only a small yellow circle behind the CalMac lion to remind us of that unique yellow of the Caledonian fleet over so many years. In due course I made sure that that colour was recaptured exactly for the funnel of my steam yacht Galatea.

In 1969 the daily sailings from Bridge Wharf were abandoned; no more were hordes of Glaswegians clamouring to surge aboard. Changing habits had taken their toll. 1970 was a year of change with the closure of Bridge Wharf. The Mary found herself based at Gourock undertaking mainly afternoon cruises. On Mondays she went to Arran via the Kyles — in my view the finest of all the sailings and on Saturdays went around Ailsa Craig. I often wondered how those lighter ribs stood up to it! By 1971 the glorious Duchess of Hamilton had gone and with her, in all honesty, some things which the Mary could never match. I can vividly recall a sparkling day on the Duchess as she creamed along between Rothesay and Largs on a motionless sea at 20 knots and not even a tremor on the surface of the glass of water which lay before me. Although I enjoyed sailings on the Mary to Inveraray, Lochranza, Campbeltown and Brodick it was not what she was built for and the old lady was all too plainly struggling a bit. In contrast to her heyday when all vessels gave way to the flagship, I can remember her having to lay off Brodick for the best part of an hour to allow the car ferry Clansman access to the pier.

To fit her out for her mainline cruising role she had had an extensive internal refit. The deck lounge had been refurbished, the main deck forward was converted to a cafeteria, the bar was moved from the lower deck near my cabin and became the lounge on the main deck aft. A restaurant was created on the lower deck forward. Sadly this was little used as both crowds and eating patterns declined.

In the seventies we sensed that great austerity was coming. Cruising was no longer the attraction it had been and in any case the Mary could not last for ever. She could never be replaced. I used to harbour a fantasy that the Maid of the Loch might be dismantled and brought overland to the Clyde. Suitably modified, she would have been about the right size for the traffic. In 1974 with the Waverley gone — as it happens to a quite different life, the Mary was the last survivor of the great days and her timetable combined bits of almost all of the rosters of the old days which meant more up-river work and dazzling, ingenious, dashes around the lochs, round Bute and to Arran in the Jeanie Deans' footsteps. In 1976 with a grant from Strathclyde Region like the Maid of the Loch — and my lips are sealed about my part behind the scenes in bringing that about — she followed the Waverley back to Glasgow and sailed to the Kyles, but no longer every day.

In 1977 came the news we feared and expected. I was aboard with my family on the night of 12 September; we sailed from Largs to

Rothesay on the Final Showboat Cruise. She went out with style. The skies opened symbolically as we went ashore and the Mary slid off into the mists and the night. She was succeeded as a cruise boat by the Glen Sannox and that of course is another story.

Now a veteran herself, Glen Sannox was re-engined and refurbished, with provision for tables and 'Martini umbrellas' on the car-deck for cruising, and modern catering facilities. The great cruising days were certainly over when a converted car ferry was all that remained. Mind you, criticised as ugly in 1957, Glen Sannox was now considered relatively graceful. Modern ferries world-wide appear to be built in continuous lengths and chopped off at bow and stern as required! Only the Tor Britannia and Tor Scandinavia of the seventies which sail to Sweden have made any pretence to beauty in recent times.

For ten years the Queen Mary lingered on in static limbo amidst rumours of disintegration, including the loss of her funnel. She was saved by the ill-luck which befell the Caledonia, lost in a fire on the Thames. She was acquired by Toby Restaurants Limited in December 1987. In dry dock at the Chatham Dock Yard in Kent and after massive internal conversion involving some 65,000 man hours and at a cost of £2,000,000 (30 times her cost when new), she made her way from the Medway to the Thames. Even without funnels and mast, clearances were very tight and with her bow riding too high in the water 20 additional tons of concrete had to be laid below the water line. She sports two funnels once again somewhat marred by the Toby colours and she has an unfortunate construction — a sort of mini-portakabin — on top of that lovely curved aft staircase which mirrored the focsle and the after castle. Still she is there, some of her internal grace remains and there are some excellent pictures and documents for the visitor to brouse over.

In a brochure produced by her brewery owners to celebrate her new life both Richard Orr and myself recalled a grand and regal lady in her prime. She was truly Glasgow's own. I toast her every morning in coffee from my Queen Mary mug, and in the evenings occasionally with an exquisite Springbank or Longrow malt from Campbeltown, latterly her furthest port of call.

Wider Horizons — Lakes and Steamers

In a sense it has been all downhill for me since the fifties! A career in education on both sides of the Border has had its moments, but never the sustained pleasure of my life as a purser. The consolation is that I was, without doubt, just in time for the experience of a lifetime. In retrospect there is little doubt that the fifties represented the sunset of the great days of cruising on the Clyde. There was change in terms of the ships and the holidaying habits of the folk who sailed 'doon the watter'. But great steamers were there, crowds were still flocking to the resorts and it was possible to cruise to a different destination every day or sample a wide range of cafe, afternoon and evening cruises.

By the next decade, there was a feeling of all-pervading decline as a succession of legendary steamers made their way one-by-one to the breakers. By the early seventies only Queen Mary II and Waverley remained on the Clyde, with Maid of the Loch on Loch Lomond. Increasingly it was subsidies that kept them going, but by the end of the decade cruising was effectively reduced to some excursions by the Glen Sannox whose main role was on winter ferry services and as summer 'emergency' vessel. Piers fell into disrepair, and short car ferry crossings became the order of the day.

While interest remained in the newer vessels, the glamour was gone. In the name of economy and, it must be admitted, efficiency, ships became slower; correspondingly, journey times lengthened. The victory of the diesel engine was complete. Fortunately, as has happened more recently with motor-car engines, these have become noticeably quieter with less vibration. Ferries such as the Lord of the Isles, Isle of Arran and Isle of Mull have covered accommodation which is quiet, warm and comfortable. Like cross-channel ships they have become mini-liners. Folk must be less hardy now — the spacious open decks of the cruising days have gone to be replaced by odd corners usually near the stern with little forward view. Bridges are now enclosed right out to the wings — no

162

need now for a Sou-wester and an oilskin and a far cry from the skipper and mate lashed by the elements, trying to see round the funnel of the Prince Edward.

Passengers and tourists have gained some comfort but in my view lost some of the quality of life. They visit towns which first gained from improved roads and then lost out to the consequences — if you can drive to Campbeltown and Tarbert, you can drive to Bournemouth and the Dordogne. Wider horizons bring their downside too. Probably more Scotsmen use cross-Channel ferries than those of the Clyde and Western Isles. By the same token, many more American and European visitors come to Scotland but not enough to compensate.

I watched the changes from different vatage points. My career took me to Renfrewshire where I continued to visit schools in Greenock and Gourock, frequently as a pretext for seeing what was afoot on the Clyde. It blessed me for five years during the seventies with an excuse to visit Argyll from time to time and to sail to Mull, Colonsay, Coll, Tiree and Islay. Incidentally the latter has the ideal ratio of schools to distilleries — about three to one! Wider horizons have brought experience of the MacBrayne end of what is now CalMac. There are tales to tell of education in the Isles and of characters as extravagant as any on the steamers. My journeys meant meeting old shipmates who made it clear that they regarded my job in educational administration as something of a come-down from junior purser on the Queen Mary.

Another perspective came from taking up sailing as a pastime. This was a natural progression — steam traditionally has to give way to sail. I started off with Loch Long Number 95 Iris — a wooden long-keeled day-boat of the type which I had admired from the decks of the Jeanie Deans off Gourock and Hunter's Quay. Perhaps she had too many coats of varnish by the time I had her — we came last in every race we entered. Once when racing off Largs we were swamped by heavy seas. A passing American submarine support-vessel pumped us out and presented us with a bottle of Johnny Walker to stave off hypothermia. Iris was followed by Skua, a Hunter Europa, still to be seen at Sandbank. This 19-footer had a tiny cabin, basic domestic arrangements, and could sail like a witch. In spite of her diminutive size, we explored parts of the outer firth which I had never seen from the more secure vantage point of a steamer. Basking sharks look quite terrifying from a deck eighteen inches above the surface of the sea. Skua had a tendency to tack up and down just off Rothesay and Dunoon piers. Old habits die hard.

There followed a hard apprenticeship in the skills of passage-racing at the hands of two merciless skippers. Sandy and Ron, both of whom would go to any lengths to race with any vessel on the horizon. They would have flourished as steamer skippers in the 1860s, racing for every pier. With the former I had an unforgettable West Highland Week based

The Waverley at Rothesay, 1993

at Oban. In the usual August weather, we never even saw Lismore and Kerrera, let alone Mull. We blew out spinnakers with gay abandon at £2000 a time while others ran for shelter with reefed mainsails and storm jib.

Ron is the kindest and mildest of men who undertook a complete transformation at the starting gun. In the seventies he won virtually every race he entered with his home-built folk boat rumoured to be constructed of surplus desk lids from local schools. He caused heartache to cheque-book skippers seeking to buy their way to success with individual sails costing more than his entire vessel.

I am sure he would have inspired Bram Stoker or R.L. Stevenson to create Dracula or Dr Jekyll and Mr Hyde had he been around in their time. Having enticed hapless crewmen aboard with winsome words and the best food in the fleet, he would berate, castigate, exhort, flagellate with words and gestures both bloodcurdling and specific. Terror ruled absolute. I spent a whole leg of the Tobermory race, from Crinan at 4am until crossing the line 14 hours later, drenched on the foredeck, whistling sails up and down at the whim of the master, cursed the while and starving to boot; we won our class of course. Cross the line and Ron was mild, inoffensive, diffident even. He was eventually discouraged by the well heeled mafia of the Clyde Cruising Club — handicapped into mediocrity in terms of results. His was a management style which would have led only to the industrial tribunal today!

Eventually it all paid off. I managed to buy my own Contessa 26, Charisma, recently seen lying at Tighnabruaich and looking as graceful as ever. We won as often as we lost before concluding that the Clyde was meant for cruising rather than for racing — as I suppose in their time the skippers of the paddlers had. Voyages to Swine's Hole in Loch Goil, near Carrick Castle, and to Caladh Harbour at the mouth of Loch Riddon were the order of the day. Caladh, a secure sandy-bottomed anchorage between a little island and the coast is my favourite anchorage. Walk to the end of the island and you can see everything which passes through the Kyles. You can lie snug on your anchor, secure in any amount of wind.

By the time that circumstances took me to Suffolk in 1979 there was precious little left to see on the Clyde. Apart from the ferries only the Waverley was still steaming, now in the hands of the Paddle Steamer Preservation Society and with the whole firth to cruise on her own. Her continued survival ensures that there is a priceless link with the past and all its splendours. My children and countless others have seen and heard the evocative beat of paddle-wheels and witnessed pistons pounding. I hope that in due course my grandchildren will too. That section of the bow which I painted in 1957 still looks rather well. In truth she is in better shape now than she was then, much of her so lovingly renewed that a great deal of the original 1947 vessel must have gone. She appeared from time to time in Suffolk on her annual round Britain cruise, and I made sure that youngsters there enjoyed a unique experience. Their parents came aboard too to relive trips by paddle-steamer to Margate and Southend.

Suffolk means Felixstowe in ferry terms, and the passenger vessels there became a new source of interest for me. At that time the Townsend ferries to Zeebrugge were the sisters Viking Voyager and Viking Viscount, one or other of which left Felixstowe like clockwork every eight hours, 24 hours a day. They crossed in mid-voyage exactly halfway, a hundred yards apart. You really could set your clocks by them. At 7000 tons they were much bigger than Clyde vessels, but small by the standards of the 40,000 tonners in use today. With a marine-band receiver one could 'eavesdrop' on their VHF, and the captains and the local pilots became friends on the other. Impressive too was the impeccable English of the skippers of the Dutch vessels on the Harwich Hook of Holland service. The Koningen Juliana, a graceful vessel by today's standards, left Harwich at 10pm every evening — it was a real treat to watch her sail past, lights ablaze on a soft Suffolk evening. A fine vantage point was the pub at the end of the Shotley Peninsula, beside HMS Ganges. From there too one could see Dana Anglia (star of the appalling *Tri-Angle* TV soap of the eighties) and the slick Tor vessels which sailed to Gothenburg. It was all a far cry from the promenade at Dunoon Pier in the late forties, but there was something of the excitement and the bustle.

One evening when we switched on to 'hear out' the Zeebrugge ferry we came upon drama instead. The European Gateway, a freight and vehicle vessel owned by Townsend, had collided in clear conditions with the incoming British Rail train ferry and had capsized, drifting onto a sandbank. It was the first great ferry accident, eclipsed in recent times only by the Herald of Free Enterprise disaster, and it fully illustrated the vulnerability of their design. We listened as the crews of the tugs heroically plucked passengers (mainly lorry-drivers) and crew from the water, reducing the loss of life to a handful. Thereafter it took a huge crane from Rotterdam many weeks to raise Gateway. Repaired and modernised, she now sails in the Baltic, her identity well concealed by a new name.

Events took us next to Humberside, where there was the excitement of watching the great North Sea ferries, enter a sealock twice a day at Hull, where those vast ships — the Norsea and the Norsun are 31,598 gross tons — have less than a foot to spare on either side. They don't even scrape the paint work. In 1987 the Norsea was the last great passenger ship ever built in Glasgow. Sadly, she may remain so. At the inaugural lunch, my daughter was shocked to see a Royal Princess putting on her make-up at table and smoking cigarettes between courses! Her identity shouldn't be too difficult to surmise. Tickets on this route include all the food you can eat from a splendid Scandinavian table — a far cry from six shillings for lunch and tickets for the second sitting available from the purser's office!

A business trip to New Zealand widened my horizons in an unexpected way. I escaped from work and visited the South Island to fish and to climb, and in Queenstown on Lake Wakatipu, I came upon the magnificent coal-fired twin-screw steamer Earnslaw built in 1912 and still going strong. I abandoned all else and sailed on her for three successive days, investigating her story.

She now sails exclusively as a tourist attraction on that most beautiful of lakes — the Loch Lomond of New Zealand. Her story is an antipodean version of Prince Edward's with a happier ending. Steamboats came to Lake Wakatipu in 1863, and the railway to Kingston in 1878. Soon railway steamers were serving the lakeside hamlets and sheep-farms. In 1910 it was decided to build a new ship which could exceed 16 knots and carry cargo and 1000 passengers. She would be the biggest ship ever built in New Zealand. The contract was won by the firm of J. McGregor & Co. of Dunedin, who built her in their yard, dismantled her for rail transport to Kingston and reassembled her there. She became an institution, and with no lakeside road (it is still partly dust-track) until 1962, she served faithfully, carrying livestock, farm supplies and passengers, including a few tourists. Sheep stations could summon her as she passed by lighting fires on the shore; three fires meant a death. The story goes that one farmer lit three, and when the Earnslaw dashed in to ask who was dead, the reply was 'Me! I'm dying of thirst, the beer has run out!'.

With the coming of the roads, Earnslaw seemed doomed. At the very least it would be diesel-engines and modernisation. But an enterprising company Fiordland Travel saved her intact. Surveys showed that after more than 60 years in the cold unpolluted fresh water of the Lake she was as good as new. Today she carries tourists who thrill to the thick smoke from her original locomotive-type boilers, and twin 500hp triple expansion engines which carry her along at a cruising speed of 13 knots.

Her decks and fittings are delightfully Edwardian, the views spectacular and the crew typical New Zealander — Scottish backgrounds, friendly and helpful. A lady reminiscent in style and figure of Mrs Mills plays a piano under a canopy on the main deck, leading to impromptu dances and singsongs. Hearing my accent she launched into *Loch Lomond* and incredibly *Haste Ye Back*. The tears rolled down my cheeks with a mixture of homesickness and frustration for what might have been on Loch Lomond.

When we docked at Mount Nicholas, a sheep station on the grand scale with literally tens of thousands of sheep, we were treated to a sheep-shearing exhibition by a virtuoso performer clad in check shirt, jeans, and leather apron. He looked somehow familiar, as indeed he should have. He was none other than the Earnslaw's purser. It was one thing to combine pursing with stewarding on the Prince Edward but this was doubling up on an altogther grander scale. We enjoyed a comparison of notes which resulted in a trip to the bridge and hands on the telegraphs — like so many on the Clyde, made by Chadburns of Liverpool. I learned that Earnslaw had had an open bridge until as recently as 1982, although the weather is kinder there for most of her ten-month season.

There is a little bit of the fifties still alive in the nineties, albeit on the other side of the world. Curled up on the stern, with a magnificent salad from the cold-table, the smell of steam in the nostrils, the sound of the piano playing Scottish medleys above, and the range of hills known as the 'Remarkables' purple-ridged in the background, I felt almost as if I was back sitting on the aft deck of the Jeanie Deans again with Dolly, Roddy, and Neil as we cruised serenely round Bute. The only things missing were the paddles.

Sadly it is not possible to visit New Zealand on a regular basis so if you want to get some idea of what life was once like on Loch Lomond the place to be is the Lake District where I now have the good fortune to live. There are real passengers ships on Ullswater and Windermere and a steam launch on Lake Coniston. It is a treat to sail on them during seasons much longer than the Clyde could manage — March to November, and to watch them being lovingly repaired and refurbished in the winter months, where the atmosphere is just as it was in Balloch when the

Prince Edward and Princess May were laid up, or at Bowling in the old NB days of the Lucy Ashton and the Jeanie Deans.

The vessels are all of great antiquity, the youngest being almost as old as myself. They no longer carry cargo to the hamlets on the lakeside, but on busy days they provide a pleasant alternative to the overcrowded roads. The Raven and the Lady of the Lake ply Ullswater. The Lady is a screw driven steamer built in 1877 by Seath of Rutherglen with a speed of 12 mph. She has a graceful slender hull with a clipper bow. She has survived two sinkings and a major fire to sail serenely on, albeit with diesel engines and a small modern funnel. To watch her between Glenridding and Howtown with her pale green hull, white topsides and red funnel is a sight not to be missed. Her sister Raven is a mere stripling, 12 years younger and like the Lady built of iron, not steel. She too now has diesel engines and has lost her original funnel to the dismay of the purists, replaced with one too far aft to be quite right. She is trim, endearing and carries that aura of timelessness that defies definition. You can turn the clock back on Ullswater, cared for by the friendliest crews to be found anywhere. In winter you find them with dungarees on, acetylene cutter in hand, repairing the ravages of time and the previous summer. They always have a moment for a word with us as we brave the snell winds on the lakeside, wrapped up in our Barbours and winter woollies.

Windermere is the biggest of the lakes, and fittingly so are its steamers, alas all now with diesel engines. They were built as railway steamers connecting with services at lakeside where the branch line to Haverthwaite is now run once again with steam trains. The oldest is Tern built in 1891 in Essex. She can carry 608 passengers, and has a beautiful hull with a bow shaped like that of a Red Indian canoe of the Hollywood ilk. Her saloons are beautiful and elegant. She celebrated her centenary by having an odd stumpy funnel, which she gained in 1958 when converted to diesel, replaced by a tall elegant bell-topped replica of the original. The stumpy one used to give passengers many a surprise since it contained the door to the engine-room from which engineers would emerge quite unannounced.

The sisters Teal and Swan were built in 1936 and 1938 respectively. They were built at Barrow, but like the Maid of the Loch, reassembled at the lakeside. They were very different from what had gone before. Built as motor ships, with a speed of 12mph and a capacity of 600, they were like big sisters of the Countess of Breadalbane built for Loch Awe at the same time, 45ft longer and with twice the tonnage, they would have dwarfed her. Like her, they had exhausts instead of funnels. To this day their immaculate white cruiser sterns are dirtied by the grime from the water level exhausts. Like the Countess they now have full-width deck shelters. Perhaps someone should take their owners since 1993, the Bowness Bay Boating Company, to see the Countess Fiona at Balloch —

they now have twin funnels which add little to their appearance.

Teal and Swan are great to sail on, with open decks and modern carpeted saloons. They call at Ambleside, Bowness and Lakeside. The last run down the lake in the evening is uncannily like the Maid of the Loch cruising serenely into Balloch in the gloaming, although without Donald's son holding up the oil lantern from his boat attached to the buoy. As at Ullswater, the service and courtesy are of a high standard, and there is the same feeling of joining a family as there once was on Loch Lomond.

Perhaps the most remarkable of all the vessels in Cumbria is the SY Gondola which sails on Lake Coniston, courtesy of the National Trust. She was built in 1859 in Liverpool and is unique in appearance. Her bow has an enormous overhang with a figurehead in gold leaf. The saloons are as they were in Queen Victoria's time — plush red seating, rich carpets and ornate panelling and beautiful curtains. There is nothing quite like sitting aboard her, being borne along like an oriental potentate across the waters of this exquisite lake. You do so in silence as the steam engine, which can be glimpsed through yacht-like deck hatches, is smooth and silent. The open bridge is above, with the funnel right aft, tall and at a rakish angle. No other boat looks like Gondola. The name is apt. What completes the sense of wonder is to learn that she lay derelict during the Second World War, was then converted into a houseboat and allowed to rot virtually beyond repair. In 1978 a miracle of restoration was achieved by the National Trust.

The home of the private steam yacht is Windermere, where some of the most elegant are still preserved at a working museum near Bowness. Osprey and Bat epitomise them, with elegant engines, yellow funnels, magnificent brasses, and carpeted saloons with their own tea-sets, wicker chairs and trumpet-gramophones. They can still muster a fair turn of speed, and look their best when their owners don Edwardian dress and set off to cruise on a fine calm day. I coveted these beyond bearing — so exquisite, so unattainable.

Then I learned that it was possible to have a miniature replica built even today, with a hull as graceful, a tiny engine, a yellow funnel, and plenty of mahogany and brass to complete the illusion. Even more remarkable, at 16 foot in length it could be trailed to the lake of one's choice.

And so it was that my wife and I made our way to Port Dinorwic on the Menai Straits where a magician called Glynn Lancaster Jones constructs such craft to order. We soon laid a firm order for Galatea — a good Clyde name, her hull to be dark blue, her funnel Caledonian Steam Packet yellow. The engine was to be a Stuart Turner single cylinder, based on an Edwardian design. It had been built by a retired ship's engineer in Liverpool and was perfect in every detail, with the cylinder green with gold lines and a mass of copper and brass pipes and fittings. There would be a Lune Valley boiler, coal-fired of course, and wheel-steering, although the bridge was certainly behind the funnel! A small shovel of coal every ten minutes or so was the extent of the stoking required. The main thing, apart from idling along at five knots enjoying the view, was to make sure there was enough water in the boiler to prevent an explosion. An eye was always needed for the sight-glass.

Galatea has been a great success. She has sailed mostly on her home waters of Ullswater, and more recently on the Norfolk Broads. There she has become a tourist attraction in her own right. Raven and the Lady of the Lake make extravagant detours to allow passengers a clear view. We feel obliged to put on a show, blowing off steam, and exercising the steam whistle. We are seldom alone when raising steam at the jetty at Glenridding — we can attract a crowd pretty quickly, ranging from old salts who tut-tut at our methods, to wide-eyed youngsters who have never seen live steam in their lives. On such occasions I like to pose as a cross between Captain Crawford and Chief Engineer Maclean, with a touch of seasoned seaman thrown in. My wife is allowed to pose as stoker and deckhand.

Galatea has ventured north of the Border to the annual steam rally on Loch Awe, which centres on Lady Rowena, a peat-burning steam launch which carries passengers from the pier at Loch Awe, once home to the Countess of Breadalbane. A sail on her is well worth having. Her crew of two are characters to match any on the Clyde or Loch Lomond. Galatea retraced the paths of the Victorian steamers on the Loch. She managed four knots for eight miles or more to Portsonachan Hotel for lunch, and then back to Loch Awe for afternoon tea. It was a far cry from my first day as a purser on the Prince Edward, but it had the same ingredients — a loch, the magic of steam, Edwardian elegance, enduring scenery and a fine malt to end the day. My thoughts drifted pleasantly back to the Talisman, the Jupiter and the Jeanie Deans, the latter as she approached Craigendoran on a balmy evening in the Glasgow fair in the fifties. It was sunset on the Clyde.

The Fleet List

Abbreviations:
P.S. — Paddle-Steamer
T.S. — Turbine-Steamer
M.V. — Motor Vessel
D.E.P.V. — Diesel electric paddle vessel
S.Y. — Steam Yacht
T.S.S. — Twin screw steamer
* — Still in service
** — In static use or laid up

1. Caledonian Steam Packet Co.
Fleet in the Fifties —
Traditional Vessels

Name: P.S. Caledonia
Builder: Wm. Denny's, Dumbarton
Launched: 1934
Length: 230ft
Tonnage: 624
Maximum passenger capacity: 1766
Description: Paddle-Steamer, concealed paddle-boxes, single large elliptical funnel, triple expansion diagonal engines, coal fired originally, oil fired 1955. Speed on trial 17.2 knots
Routes with which primarily associated: General excursions, especially from Ayr. Ferry Services: Arran. 1954-1964 Ayr Excursion Steamer 1965-1969, Craigendoran Steamer in succession to Jeanie Deans. War Service as HMS Goatfell minesweeper and escort ship.
Comments: A great favourite with excellent passenger accommodation above and below decks. Strong and powerful looking, a mainstay of

the Arran run in the days before car ferries, when Lamlash and Whiting Bay were still open. In the fifties she kept the Ayr excursions popular and proved successful at the home of the NB Steamers under Donald Crawford's command in the late 1960s.

Withdrawn: 1969, sold in 1970 to become the Old Caledonia floating pub/restaurant on the Thames. Destroyed by fire, 1980.

Sister vessel: Mercury, built by Fairfields — lost while minesweeping, 1940.

Name: P.S. Duchess of Fife
Builder: Fairfield Shipbuilding and Engineering Co. Glasgow
Launched: 1903
Length: 210ft
Tonnage: 336/329
Maximum passenger capacity: 1101
Description: Paddle-steamer typical of her era, with lovely paddle-boxes and single tall funnel. Triple expansion twin crank diagonal engines, coa- fired. Speed on trials: 17.55 knots.
Routes with which primarily associated: All the Clyde routes; in the early fifties on the Millport station. During the First World War, as HMS Duchess, a minesweeper at Grimsby and Devon. Second World War — training ship on the Forth.
Comments: A grand old lady, and a graceful example of the great turn of the century upper-firth paddler. A favourite at the end at Millport, her bell is now the fog-bell on Millport Pier.
Withdrawn: 1953, broken up Port Glasgow.
Sister vessel: Quasi-sister to Duchess of Montrose 1902.

Name: T.S. Duchess of Hamilton
Builder: Harland & Wolff, Glasgow
Engines: Harland & Wolff, Belfast
Launched: 1932
Length: 272ft
Tonnage: 795/801
Maximum passenger capacity: 1918
Description: In many eyes, the most graceful and elegant of the great Clyde turbines; two slender funnels, perfectly proportioned upper decks, and a cruiser stern. Three direct steam turbines driving triple screws, coal-fired, oil-fired from 1956. Trial speed: 20.65 knots.
Routes with which primarily associated: Pre-war largely on excursions from Ayr, Troon and Ardrossan. Post-war with the Duchess of Montrose, the mainstay of day-cruises from Gourock. Associated particularly with the Lochranza/Campbeltown service. War Service — troop transport, mainly Stranraer-Larne and the Clyde.

Comments: The Duchesses were the greyhounds of the fleet. The Hamilton could be distinguished by the cross-tree on her main mast and four windows in a group in front of the engine-room gap; the Montrose had three. With Fergie Murdoch as skipper, she could take on anything in the fifties and win. Probably had the edge on the Montrose, but both had their ardent supporters.

Withdrawn: 1970 and languished until 1974 with prospects of floating restaurant status in Glasgow. Scrapped at Troon.

Sister vessel: Duchess of Montrose, Wm. Denny's, Dumbarton 1930.

Name: T.S. Duchess of Montrose
Builder: Wm. Denny's, Dumbarton
Launched: 1930
Length: 273ft
Tonnage: 806/792/795
Maximum passenger capacity: 1937
Description: Similar to her sister in appearance and equally popular. Her trial speed was 20 knots, fractionally slower than her sister. She was the high point of Denny's production of greyhound turbines.
Routes with which primarily associated: Pre-war excursion from the upper Firth round the lochs, round Arran, Ailsa Craig, Stranraer and Inveraray. Post-war associated with Inveraray, and Arran via the Kyles. Spent the war, outside the boom, on the Wemyss Bay-Innellan-Rothesay route. Tommy Morgan the comedian had a song about how Hitler would never sink her!
Comments: One of the great sights of the fifties was to see both Duchesses leave Gourock around 9am for a whole day's cruise — up to a hundred miles of smooth silent delight. The Montrose had her staunch supporters. A day to Inveraray when Loch Fyne was looking its best could match anything in the golden age of the steamers. In the early thirties a worthy rival for the LNER flyer Jeanie Deans.
Withdrawn: 1965 — broken up in Belgium.
Sister vessel: Duchess of Hamilton, Harland & Wolff, Glasgow.

Name: P.S. Jeanie Deans
Builder: Fairfield Shipbuilding and Engineering, Glasgow
Launched: 1931
Length: 258ft
Tonnage: 635/814/840
Maximum passenger capacity: 1480
Description: Elegant traditional paddle-steamer. First with both funnels forward of the paddle-box, being initially of different heights. Post-war, she resembled Waverley in funnels and deckhouses. Triple-expansion three-crank engines, double-ended boilers; converted to oil-fired

in 1957. Speed on trial: 18.5 knots.

Routes with which primarily associated: Pre-war all-day excursions from Craigendoran to Arran, Ayr, Girvan and Ailsa Craig. Later on Arrochar/Three Lochs Tour run. After 1950 most often on the Round Bute cruise from Craigendoran. War service as minesweeper and anti-aircraft vessel in the Thames.

Comments: Built as LNERs response to Duchess of Montrose, she became the flagship of their fleet; the biggest and the fastest. Held her own in races and became by the fifties one of the most popular ships in the Clyde. After conversion to oil-burning, a real flyer again in the right hands. Her withdrawal was the end of an era.

Withdrawn: 1964, to sail as Queen of the South on the Thames. Unsuccessful and towed to Antwerp for scrap, 1967.

Name: P.S. Jupiter
Builder: Fairfield Shipbuilding and Engineering, Glasgow
Launched: 1937
Length: 231ft
Tonnage: 642
Maximum passenger capacity: 1509
Description: Paddle-steamer with two funnels, concealed paddle-box, cruiser stern. Built for ferry/winter services, with deck space for cars. Triple expansion diagonal engines, one double-ended boiler, coal burning, oil from 1957. Speed on trial: 17.5 knots, seldom reached again.

Routes with which primarily associated: Ferry services from Gourock and Wemyss Bay. Relief on the Arran run. In the fifties, the Cumbrae Circle Cruise, and Sunday excursions to Lochgoilhead. War service as HMS Scawfell, minesweeping and anti-aircraft defence: Channel, East Coast, Holland.

Comments: A workhorse of the fleet in the days before car ferries, faithfully carrying passengers, cargo, cars, summer and winter. In the fifties, supplanted by the new ferries, and relegated to afternoon cruises and Saturdays on the Rothesay run. Awkward to handle, but a great crowd-mover. Every inch a real steamer.

Withdrawn: 1957, scrapped 1961.

Sister vessel: Juno, Fairfield Shipbuilding and Engineering, 1937 as HMS Hellvellyn, bombed and sunk in the Thames 1941.

Name: T.S. Marchioness of Graham
Builder: Fairfield Shipbuilding and Engineering, Glasgow.
Launched: 1936
Length: 231ft
Tonnage: 585

Maximum passenger capacity: 1300

Description: Turbine steamer with four turbines driving two screws through single reduction gearing. Single funnel, high bridge, with space behind for cars, single deckhouse aft. Purposeful rather than graceful. Coal-burning. Speed on trials: 17 knots.

Routes with which primarily associated: Built for the Ardrossan/Arran run, and as Arran winter boat; spent most of her life there either as mainstay or assisting. Post-war Ayr excursion steamer until succeeded turbine Glen Sannox in 1954 on Arran run until new car ferry Glen Sannox came in 1957. Spent two seasons on excursions.

Comments: After the Atalanta of 1906, built by John Brown of Clydebank, the only single-funnelled turbine steamer. Although used on excursion work, mainly remembered for the Arran run. A comfortable, homely unsung hero of the fleet. The coming of car ferries spelled the end for her. The last coal-fired steamer on the Clyde.

Withdrawn: 1958. Converted to diesel, remodelled and sailed in Greece under different names until laid up in 1970 and scrapped 1975.

Name: P.S. Marchioness of Lorne

Builder: Fairfield Shipbuilding and Engineering, Glasgow.

Launched: 1935

Length: 207ft

Tonnage: 427

Description: A paddle-steamer with triple expansion diagonal engines, coal-fired. She had a single squat funnel and concealed paddle-boxes. She looked like a small, low Caledonia. Her trial speed of 15 knots was never again attained, 12 being her maximum.

Routes with which primarily associated: Built for the Holy Loch run, her lack of speed did not matter too much as she was easy to handle at the many small piers. Transferred to the Millport Station in 1953, she survived only one season.

Comments: A tidy little steamer dogged by her lack of pace — she only once met her contract speed. Comfortable on the Holy Loch run. Her withdrawal in favour of small vessels like Ashton and Leven caused a near riot. Too slow for the Millport/Wemyss Bay run.

Withdrawn: 1952, broken up in 1955, Port Glasgow.

Name: T.S. Queen Mary/Queen Mary II **

Builder: Wm. Denny's, Dumbarton

Launched: 1933

Length: 263ft

Tonnage: 870/918/1014

Maximum passenger capacity: 2086

Description: Broad, capacious, triple screw direct drive turbine-steamer with ample covered accommodation. Built with two sturdy funnels; in 1957, one modern oval funnel, when reboilered and converted to oil-fired. Speed on trial: 19 knots, seldom 18 thereafter.

Routes with which primarily associated: Built for the 'doon the watter' sailings from Glasgow, she spent most of her life on this run, with the 10am sailing to Arran pre-war. Until the service reduced in the fifties to the 11am to Rothesay and Tighnabruaich from 1970, she was the sole Gourock cruise steamer on day-cruises to Campbeltown, Inveraray etc. Popular on charters.

Comments: Glasgow's favourite steamer, stately rather than speedy, and flagship of the fleet in the fifties. Set new standards in passenger comfort which kept her in service as the last turbine steamer on the Clyde, and the last Caledonian cruise steamer.

Withdrawn: 1977, and after attempts to keep her on static display on the Clyde, finally opened in 1989 as a Toby Restaurant on the Thames Embankment, complete with two original funnels.

Name: D.E.P.V. Talisman
Builder: A. & J. Inglis, Pointhouse, Glasgow.
Launched: 1935
Length: 223ft
Tonnage: 544
Maximum passenger capacity: 1252

Description: Not really a steamer! Unique diesel electric paddle engines, austere hull with conventional paddle-boxes and a single tall slightly elliptical funnel, cruiser stern. English Electric diesel engines replaced with British Polar in 1954. Speed on trials: 17.25 knots. After 1954, 15 knots.

Routes with which primarily associated: Pre-war the principal Craigendoran runs to Rothesay and Kyles of Bute. From 1954 she took over the Millport station, with Cumbrae Circle Cruise. War service as HMS Aristocrat, anti-aircraft ship in Thames, on the Dieppe raid and Normandy beaches.

Comments: Although her pioneering machinery gave endless trouble, she was a survivor because of her great fuel economy and ability to be put into service quickly (no steam to raise). Noisy and rattly, she won her way into the affections of folk by her quaintness and her longevity. Nearly scrapped in 1939 and 1953.

Withdrawn: 1966, broken up at Dalmuir, 1967

Name: P.S. Waverley *
Builder: A. & J. Inglis, Pointhouse, Glasgow
Launched: 1947

Length: 240ft
Tonnage: 694
Maximum passenger capacity: 1350
Description: Paddle-steamer with her triple expansion engines built by
  Rankin and Blackmore, and a double-ended boiler, coal-fired until
  1957. She has two funnels, conventional paddle-boxes, a nice raked
  stem, and a neat cruiser stern. Deckhouses resembled those of post-
  war Jeanie Deans. Speed on trials: 17 knots.
Routes with which primarily associated: At first mainly the
  Arrochar/Tighnabruaich cruise, but with excursions to Arran, Round
  the Lochs and up river etc. In the 1970s as the last surviving paddler,
  she undertook a wide range of excursions. Now sails on the Clyde,
  and round the coast of the United Kingdom.
Comments: The last sea-going paddle-steamer in the world, and the only
  post-war steamer on the Clyde. A rival of the Jeanie Deans in the
  fifties, and later performed well, even on the turbine runs to
  Campbeltown and Inveraray. Now a living legend preserved for our
  pleasure by the Paddle-Steamer Preservation Society and the Waverley
  Steam Navigation Company, together with the Balmoral. Still going
  strong.

2. Caledonian Steam Packet Co.
Motor Vessels

Name: M.V. Cowal
Builder: Ailsa Shipbuilding Co. Troon
Launched: 1954
Length: 179ft
Tonnage: 569
Maximum passenger capacity: 650
Description: Car ferry — capacity 34 cars, on car deck reached by
  hoists. Passenger accommodation forward of the hoist on the prome-
  nade deck. Single funnel. Twin screws. British Polar diesel engines.
  Speed: 15 knots.
Routes with which primarily associated: Car ferry routes:
  Gourock/Dunoon, Wemyss Bay/Rothesay, occasionally Arran and
  Millport. 1970-72 new route from Fairlie to Brodick and Tarbet, super-
  seded by Lochranza-Claonaig (Kintyre) ferry.
Comments: One of the three ABC car ferries which brought about a revolution in the fifties — from planks for cars to lifts; cargo now
  wheeled aboard. Efficient but too small, and lifts terribly slow.

Modernisation at a price and lacking in elegance.

Withdrawn: 1977, sold to Greece, but never used. Scrapped 1984.

Sister vessels: Arran: 1954, Wm. Denny. In 1962 transferred to MacBrayne for West Loch Tarbert/Islay run. In 1974 altered to stern loading, with lifts and aft superstructure removed. Returned to Clyde in 1974 when Pioneer took over Islay run. Withdrawn 1979. Bute: 1954. Ailsa Shipbuilding Co. After service on Clyde routes, assisted in the 70s Mallaig/Armadale and Small Isles service. Withdrawn 1979.

Name: M.V. Maid of Argyll *?
Builder: A.& J. Inglis, Pointhouse, Glasgow
Launched: 1953
Length: 153ft
Tonnage: 509
Maximum passenger capacity: 627
Description: Twin Screw diesel passenger vessel, (engines, British Polar) single oval funnel, tripod masts. Speed: 15 knots.
Routes with which primarily associated: In the fifties, Craigendoran and Rothesay; Saturdays: Arrochar. Evening and cafe cruises. Later to share rosters with other Maids — service runs, morning and afternoon cruises. In spring 1970, the Ardrishaig mail run.
Comments: The Craigendoran Maid appropriately built by Inglis, gave yeoman service for over 20 years. In the fifties with her sisters, carried out the essential runs and cruises for which the traditional steamers were too costly. A great comedown in quality of life for the day-tripper.
Withdrawn: 1974 and sold to Greece as City of Piraeus, greatly modernised and more luxurious; last seen on day trips to Hydra, Poros, Aegina.
Sister vessels: Maid of Ashton*: 1953. Yarrow of Scotstoun (first for them on the Clyde). Associated with Holy Loch run. Withdrawn 1971 to become the Hispaniola club on the Thames.
Maid of Cumbrae*: 1953. Ardrossan Dockyard Ltd. In 1972 altered to mini stern-loading car ferry to use new Dunoon Linkspan. Withdrawn in 1977 then employed on Naples to Capri/Sorrento service.
Maid of Skelmorlie*: 1953. A.& J. Inglis. In fifties on Wemyss Bay, Rothesay, Largs run and cruises. Withdrawn 1973 converted to small car ferry and now with the Maid of Cumbrae at Capri and Naples.

Name: M.V. Countess of Breadalbane **
Builder: Wm. Denny's, Dumbarton
Launched: 1936
Length: 95ft

Tonnage: 106
Maximum passenger capacity: 200
Description: Small twin-screw motor vessel with two Gleniffer diesels. No funnel, waterline exhaust, observation lounge on promenade deck, with bridge and landing platform above. 1983/1989 alterations to full width deck shelter and funnel just aft of the wheelhouse. Trial speed: 10.5 knots. After new engines, 1956: 12 knots.
Routes with which primarily associated: 1936-52, Loch Awe cruises; 1952-71, Holy Loch, link services and short cruises; 1972-78, Kilmun, Blairmore etc. Ritchies' Ferries; 1978-79, cruises from Mull to Staffa/Iona; 1982-89, Loch Lomond
Comments: Ubiquitous cruise/ferry vessel on Loch Awe, the Clyde, and Loch Lomond. Renamed Countess of Kempock, 1972, and Countess Fiona, 1982. A great advert for Denny's and still in existence at Balloch, perhaps to sail again.

Name: M.V. Glen Sannox
Builder: Ailsa Shipbuilding Co., Troon
Launched: 1957
Length: 257ft
Tonnage: 1000/1107
Maximum passenger capacity: 1100
Description: Biggest and fastest of the new car ferries, a twin screw motor vessel with Sulzer diesel engines (replaced with Wichmann, 1977). Low at the stern, with a high superstructure forward containing passenger accommodation and a single funnel. Her midships lift was hydraulic and excruciatingly slow. Her speed of 18 knots compensated to an extent. 1970, altered to stern-loading, deck crane removed.
Routes with which primarily associated: 1957-70, Arran-Brodick, Ardrossan (replaced by M.V. Caledonia); 1970-77, Wemyss Bay-Rothesay-Gourock, Dunoon. From 1977: combined cruise/car ferry ship, and latterly winter boat on the Oban/Craignure run.
Comments: At first resented as new and ungainly, Glen Sannox became as popular as the traditional steamers. Her wide decks and passenger space made her suitable for cruising. A great winter boat on the Arran and Mull runs.
Withdrawn: 1989, left Clyde under Panamanian registration with the graceless name of Knooz.

Name: Ashton/Leven
Builder: Wm. Denny's, Dumbarton
Launched: 1938
Length: 63ft

Tonnage: 39
Description: Twin screw Gleniffer diesel launches.
Routes with which primarily associated: 1938 Empire Exhibition from Bridge Wharf. In 1940s, Gourock-Dunoon and then settled down on the Largs-Millport ferry service in the fifties.
Comments: Very basic transport, and decidedly lively.
Withdrawn: Ashton: 1965, sold to Roy Ritchie as Gourockian. Leven: 1965, sold to Brixham as Pride of the Bay.

3. The MacBrayne Presence in the Fifties

Name: T.S. King George V
Builder: Wm. Denny's, Dumbarton
Launched: 1926
Length: 261ft
Tonnage: 797/801/815
Description: Turbine steamer, twin screw with six Parsons turbines through single reduction gear. Oil-fired from 1951. The first modern turbine with two elegant funnels, modern deck shelters; near sister to the Duchesses. Trial Speed: 20 knots.
Routes with which primarily associated: Until 1935, Campbeltown or Inveraray run, then passed to MacBraynes and became the Oban to Staffa and Iona cruise steamer, with short spells on the Clyde on the Ardrishaig run. War service — six trips to Dunkirk with D.S.Cs for the Captain and Chief Engineer.
Comments: Seen on the Clyde only in the fifties early in the season; a great favourite on the Iona run. Looked splendid in the red and black funnel of her owners; one of the best of all the great turbines.
Withdrawn: 1974, towed to Cardiff, where she was damaged by fire during conversion to a floating restaurant, 1981. Scrapped, 1984.

Name: M.V. Loch Fyne
Builder: Wm. Denny's, Dumbarton.
Launched: 1931
Length: 210ft
Tonnage: 754
Maximum passenger capacity: 1202
Description: First diesel-electric vessel in the UK, rather sturdy in appearance, with two dumpy funnels too far apart, the forward one a dummy. First vessel with direct bridge control of her Davey Paxman engines. Speed on trial: 16.5 knots.

Routes with which primarily associated: Oban excursions in summer, and the Ardrishaig run on the Clyde in winter — all year round after Saint Columba was withdrawn in 1958. War-time saw her on the Ardrishaig run from Wemyss Bay.

Comments: Not a real steamer, noisy and rattly, but nonetheless popular. Undertook MacBraynes last run on the Clyde on 30th September, 1969 — ending 120 years of tradition, and the final victory of road transport to Loch Fyne.

Withdrawn: 1969, laid up at Faslane, scrapped, 1974.

Name: T.S. Saint Columba
Builder: Wm. Denny's, Dumbarton
Launched: 1912 (rebuilt 1936)
Length: 270ft
Tonnage: 795/827/851
Maximum passenger capacity: 1800 (post 1936)
Description: Triple screw direct drive steam turbine, converted to oil 1937. Originally Queen Alexandra with two funnels, transformed by MacBraynes in 1936 into a mini Cunard Queen Mary with three elliptical stepped funnels and an extended upper deck. The only three-funnelled coastal ship ever in the UK. Speed on trial: 21 knots. (1911)
Routes with which primarily associated: From 1936 Glasgow-Ardrishaig (the Royal Route) in the footsteps of the illustrious Columba. Like her she left at precisely 7.11am (except Sundays). From 1947, Gourock to Ardrishaig in summer season. During First World War as Queen Alexandra, she rammed and sunk a U-boat. Second World War — boom defence HQ ship, Albert Harbour.
Comments: At full speed in the Kyles, there was nothing in the fifties to match this three-funnelled lady. Her sharp stem cut through the waves like a knife. A MacBrayne loner on the Clyde.
Withdrawn: 1958

4. Pre-war Steamers

Name: P.S. Lucy Ashton
Builder: T.B. Seath, Rutherglen
Launched: 1888
Length: 190ft
Tonnage 271
Maximum passenger capacity: 903
Description: Paddle-steamer built with single diagonal coal-fired

engine, replaced with a compound diagonal built by A.& J. Inglis —
1962. Single funnel, bridge behind — a classic Victorian spectacle.

Routes with which primarily associated: Gareloch piers from
Craigendoran. During the Second World War, called without relief at
Craigendoran, Helensburgh, Gourock, Kilcreggan, Kirn and Dunoon,
covering nearly 150,000 miles.

Comments: The ultimate survivor, nearly scrapped before both World
Wars. With Queen Mary II maintained all the war-time passenger services above the Dunoon/Cloch boom.

Withdrawn: 1949, and served as the first experimental jet-propelled
vessel in the world before being scrapped.

Name: P.S. Glen Sannox
Builder: J. & G. Thomson, Clydebank
Launched: 1892
Length: 265ft
Tonnage: 610
Description: Classic Victorian paddle-steamer with compound diagonal
engines, coal-fired. Two long slender funnels, behind ornate paddle-
boxes. Long slender hull, yacht-like stern. Speed on trial: 19.23 knots.

Routes with which primarily associated: Ardrossan/Arran run.

Comments: Glasgow and South West Railway built her as a great rival to
the Duchess of Hamilton (1890) of the Caledonian Company, in the
days of 80-minute dashes from Glasgow to Brodick by train and
steamer.

Withdrawn: 1925 to be replaced by the turbine steamer Glen Sannox.

Name: T.S. Glen Sannox
Builder: Wm. Denny's, Dumbarton
Launched: 1925
Length: 250ft
Tonnage: 690
Maximum passenger capacity: 1622
Description: Triple screw turbine steamer with three direct drive tur-
bines. She resembled the earliest turbines, virtually a sister of Duchess
of Argyll 1906. Two funnels on a short upper deck and old-fashioned
but graceful counter stern. A flyer with trial speed of 20.75 knots.

Routes with which primarily associated: The Arran routes —
Brodick, Whiting Bay, Campbeltown from Ardrossan, and every summer until 1963. War-time Arran steamer all year round.

Comments: Old-fashioned looking, she had limited accommodation for
busy Arran summers but she epitomised the Clyde in its heyday, with
a great turn of speed until the end. First major victim of modernisation
and the car ferry revolution.

Withdrawn: 1953, scrapped in Ghent, 1954

Name: T.S. King Edward
Builder: Wm. Denny's Dumbarton
Launched: 1901
Length: 150ft
Tonnage: 502/551
Maximum passenger capacity: 1966
Description: First turbine passenger steamer in the world, a history-maker. Had five screws originally but altered to three with direct drive from three turbines. Long and lean, with small upper deck and two funnels. Speed on trial: 20.483 knots.
Routes with which primarily associated: Until 1927, day cruises on the lower Firth, often to Campbeltown. 1927 took up the 10am run from Bridge Wharf to the Arran Coast. In 1933 when Queen Mary took over this run, she took the 11am to Tighnabruaich. In the First World War, a troopship and then ambulance ship in the White Sea. A troop tender in the Clyde during the Second World War.
Comments: A historic vessel which altered the Clyde scene with a succession of swift turbines following for the long distance routes. Only Jeanie Deans of the paddlers challenged their supremacy. One of her turbines is preserved at the Glasgow Transport Museum as is her ship's bell. A fitting up-river consort for Queen Mary II.
Withdrawn: 1952, scrapped at Troon.

5. Loch Lomond Steamers
(Loch Katrine, Loch Awe)

Name: P.S. Prince Edward
Builder: A & J. Inglis, Pointhouse, Glasgow and Balloch
Launched: 1911/1912
Length: 175ft
Tonnage: 304
Description: Edwardian paddle-steamer with compound diagonal steam engines, haystack boiler, coal-fired. Low graceful, with white slatted paddle-boxes and one long raked funnel with the bridge behind. She lost her mast in the thirties. Speed: 15 knots.
Routes with which primarily associated: Loch Lomond services from Balloch to Balmaha, Luss, Rowardenan, Tarbet, Inversnaid and Ardlui.
Comments: In the fifties a beautifully maintained relic of a by-gone age.

What an attraction today if she had been preserved! The biggest vessel on the Loch until 1953, and arguably the biggest the loch could take.

Withdrawn: 1954, broken up at Balloch, 1955.

Sister vessels: Near sisters were the Prince George and Princess May built by A & J. Inglis in 1898 with single diagonal engines. Prince George scrapped 1942; Princes May 1953.

Name: P.S. Maid of the Loch **
Builder: A. & J. Inglis, Pointhouse, Glasgow and Balloch
Launched: 1953
Length: 193ft
Tonnage: 555
Maximum passenger capacity: 1000
Description: Modern paddle-steamer with compound diagonal engine and navy boiler by Rankin and Blackmore. She has a raked stem and cruiser stern, ample deckhouses, and a single yellow funnel, her hull being white. The paddle-boxes are traditional, slatted, with Celtic decoration. Upper works are in aluminium.
Routes with which primarily associated: Loch Lomond, Balloch to Balmaha, Luss (from 1980) Rowardenan, Tarbet, Inversnaid, Ardlui.
Comments: The biggest inland vessel built in Britain, and the last paddler to be built. In the fifties in her prime she gave a luxurious service to a wide range of tourists. In the 60s and thereafter a constant struggle for viability, despite subsidies from local authorities — a victim of accountancy.
Withdrawn: 1981. Sold to various owners, finally Dumbarton District Council. In a sorry state, there are hopes of a full or partial restoration.

Name: Sir Walter Scott *
Builder: Wm. Denny's, Dumbarton
Engine: Matthew Paul
Launched: 1900
Length: 110.6ft
Tonnage: 115
Description: A single screw steamer with her original triple expansion engine; boilers renewed in 1956, fired with smokeless fuel. Neat hull with counter stern and single white funnel behind the bridge; two pleasant saloons. Decidedly slow.
Routes with which primarily associated: Loch Katrine, Trossachs Pier and Stronachlachar.
Comments: The only surviving screw steamer sailing in regular passenger service in Scotland.

Name: S.Y. Lady Rowena *
Builder: C.H. Breaker, Bowness-on-Windermere
Launched: 1927
Length: 36ft
Maximum passenger capacity: 30
Description: Reversing the normal trend — originally a motor yacht, Water Lily, on Lake Windermere until 1973. Converted to steam by Harry Watson in 1984 with a Sisson replica compound engine, and peat-fired boiler. Taken to Loch Awe, 1986. Plain white hull with funnel on top of boiler near the bow; saloon behind.
Routes with which primarily associated: Loch Awe-Portsonachan, Taychreggan, Dalavich and Ardanaseig.
Comments: A pleasant throwback to 19th-century steaming on a beautiful loch, deserted since the departure of the Countess of Breadalbane in 1952.

6. Lake Steamers — England and New Zealand

Name: T.S.S. Earnslaw *
Builder: J. McGregor & Co., Dunedin, New Zealand
Launched: 1912
Length: 160ft
Maximum passenger capacity: 1000
Description: Twin screw steamer with two 500hp triple-expansion engines, two locomotive-style boilers, coal-fired. A sturdy broad white hull with deck shelters, a high red and black single funnel, and a mast and derrick forward.
Routes with which primarily associated: Lake Wakatipu, South Island, New Zealand. For many years service runs from Kingston to Queenstown and hamlets in between. Now cruises from Steamer Wharf, Queenstown and calls at Mount Nicholas, Sheep Station.
Comments: A world away, a vessel lovingly preserved which has a history matching the Loch Lomond steamers, and a major tourist attraction. A must for visiting steamer-buffs.

Name: M.V. Lady of the Lake *
Builder: T.B. Seath, Rutherglen
Launched: 1877
Length: 97ft
Maximum passenger capacity: 220
Description: A beautiful Victorian hull with graceful stern, single semi-

modern funnel. Steam engine replaced in 1935 by Crossley diesels and in 1979 by Kelvins driving twin screws. Speed: originally 12mph, now 11mph.

Routes with which primarily associated: Ullswater, Glenridding to Howtown.

Comments: A real treat with elegant saloon and a timeless grace. Lake travel as it used to be.

Name: M.V. Raven *
Builder: T.B. Seath, Rutherglen
Launched: 1889
Length: 112ft
Maximum passenger capacity: 284
Description: Twin screw motor vessel, originally with steam engines. In 1935, diesel engines (National Gas and Oil Engine Co.) were fitted which lasted until replaced with Thorneycrofts in 1964. Original funnel replaced with a dumpy one too far aft — quaint but endearing. Speed: 11mph.
Routes with which primarily associated: Ullswater, Glenridding, Howtown, Pooley Bridge.
Comments: See Lady of the Lake! 100 years plus and still going strong.

Name: M.V. Tern *
Builder: Wm. Forrest, Wyvenhoe, Essex
Launched: 1891
Length: 140ft
Tonnage: 120
Maximum passenger capacity: 608
Description: A twin screw motor vessel with two Gleniffer diesels fitted 1958. Originally steam engines which gave 140 rpm making her smooth and silent. Two Victorian saloons give a touch of luxury. She has a unique canoe-shaped bow and a replica of her original tall funnel in dark green. Speed: 12mph.
Routes with which primarily associated: Windermere, Lakeside, Bowness, Waterhead (Ambleside)
Comments: The beauty of Windermere from the deck of a Victorian relic — who could ask for more?

Name: M.V. Teal *
Builder: Victor Armstrong, Barrow and Lakeside
Launched: 1936
Length: 136ft
Tonnage: 251
Maximum passenger capacity: 612

Description: Twin screw motor vessel with two Gleniffer diesels. A scaled-up version of Countess of Breadalbane, with similar deck shelters, now upgraded like hers to full width and well-appointed. Still no funnel — just exhausts at water level.

Routes with which primarily associated: Windermere-Lakeside, Bowness, Waterhead (Ambleside).

Sister vessel: M.V. Swan *, Vickers Armstrong, 1938

Name: S.Y. Gondola*
Builder: Jones Quiggan, Liverpool
Launched: 1859
Length: 84ft
Maximum passenger capacity: 225
Description: Unique steam launch with long overhanging bow, curved deckhouses over a Victorian saloon, and a long sloping funnel aft with an open bridge in front. Two twin cylinder engines and a locomotive-type boiler.
Routes with which primarily associated: Cruises on Lake Coniston and to Brantwood.
Comments: Defies description — beautiful but unique, saved from dereliction and restored to full sumptuous luxury. The imagination can easily transport you back a century and more.

Name: S.Y. Galatea *
Builder: Glyn Lancaster Jones for the author
Launched: 1991
Length: 16ft
Tonnage: 900lbs
Maximum passenger capacity: 4
Description: Single screw steam launch. Glass fibre hull with graceful counter stern, woodwork in mahogany. Lune Valley boiler, coal-fired in brass surround. Stuart Turner SA single cylinder 1.5hp engine, built by R. Thorogood. Single funnel Caledonian Steam Packet yellow. Steam whistle and Windermere Kettle. Speed on trial: 5 knots.
Routes with which primarily associated: Ullswater, Loch Awe, Norfolk Broads.
Comments: Master of a steamer at last!
Sister vessels: Sixteen of the Mariamne Class.

Further reading

Clyde River and Other Steamers 4th. edition, Duckworth and Langmuir, Brown Son & Ferguson 1990

Clyde Steamer and Loch Lomond Fleets, Peter Milne, Ian Allan 1955

Clyde Coast Pleasure Steamers, E. C. B. Thornton, T. Stephenson and Sons 1968

Clyde Passenger Steamers 1812-1901, Cpn. James Williamson, Strong Oak Press 1987 (reprint)

Clyde River Steamers 1872-1922, Andrew McQueen, Strong Oak Press 1990 (reprint)

The Victorian Summer of the Clyde Steamer, Alan Paterson, David and Charles 1972

Classic Scottish Paddle Steamers, Alan Paterson, David and Charles 1982

The Caledonian Steam Packet Co. Ltd., Ian C. McArthur, Clyde River Steamer Club 1972

Clyde Pleasure Steamers — An Illustrated History, Ian McRorie, Orr and Pollock 1986

To the Coast 100 Years of the C.S.P Co., Ian McRorie, Fairlie Press 1989

Clyde Piers, McRorie and Monteith, Inverclyde Libraries 1982

Millport Pier Album, Alastair Chisholm, St Maura Press 1992

Birth of a Legend — Waverley, Paddle Steamer Preservation Society 1987

Craigendoran Steamers, Alan Brown, Aggregate Publications 1979

Talisman Solitary Crusader, Alan Brown, Aggregate Publications 1980

Queen Mary, Richard Orr, Caledonian MacBrayne 1976

Maid of the Loch, Robert Cleary, Caledonian MacBrayne 1979

Steamers of the Clyde (illustrated), Stromier and Nicholson, Scottish Field

Song of the Clyde, Fred Walker, Patrick Stephens 1984

Clyde Steamers Remembered, Paddle Steamer Preservation Society 1994

Days at the Coast, Robert Preston, Stenlake 1994

Caledonian MacBrayne — The Fleet, Ferry Publications 1994

Waverley, Waverley Excursions 1994

Clubs

Clyde River Steamer Club
Regular meetings in Glasgow and a wide range of excellent and readable material. Secretary: Mr Eric Schofield, 67 Atholl Drive, Giffnock, Glasgow G46 6QW.

Paddle Steamer Preservation Society
Volunteers support Waverley, Kingswear Castle and Balmoral. Scottish Branch Secretary: Wilfred Gellatly, 64 Inveroran Drive, Bearsden, Glasgow G61 2PN.

Excursions

Waverley Steam Navigation Company, Anderston Quay, Glasgow G3 8HA.